MORMONISM (OR THE CHURCH OF JESUS CHRIST OF LATTER-DAY SAINTS)

MORMONISM (OR THE CHURCH OF JESUS CHRIST OF LATTER-DAY SAINTS)

WHAT EVERYONE NEEDS TO KNOW®

TERRYL GIVENS

OXFORD
UNIVERSITY PRESS

OXFORD
UNIVERSITY PRESS

Oxford University Press is a department of the University of Oxford. It furthers the University's objective of excellence in research, scholarship, and education by publishing worldwide. Oxford is a registered trade mark of Oxford University Press in the UK and certain other countries.

"What Everyone Needs to Know" is a registered trademark of Oxford University Press.

Published in the United States of America by Oxford University Press
198 Madison Avenue, New York, NY 10016, United States of America.

Library of Congress Cataloging-in-Publication Data
Names: Givens, Terryl, author.
Title: Mormonism : what everyone needs to know / Terryl Givens.
Other titles: What everyone needs to know.
Description: New York : Oxford University Press, [2020] |
Series: What everyone needs to know | Includes index.
Identifiers: LCCN 2020008080 (print) | LCCN 2020008081 (ebook) |
ISBN 9780190885083 (hardback) | ISBN 9780190885090 (paperback) |
ISBN 9780190885106 (updf) | ISBN 9780190885113 (epub)
Subjects: LCSH: Church of Jesus Christ of Latter-day Saints. | Mormon Church.
Classification: LCC BX8635.3 .G575 2020 (print) |
LCC BX8635.3 (ebook) | DDC 289.3—dc23
LC record available at https://lccn.loc.gov/2020008080
LC ebook record available at https://lccn.loc.gov/2020008081

1 3 5 7 9 8 6 4 2

Paperback printed by LSC Communications, United States of America
Hardback printed by Bridgeport National Bindery, Inc., United States of America

To Dan and Maureen

Humor is a prelude to faith and laughter is the beginning of prayer.

—Reinhold Niebuhr

CONTENTS

10 Conflicts and Challenges 229

1

WHAT EVERYONE NEEDS TO KNOW ABOUT MORMONISM (OR THE CHURCH OF JESUS CHRIST OF LATTER-DAY SAINTS)

Let's start with the name: What to call them?

It is often the case that a word originally invoked as a term of derision comes to be tolerated—or even embraced—by the group to which it is attached. "Yankee" was not a complimentary label in the revolutionary era but came to be accepted by Americans without protest; "Shakers" and "Quakers" were similarly far from affectionate terms when first employed in reference to the physical manifestations of their spirit-filled meetings. Those nineteenth-century Christians who believed the Book of Mormon to be a new revelation from God were called "Mormonites" and later "Mormons" in derisive allusion to their belief in their Book of Mormon. Joseph Smith and fellow believers at first resisted the nickname, but it did not take long before he and his followers began referring to themselves with the same word.

Officially, the church was denominated the Church of Christ at its 1830 founding. However, that name was also employed by other groups in the restorationist movement of the early nineteenth century. In 1834, the name was changed to the Church of the Latter-day Saints. This appellation reflected the millenarian preoccupation of many nineteenth-century Americans and the Mormons in particular. Numerous revelations to Joseph Smith had emphasized that he was initiating the final dispensation, the "Dispensation of the Fulness of Times," and that the Lord's return was imminent. These followers of Christ, as distinct from the disciples of the *early* church (denominated "saints" in the New Testament), were gathering in the "*Latter* Days." The term for "saints," in the New Testament, means "consecrated ones." Hence, a saint was called or challenged or invited to be holy. The name denoted an aspiration, not an accomplishment.

Other permutations on the name followed, but in 1838 a revelation definitively established the official body as the Church of Jesus Christ of Latter Day (soon spelled Latter-day) Saints. The name reflected a scriptural injunction that had until then been followed only erratically. In the Book of Mormon, a prophet asks how followers of Christ should call themselves. In reply, the risen Lord replies: "how be it my church save it be called in my name?" (3 Nephi 27:8). Consequently, the new name complies with scripture while emphasizing the church as a modern counterpart to the early Christian disciples.

Mormonism, however, has been the dominant moniker if for no other reason than simplicity. "Mormon" rolls off the tongue—and into print—so much more readily than "member of the Church of Jesus Christ of Latter-day Saints." In recent decades, the church's leadership has from time to time attempted to turn back the clock, appealing to members and media outlets alike to employ the full and proper name as a sign of respect and deference. This has happened concurrently with efforts, in the face of frequent misrepresentation, to emphasize the Christ-centered nature of the church. When Russell M. Nelson assumed the presidency in 2018, he renewed calls for a course correction. These most recent calls have offered "The

Church of Jesus Christ" as an acceptable shorthand for the full title, rather than the previous alternative, "the LDS (for Latter-day Saint) Church." How this will play out in the academy is uncertain. "Mormon studies" and "Mormon history," for example, are solidly entrenched as subdisciplines and are part of common cultural parlance. The church's decision to rebrand its most famous cultural entity as "The Tabernacle Choir at Temple Square" is proof that this is a renaming venture with real teeth. Institutional efforts will require the cooperation of media, academics, and a wider public if a historical trend of a century and more is to be reversed.

In that spirit, this book will generally refer to the "Church of Jesus Christ" and to the church's members as "Latter-day Saints" or "Saints," with the understanding that the terms "Mormonism" and "Mormons" may occasionally need to be used either to refer to a more amorphous cultural entity that transcends the institution or to be consistent with historical context.

2
HISTORY

What is the Church of Jesus Christ of Latter-day Saints?

The Church of Jesus Christ is a Christian denomination founded in 1830 by Joseph Smith. Neither Catholic nor Protestant, Latter-day Saints believe their church was founded as a "restoration" of original Christianity, when God directed Smith to preach the fullness of the gospel, in an organization roughly modeled on New Testament forms, performing saving sacraments with authority bestowed on him by angelic messengers. The distinctive hallmark of the church was the Book of Mormon, which Smith published shortly before the church's founding. It made these early saints a "people of the Book," like the Jews, Muslims, and other Christians. The Book of Mormon singled them out as a unique branch of Christianity and gave the group its popular moniker, and its miraculous translation from gold plates was heralded by believers as the most conspicuous sign of Smith's prophetic vocation and authority. Though believers in Jesus Christ as Savior, they espouse a body of doctrine that is often quite distinct from those of their Christian peers.

Smith preached a doctrine of "gathering," and his people flocked to gathering sites in Ohio and later Missouri. Fleeing persecution, they settled in Illinois, where they built a temple based on Old Testament precedent, grew by thousands, and created a prosperous community (Nauvoo). In

1844 Joseph Smith was martyred, the Saints were forced into exile, and they settled after a long trek in the Valley of the Great Salt Lake.

After decades in relative isolation, they abandoned the practice of plural marriage, which had heightened their cultural and religious marginalization, ceased their practice of "gathering to Zion," and began their march toward becoming an international, worldwide community. Today they number in the millions, with members in some 170 countries and principalities.

What circumstances gave rise to the birth of the Church of Jesus Christ?

The intense human craving for relief from the fears of death and damnation has given rise to many cataclysms and innovations in the history of Christianity. In traditional Catholic belief, salvation comes from belonging to the true church, receiving its sacraments from authorized administrators, and living faithfully. Those conditions provide a degree of assurance that may fall short of absolute certitude but is as close to a guarantee as is possible in this world. Providing such assurance was a conspicuous function of the Catholic Church.

That role was radically undermined by the Protestant Reformation critique of the church sacraments as the necessary channels through which grace is administered, and of the role of human effort in securing salvation. In the Protestant world in which Joseph Smith grew up, an emphasis on the sinful self and the horrors of hell left many seekers anxious for the state of their souls. A popular eighteenth-century anthology, *Collection of English Prose and Verse*, captured the religious terrors that had become increasingly common. One contributor agonized over "the vast uncertainty I am struggling with . . . the force and vivacity of my apprehensions; every doubt wears the face of horror, and would perfectly overwhelm me, but for some faint gleams of hope, which dart across the tremendous gloom. What tongue can utter the anguish of a soul suspended between the extremes of infinite joy or eternal misery. . . . I tremble and shudder."[1]

When the waves of revivalism that originated in the Second Great Awakening of the early nineteenth century swept over the upstate New York of Joseph Smith's youth, he found himself, along with thousands of others, consumed by anxiety about the state of his soul. The new tradition founded by Martin Luther in sixteenth-century Europe had been born out of a similar worry. "My situation was that, although an impeccable monk, I stood before God as a sinner troubled in conscience, and I had no assurance that my merit would assuage him."[2]

A century before Joseph Smith, John Wesley wrote: "I felt that I did trust in Christ, Christ alone for salvation, and an assurance was given me, that he had taken away my sins, even mine, and saved me from the law of sin and death."[3] So too, in 1820, Joseph Smith was pursuing spiritual relief. As he recorded in his own hand, "at about the age of twelve years my mind become seriously imprest with regard to the all importent concerns for the wellfare of my immortal Soul . . . and I felt to mourn for my own sins and for the sins of the world. . . . therefore I cried unto the Lord for mercy for there was none else to whom I could go and to obtain mercy and the Lord heard my cry in the wilderness."[4] The founding of the church was still a decade away, but a combination of historical developments in Protestant thought, the immediate catalyst of revivalism, and his own spiritual insecurities led Smith to his first encounter with heavenly beings and set him on the path toward the founding of a new religious tradition.

What was the First Vision?

Young Joseph Smith grew up in an environment rife with vigorous religious evangelization. Like thousands of his contemporaries, he struggled to discern a true path amid the conflicting claims of the Protestant world around him. Struck by the passage in the New Testament book of James that encouraged the spiritually bewildered to seek wisdom through prayer, Smith did so in an isolated wood near his home in upstate New York. On that spring 1820 morning, as he would only relate to a public audience years later in one of several accounts he gave, he experienced a heavenly visitation, or vision, of God and Jesus Christ. When the Father and the Son appeared to him, his principal objective was to receive an assurance of his own standing before God. In that vision, Jesus Christ told Smith that his sins were forgiven. This personal experience of God's healing love and forgiveness affected him deeply. In this regard, his experience mirrored that of many others who received through personal intimations or dreams or visions the "assurance" they so desired. Smith's experience was an intensely personal one, which he at first did not even share with his family.

During this divine visitation, he learned that the world was mired in sin, a revelation that he would later elaborate into the doctrine of Christian apostasy—the belief that churches had diverged greatly from the teachings and practices of earliest Christianity. He received only the vaguest allusion to future events in which he might have a role. The Lord said he would soon "bring to pass that which hath been spoken by the mouth of the prophets and apostles."[5] For the present, however, Smith clearly experienced the event as a divine encounter of purely personal import.

Finally, Smith gained personal experience of the reality and power of petitionary prayer, of God and Christ's physically incarnate form, and of their existence as distinct, divine beings. It was only with the advantage of hindsight that Smith's 1820 vision was seen by members to launch a new era and the foundations of a church. For some years he continued to understand the vision as largely personal. Years later, he dated the commencement of his ministry to the 1827 recovery of the gold plates leading to the Book of Mormon, not to his 1820 theophany.

Why did Smith write differing accounts of his First Vision?

In the summer of 1832, Smith dictated his first history. At the time, his followers were few and his impact on the national scene negligible. The church's experience of religious intolerance was limited to a few skeptical ministers and mocking neighbors, though in one vicious attack Smith had been tarred and feathered earlier that year. Smith initially considered the First Vision to be a private, personal conversion experience and not directly relevant to the institutional history of the church.

Mere months after Smith produced the brief 1832 history, the world of the Latter-day Saints tipped upside down. In April 1833, a mob of three hundred assembled to demand the expulsion of Mormons from Jackson County, Missouri—the site of the Saints' first presumed New Jerusalem. By 1836, the immigration of thousands more Latter-day Saints created tensions and fears, and opponents forced them to flee northward again to Caldwell County and other places of refuge. In 1837, bank failure back in Kirtland, Ohio, along with other factors, precipitated large-scale hostility toward Smith, who fled for his life with the dawning new year. When he joined the Saints in Far West, Missouri, he found the nightmare scenario of exile about to repeat itself.

At the same time, LDS membership had exploded to nearly twenty thousand. Mission work had spread to Canada and across the Atlantic to the British Isles. The movement founded by Smith had grown from a local phenomenon to an aspiring and hotly controversial player on the international religious scene. Recent history as well as public debate gave new meaning to his earliest vision: it was no longer a conversion narrative of merely personal significance; it had become the de facto basis of his claim to authority and the foundation for his teaching that only a divine restoration could remedy a universal apostasy.

In his new account of the experience, however, are found the same four key elements that were the core of his original 1832 narrative: personal spiritual turmoil, a quest for religious truth, divine assurance of a generalized apostasy, and an intimation of some kind of coming restoration. In his 1832 version, he was (1) concerned "for the welfare of [his] immortal soul"; (2) "search[ed] the scriptures" for direction; (3) felt the Christianity of his day "had apostatized from the true and living faith"; and (4) learned "none doeth good no not one they have turned asside from the gospel." He was promised the Lord would "bring to pass that which hath been spoken by the mouth of the prophets and Apostles."[6]

In the greatly expanded 1838 version, he repeats these points with more background and elaboration: he says that (1) his mind was being "called up to serious reflection and great uneasiness"; (2) he struggled to "come to any certain conclusion who was right and who was wrong" and searched the Bible for guidance; (3) he wondered if the entire Christian world was "all wrong together" and had determined that all their creeds were based not on true doctrines but "the commandments of men"; and (4) he was directed to remain aloof from the churches that existed, with instructions "which I cannot write at this time."[7]

In the 1832 account, he mentions "the Lord" appearing and then "the Lord" addressing him; in 1838, he indicates that the Father appeared and introduced the Son as he did in the New Testament account of Christ's baptism. Some observers see here a disturbing contradiction: did one or two personages appear? Latter-day Saints scholars suggest that either the first account is referring to two beings, using the same designation of "Lord," or, given his 1832 emphasis on his personal quest for salvational assurance, the joyful words of the Savior, "thy sins are forgiven thee," eclipsed any mention of the Father's presence.

In any event, by 1838, Smith was complaining of "the many reports which have been put in circulation by evil disposed and designing persons in relation to the rise and progress of the Church of Latter day Saints." The second, more detailed narrative was meant to provide a firmer foundation for his divine calling and authority to inaugurate a new era in Christian history. It would be canonized as scripture in 1880. Given the widely varying historical circumstances, purposes, and dates of composition, perfect consistency might be grounds for more suspicion than the divergences of the several accounts.

Is there more than one "Mormonism"?

Frequently on the death of a great leader the institution he or she founded splinters. This has been true of military leaders like Alexander the Great and Genghis Khan and religious figures like Mohammed—and Joseph Smith. During Smith's lifetime, his charismatic leadership was sufficient to forestall successful schisms. However, on his death he left mixed signals about a successor—or a process for selecting a successor. Several claimants for the position emerged.

Weeks after Smith's death, a public meeting was convened in Nauvoo to decide the succession question. No one presumed to fill Joseph Smith's shoes or inherit his title of Prophet. Sidney Rigdon, the church's most powerful orator, stood and claimed the right to serve the church as "guardian." That afternoon, Brigham Young arose and asked the throng of thousands if they wished to choose a prophet or a guardian. When no support emerged, Young declared that Smith had conveyed to the Quorum of the Twelve Apostles the authority (or "keys of the kingdom") to preside over the church and promised to build on the foundation Smith had laid. Smith had, in fact, declared that quorum equal in authority to the presidency of the church, so Young's position as head of that quorum suggested to most Latter-day Saints that he possessed the authority to succeed Smith. In later narratives of the occasion, many who had been in the audience claimed that Young had been transfigured as he spoke, in voice and person, into the likeness of Joseph Smith. Rigdon declined an opportunity to speak further, and the assembly voted overwhelmingly to support Young and the Quorum of the Twelve Apostles.

Brigham Young had several advantages going into the Nauvoo public meeting that August, but principal among them was his combination of on-scene presence and steadfast prominence in church service. Rigdon had once shared comparable stature but had been publicly disavowed by Joseph Smith almost a year earlier. For years Smith had questioned Rigdon's loyalty to him and his commitment to the growing church. In the aftermath of the 1844 public meeting, a number of other claimants began to emerge. Young's strained relations with the prophet's wife, Emma, and his support for the unpopular and guarded practice of polygamy were two strikes against him. The Smith name, claims to angelic calling, public opposition to plural marriage, and purported letters and blessings given personally by Joseph Smith were all reasons advanced by one or more claimants to challenge Young's right to leadership.

The most successful challenge to Brigham Young initially came from James Strang, a recent convert who could claim formidable support for his position. He had a letter of appointment he said was in Joseph Smith's hand, claimed angelic visitations as confirmation of his calling, and had a scriptural record that (like Smith's Book of Mormon) he claimed to have translated, and within a short time a press to promulgate his message. He would go on to form his own church, move his followers to Michigan, and practice plural marriage. He was eventually murdered by some estranged disciples. By the end of the twentieth century there were fewer than three hundred remaining Strangites.

The most numerically successful challenge, which survives to this day, was the Reorganized Church of Jesus Christ of Latter Day Saints (which became the Community of Christ in 2001). It coalesced in 1860 around Joseph Smith's son, Joseph Smith III, out of several scattered groups that had earlier rejected Young's leadership, along with the practice of polygamy. In recent years, the Community of Christ has deemphasized Smith's visions and revelations, rejected a male-only priesthood and the temple theology that dominated Smith's late thought, and in general moved much closer to liberal Protestantism. The denomination now numbers a few hundred thousand.

A myriad other restoration groups have claimed descent from Joseph Smith's teachings and authority. Most have been of short duration, and hardly any now have more than a few hundred followers, except for a number of modern polygamous groups that have no connection to the Salt Lake–based church. The fluidity, evanescence, and obscurity of some of these descendant churches make it impossible to give an exact number; some scholars say there were "fifteen important groups" and over four hundred in total.[8] The seeds for their vitality—as well as their fragmentation—were planted early on, with Joseph Smith's affirmation of continuing "direct revelation" from God as the hallmark of the "Restoration."

Modern polygamous sects aside, the Church of Jesus Christ of Latter-day Saints is the only Smithian tradition of significant size or influence that maintains a steadfast fidelity to Smith's theological contributions, so this book takes that organization as its subject.

Why were the Saints persecuted?

Opposition to Latter-day Saints took different forms, at different times, for different reasons. The circumstances could be complicated, but two issues were critical. The first was "gathering." Mere months after the church was founded, in September 1831, Smith had produced a revelation in which the Lord told him he was "called to bring to pass the gathering of mine elect" (Doctrine and Covenants [hereafter D&C] 9:11). Seeing evangelization as the gathering of God's chosen people, or spiritual Israel, was a Christian commonplace. For Smith, however, gathering meant the actual physical congregating of all converts into a particular place (initially Kirtland, Ohio, but soon thereafter Independence, Missouri, followed in turn by subsequent locations). Within a short time, thousands of Latter-day Saint converts poured into hitherto sparsely populated areas in Missouri, completely upsetting the political and social status quo. The Saints tended to conduct commerce with each other and vote as a block. In addition, they referred to the lands round about as their spiritual inheritance and to Native Americans as divinely favored people of the covenant. The Saints followed a prophet who wielded a degree of authority completely at odds with democratic institutions and a Jacksonian populist sensibility. Finally, they made extravagant religious claims involving angels, gold plates, spiritual gifts, and their own chosen status. These factors were more than sufficient to explain suspicion, hostility, and the eruption of violence in Jackson County in 1833. The Saints fled to other counties, where the cycle repeated itself twice more, culminating in violence at a polling station on Election Day at Gallatin, Missouri, in 1838. Recent research has demonstrated that many in the mob that forcibly expelled the Mormons from their Missouri settlements in the final phase of the "Missouri Wars" did so at least in part out of financial motivation, working frantically to take over land before the LDS settlers would qualify for ownership by way of preemption rights.

Another wave of persecution broke out a few years later in Nauvoo, Illinois, where the Saints had taken refuge. They had resettled on some fetid marshland in a town originally named Commerce and transformed the place into a beautiful, thriving, and populous city of over ten thousand. Amicable relations with neighbors broke down over some of the Missouri issues, but with new developments. Smith led a legal but flamboyantly conspicuous militia of thousands called the Nauvoo Legion. The Saints dominated the legal system in the city and were accused of protecting their own members from legitimate prosecution. Outsiders gained the impression that Latter-day

Saints considered themselves above the law. And when Smith ran for the American presidency in the election of 1844, his action (which may have been a tactic to acquire a more prominent platform to seek redress for past persecutions) was interpreted by many observers as an expression of megalomania and a dangerous blending of religion and political aspiration. Two final, fatal factors were rumors of a practice of "spiritual wifery" or polygamy among the LDS elite, and Smith's decision to destroy, under cover of a city council mandate, the press that was exposing the practice to the public and attacking the church's leadership. Smith was arrested, a mob formed, and days later he and his brother Hyrum were murdered. In the months following, the Saints fled continuing harassment and an actual militia bombardment for Iowa and then Utah Territory. The practice of polygamy, publicly acknowledged in 1852, would thereafter prove the central source of friction, alienation, and eventual disfranchisement of the LDS people.

What was the Hawn's Mill Massacre?

By 1838, the Saints were involved in the final and most violent phase of the "Missouri Wars." They had been expelled from Jackson County in 1833 and moved into Clay and Ray counties. Three years later, in a mass meeting held in June 1836, the citizens of Clay County demanded the Saints' ouster from the area. Again they moved north, into the new county of Caldwell—designated by the state legislature to accommodate them—and neighboring Daviess County. The church grew rapidly in the next few years, and most converts headed to northern Missouri. By 1838, the LDS population of Caldwell County reached five thousand, with a few thousand more in Daviess and elsewhere. Far West, in Caldwell County, became the church's new commercial and ecclesiastical center, soon boasting 150 permanent homes, seven grocery and dry goods stores, hotels, blacksmith shops, a printing shop, and a schoolhouse. And more converts were pouring in daily.

All the old conflicts now reappeared: old settlers were alarmed by the huge influx of strangers who were clannish, spoke of themselves as a chosen people, evangelized the Native Americans, revered a man as a prophet, and made outlandish claims about gold plates, angelic visitations, gifts of healing, and speaking in tongues. Tensions finally erupted in Election Day violence twenty miles to the north in Gallatin, Daviess County, in August 1838, when locals tried to prevent Latter-day Saints from voting. Days later Saints were ordered out of nearby Carroll County to the southeast. In October, hundreds of vigilantes forcibly evicted the Carroll Saints from five other counties to which they had fled. Latter-day Saints retaliated by attacking Gallatin and another village and expelling non-Mormons from Daviess. A skirmish at Crooked River left four dead, including one church apostle (David Patten), and reports of LDS depredations further inflamed tensions. Governor Lilburn Boggs, taking at face value reports that the Latter-day Saints were the aggressors in the conflict, responded with his infamous order of extermination on October 27. Directed to General John B. Clark of the Missouri Militia, it read in part: "the Mormons must be treated as enemies and must be exterminated or driven from the state. . . . Their outrages are beyond all description. If you can increase your force, you are authorized to do so, to any extent you may think necessary. . . . You will proceed immediately to Richmond and there operate against the Mormons." Three days later, before the order had even reached them, two hundred militia rode into Hawn's Mill, an LDS settlement along Shoal Creek in northeastern Caldwell County. The women fled to the woods with children, while the men retreated into a blacksmith shop. In a matter of minutes, the militia had shot and hacked to death eighteen men and boys. The next day, Clark surrounded Far West with thousands more militia and demanded the surrender of the Saints. Smith and other leaders gave themselves up, and their thousands of followers fled the state as religious refugees, finding a new home across the river in Illinois. This episode marked the beginning of the end for the Saints' hope to establish their Missouri Zion of prophecy during their lifetimes. The massacre was indelibly imprinted in LDS memory not just as a tragic loss of life but as an egregious state-sanctioned violation of their rights, never to find redress.

What was the Mountain Meadows Massacre?

Within a year of LDS leaders' public acknowledgment of the practice of polygamy in 1852, a moral crusade against the church by American preachers, politicians, and prominent figures quickly gained steam. The public was alternately enthralled and enraged, displaying an uneasy mix of prurient interest and righteous indignation. In 1856, the newly created Republican Party organized their platform by tying the issue of slavery to polygamy and promising eradication of those "twin relics of barbarism." The next year three federally appointed judges, feeling insulted and rebuffed in their efforts to exercise authority in Utah, returned to Washington and complained that the territory was in a state of virtual rebellion, instigated by the despotic Brigham Young. Coming soon after Washington received reports of LDS intransigence and disloyalty from a thwarted surveyor general and suspicious Indian agents, these allegations convinced President James Buchanan that federal intervention was called for. So it was that in July 1857, Buchanan ordered a federal army of 2,500 to enter the territory, seat a new governor in place of Brigham Young (Alfred Cumming, former mayor of Augusta, Georgia), and restore order.

As the troops marched westward, LDS raiders harassed them, torching grazing land, scattering the army's cattle, blocking routes, burning baggage trains, and otherwise impeding their progress. The strategy worked, and the army, now under the command of Colonel Albert Sidney Johnston, was forced to winter well short of Salt Lake Valley, at the charred site of Fort Bridger, which the Latter-day Saints (having earlier purchased it) had burned. They succeeded in bringing the troops to short rations, while avoiding actual bloodshed. The troops settled into winter quarters as the crisis simmered on. The next spring, Johnston was still intent on occupying Salt Lake City so as to humble the Saints, avenge his army's humiliation, and establish incontestable federal control. Knowing the futility of continued resistance to American troops, Young had one drastic option he was willing to consider. "President Young preached yesterday at the Tabernacle," recorded a contemporary who had weathered the eastern persecutions, "that he thought it best to move southward and if the United States were determined to send their army into the Valley without some treaty, or agreement, we would burn our houses, cut down our orchards and make the country as desolate as it was when we came here. He then called for a vote of the congregation. They all voted aye."

Thousands of refugees were soon moving southward to Provo, although the they did not burn their property behind them. Further conflict was narrowly avoided, in part by the timely intervention of skilled negotiator and friend-to-the-Saints Colonel Thomas Kane. Governor Cumming entered Salt Lake City, assumed his post, and discovered—probably to his surprise—not a mutinous horde of barbarians but a handful of respectful and decent people justly in fear for their peace and safety. With Cumming's report in hand, President Buchanan declared an amnesty. The army made a token pass through the mostly deserted city and then retired to a discreet distance, where they established Camp Floyd. The whole affair eventually wound down—but the tension and paranoia had precipitated what would become the darkest chapter in the Latter-day Saint saga.

At the height of this conflict, known as the "Utah War," in early September, the Baker-Fancher wagon train, a group of Arkansas and Missouri emigrants, headed for California. As they journeyed from Salt Lake through central and southern Utah with several hundred head of cattle, tensions arose over grazing and water sources. Rumors soon circulated that they had poisoned a well; possibly their cattle had spread anthrax they had recently contracted. Following verbal clashes in the southern Utah town of Cedar City, some in the company boasted of complicity in the Missouri atrocities against the Saints or of participation in the murder of Joseph Smith and his brother. The complex mix of wartime tensions, wounds of the past, and bad judgment all around ended in a massacre of the emigrant train by local Mormons, aided by some Native Americans. Seventeen young children were spared, but no one old enough to tell the tale survived—some 120 were killed. Prominent LDS leader John D. Lee was eventually tried and executed by federal authorities for the crime. (A few other leaders faced church discipline.) Suspicion long lingered with respect to Brigham Young's complicity, but the relevant sources point to only local LDS authorities as orchestrating the atrocity.

The Mountain Meadows Massacre, as it came to be known, was the darkest tragedy of Latter-day Saint history. It was often invoked as evidence that the Saints were a violent, bloodthirsty people. In reality, a perfect storm of events brought it about, and nothing like it ever happened again. In recent years, the church has sought reconciliation with the descendants of the Baker-Fancher wagon train by erecting a monument on the site of the massacre and publicly apologizing for this atrocity.

What was the role of folk magic in the life of the young Joseph Smith?

Cultural historians recognize the pervasiveness in nineteenth-century America of superstitious beliefs and practices that to a modern audience seem to comport strangely with Christian religiosity. Divining (or dowsing) rods were employed to find water, peep stones or seer stones were placed in hats and prompted visions of lost objects, and belief in angels, devils, and guardian spirits who watched over buried treasure was widespread. A historian of the period writes: "many Americans resorted to various forms of folk magic in expressing their religious beliefs . . . and nothing in their occult practices was regarded as contrary to accepted Christian values."[9] That culture, combined with ubiquitous reports of lost mines and buried treasure, fueled a common practice of "money-digging," in which all classes except the most intellectually progressive seem to have engaged. To this day there can be found on farms in upstate New York humanmade depressions that locals refer to as "Winchell holes," the traces of searches carried out by a nineteenth-century money-digger from Vermont.

Some historians have pointed to this context as an explanation for Smith's story involving angels, buried gold plates, and the seer stones he employed to translate them. Hostile neighbors would later testify that he had used one such seer stone in nocturnal rituals aimed at retrieving buried gold and silver. Smith did not deny having acted as a money-digger, but he insisted that he engaged in the pursuit only sporadically, reluctantly, and temporarily. In October 1825, the entreaties of wealthy farmer Josiah Stowell, together with the Smith family's poverty, led Smith to accept an offer of employment digging for a lost silver mine. He and his mother would both complain in later years that this brief employment was the real source of Joseph's reputation as a money-digger. Smith found little to be embarrassed about in what was not unusual for that time and place and readily acknowledged his past forays into the practice with frank humor. Publishing a list of questions he was commonly asked, together with his answers, he included this very topic. "Was not Jo Smith a money digger? Yes, but it was never a very profitable job to him, as he only got fourteen dollars a month for it."[10]

Why did Joseph Smith run for president of the United States?

Throughout much of the decade subsequent to the founding of their church in 1830 and later relocation to Missouri, the Latter-day Saints had experienced some of the severest religious persecution in American history. Quakers had been hanged by

Puritans in Massachusetts, Baptists had been imprisoned in Virginia, and Catholics had been victims of riots and convent burnings in Charlestown, Massachusetts. None of those cases matched the scale of the orchestrated campaigns against the Latter-day Saints. Mob action forced the LDS populace from Jackson County in 1833 and from Clay County, where they had sought refuge, a few years later. After they resettled in Caldwell and Daviess counties in 1836, the conflict repeated itself and then escalated to pogroms and armed conflict. In 1838, the governor issued an extermination order, and thousands of militia descended on LDS settlements to enforce it. Smith and other leaders were arrested and sentenced to be executed by firing squad, though the order was protested by brigadier Alexander Doniphan and not carried out. They were then imprisoned in Liberty, Missouri, during the winter of 1838–1839.

Months later the authorities allowed Smith to escape custody, and the Saints regrouped in Illinois. Over the ensuing years, Smith would lead efforts to gain redress for the massive losses of property (not to mention life) his followers had experienced at the hand of Missourians. In 1839, a delegation to Washington led by Smith was told by President Martin Van Buren: "your cause is just, but I can do nothing for you." Anticipating the next presidential election cycle, Smith sent letters to the five leading candidates—John Calhoun, Lewis Cass, Richard Johnson, Henry Clay, and Martin Van Buren—asking what their policy toward the Mormons would be. Only Calhoun, Cass, and Clay responded, and none gave an encouraging reply. This was the context for Smith's 1844 decision, made in consultation with the apostles, to run for president on an independent platform. He would not have done so, he said, if other means of safeguarding the Saints' religious and civil liberties had been available to him.

At the time, the move seemed enlightened. His candidacy would draw national attention to the Mormon cause, serve as occasion to highlight their mistreatment and persecution, and provide opportunities for zealous missionaries to promote his candidacy and the gospel simultaneously. Hundreds of missionaries, as well as most of the Quorum of the Twelve Apostles, fanned out across the country to canvass. A newly formed party, the Reform Party, held a convention in May. Delegates from all twenty-six states attended, and Sidney Rigdon was confirmed as Smith's running mate. A statement of the party platform, *Views of the Powers and Policy of the Government of the United States,* was published. Perhaps Smith's most significant proposal was compensated emancipation of slaves by 1850 (to be financed in part by reducing congressional pay). He also advocated a national bank, open borders, and prison reforms. His campaign gained more traction and favorable press than expected; the vehement opposition it attracted was not as unexpected. Smith's murder in June ended Latter-day Saints' hopes of any political solution to their travails.

Why was Joseph Smith murdered?

From the moment of the church's organization, the Latter-day Saints encountered opposition. Some of the hostility was purely religious in nature (religious persecution has long been a feature of the American experience). Latter-day Saints contributed to the problem with their rhetoric of exceptionalism and claims that Missouri was their promised land. Their abolitionist sympathies, economic clannishness, and rapid overturning of political demographics added fuel to the fire; gathering by the thousands, they achieved local political hegemony almost overnight. As the reputed author of the Book of Mormon, the source of the movement's numerous revelations, and the church's founder and prophet, Joseph Smith was the most conspicuous embodiment of the movement, and he was the target of increasing fury from pulpit and paper.

By the 1840s, an additional set of circumstances set the stage for Smith's murder. In an attempt to restore ancient biblical religious observances, including plural marriage—practiced by

Abraham, Jacob, David, Solomon, and others—sometime in the 1830s Smith began to take plural wives. Smith revealed the practice only to a small inner circle. However, rumors quickly spread, outraging the public and alarming even his devoted followers. After expulsion from Missouri, the Saints acquired unusual legal privileges associated with the establishment of their new gathering place in Nauvoo, Illinois. They ran their own law courts, and they were authorized to raise their own militia (as did many communities at the time). Most inflaming was their right of habeas corpus, permitting Nauvoo courts to assess the legitimacy of an external warrant against Joseph Smith (or any local citizen). The Nauvoo Legion regularly drilled with great public fanfare and in numbers that many deemed threatening and inconsistent with purely religious aspirations. The milita's ranks swelled to a third the size of the federal army, and their drills and mock battles drew audiences of several thousand.

When Smith announced his candidacy for the presidency of the United States in the 1844 election, he lent credibility to those who alleged he was not just a religious fanatic but a megalomaniac. His motivation may have been to find a national platform to draw attention to the past abuses of the LDS people, but combined with his religious authority, his position as mayor of Nauvoo, chief justice of the Nauvoo Municipal Court, and lieutenant general of a thousands-strong militia, it was easy to construct a narrative that judged him a threat to democratic values.

The last ingredients in the tragedy fell into place in the summer of 1844. Convinced that polygamy was equivalent to indecency, a group of dissidents initiated a hostile newspaper, the *Nauvoo Expositor*, in the city of that name. The city council, with Smith presiding as mayor, declared the paper a public nuisance and ordered the press destroyed. The question of legality aside, it was the worst conceivable public relations misstep, and the immediate outcry was furious. Within days, Smith had been arrested and jailed in Carthage, a few miles from Nauvoo. With the prophet temporarily beyond the protection of faithful supporters and the powerful Nauvoo Legion, on the evening of June 27, 1844, a mob of a hundred men with painted faces stormed the cell where Joseph and three others were held. When the smoke cleared, Joseph and his brother, Hyrum, the prophet and the church patriarch, were dead.

Was Joseph Smith crowned king before he died?

In the spring of 1844, Joseph Smith created a secret civic organization called the Council of Fifty. Some mystery remains as to the exact nature and purpose of the group, even after the recent publication by the church of the council's minutes. What does emerge clearly from the minutes is the general sense among Latter-day Saints of the Savior's imminent Second Coming and the urgency of making appropriate provisions in the realm of political governance. Indications are that the men saw their task as the creation of a kind of template for a government that would assume authority at the time of Christ's advent. Significantly, and in harmony with Smith's public professions of respect for all religions, he included some non-Mormons in the council, signifying that the millennial kingdom would have place for all faiths. At the same time, Smith had in mind an LDS exodus from the United States and the establishment of an independent commonwealth somewhere to the west. Oregon, Vancouver Island, and Texas were all considered at one time or another. Smith's candidacy for president was also a topic of discussion, and the group served as a kind of coordinating council for that endeavor.

At one point in a council meeting, Erastus Snow moved that the council "receive . . . Joseph Smith, as our Prophet, Priest & King."[11] The motion was approved unanimously. No real change in Smith's authority or prerogatives seems to have been the point. The resolution is most reasonably interpreted as intended as a recognition of Smith's spiritual preeminence as the presiding priesthood authority of the dispensation. The titles "king" and "queen" featured in temple rituals Smith had recently implemented and were evocative of biblical promises of joint heirship with Christ, and the words in the Revelation to John, about being made "unto our God kings and priests [who] shall reign on earth" (5:10). Nothing in the minutes or in Smith's place in the church thereafter suggested that the resolution had any more than ritual significance.

What was the Latter-day Saints' response to the Civil War?

Relations between the Latter-day Saints and the US government were never good through most of the nineteenth century. President Martin Van Buren refused to intervene on behalf of the Latter-day Saints after their 1838 expulsion from Missouri, along with the theft of all their goods and properties. After Joseph Smith's 1844 murder, they were forcibly evicted from Nauvoo, Illinois. Given recent history, they found entirely credible the rumors that federal troops were preparing to attack them before their planned exodus; hence their precipitous winter departure in 1846. Fleeing the United States, they arrived in Utah just as the Mexican War was resulting in that territory's incorporation into the country they had hoped to escape. For some years, the federal government largely ignored the Saints. About a decade after settlement, three federally appointed judges complained to Washington that the territory was resistant to federal authority. Added to other reports of misconduct and resistance to federal sovereignty, their complaint convinced President Buchanan that federal intervention was called for. So it was that in July 1857, Buchanan ordered a federal army of 2,500 to invade the territory, seat a new governor, and restore order.

No blood was shed, but armed conflict was only narrowly avoided, largely due to the timely intervention of wise mediators. When the Civil War broke out a few years later, the largest federal military group in the army was in Utah, two thousand miles away from the action. In the immediate aftermath of the conflicts the Latter-Day Saints had experienced, which had included expulsion from the slave state of Missouri and invasion by a federal army, it is no surprise that members of the church were quite happy to stay on the sidelines and watch the two sections of country attack one another instead of them. Young refused to raise troops to support the Union but stopped short of treason; LDS teachings affirmed the inspiration behind the Constitution and the providential role assigned the United States, however corrupt or uninspired recent administrations had been. When Abraham Lincoln asked for Young's assistance in guarding federal mail routes, he agreed. (However, he refused to permit the company raised for the purpose to serve outside the region.) Lincoln's policy of benign neglect toward the Latter-day Saints probably won many hearts. When asked what he would do about the Mormon problem, he reportedly responded by comparing them to a fallen log in a farmer's field. Sometimes, he said, it's easier to just plow around it.

In spite of official indifference, individual members fought on both sides of the Civil War. Most American Latter-day Saints came from the North, and so most of the church's combatants enlisted in the Union army.

3
POLYGAMY

Why did the Latter-day Saints practice polygamy?

Joseph Smith never left a record of his thoughts on the origin of a practice that Latter-day Saints called plural marriage, celestial marriage, or "the principle." Nor did he ever present to his people or to an incredulous world a rationale for the practice. It seems clear, however, that Smith was unlike other restorationists (like Barton Stone Thomas and Alexander Campbell) in his belief that both New and Old Testament forms and practices needed to be restored, in a great synthesis he called the New and Everlasting Covenant. Smith called bishops and twelve apostles, practiced immersive baptism and the laying on of hands for the gift of the Holy Ghost, and emphasized spiritual gifts of healing, tongues, and prophesying. But he also restored a priesthood of Aaron and of Melchizedek, established the offices of patriarch and high priest, and instituted temples and temple worship as a centerpiece of the faith. Plural marriage was also an Old Testament practice, as Smith would have been reminded when he worked through his revision of the Old Testament shortly after translating the Book of Mormon. He apparently inquired about the practice, in order "to know and understand wherein I, the Lord, justified my servants Abraham, Isaac, and Jacob, as also Moses, David and Solomon, my servants, as touching the principle and doctrine of their having many wives" (D&C 132:1).

The explanation Smith received was neither clear nor straightforward, and he did not record it until 1843, but it indicated that the Old Testament figures who married multiple wives "in nothing [sinned] save in those things which they received not of me" (D&C 132:38). Smith believed that he was commanded to enter into the practice himself, and he did so a number of times, probably beginning in the mid-1830s. It would be another decade, however, before he regularized the practice with special rites and began to teach the principle to a trusted inner circle.

DNA testing has failed to verify a single descendant of a polygamous liaison involving Joseph Smith, suggesting that sexual relations were either not central to the purposes of polygamy as he understood them or were inhibited by the need for secrecy. In any case, a kind of dynastic, or kin-building, enterprise, rather than unions for purposes of procreation, seemed to be the point. It is clear that a prime motivation for Smith was the promise of eternal relationships that included more than marital relationships.

All this changed under Brigham Young, who made the practice more general among the membership, although only men deemed worthy and financially able were allowed to take plural wives. The leadership strictly regulated the practice. Estimates vary, but it would appear that at the practice's height, half the LDS population in Utah (polygamy wasn't practiced by Saints in other locations) had had experience in a polygamous family as a child, parent, or spouse. Popular depictions to the contrary, by far the most common number of wives was two.

In the absence of scriptural rationale (rather than simple precedent) for plural marriage, various folk theologies developed. One was that, given LDS belief in the premortal existence of human spirits, there is a finite quantity of human souls. Plurality afforded opportunities to raise in a gospel-rich environment more of these spirits, who would otherwise go to nonmember households (the Book of Mormon contains the instruction to "raise up seed unto me"; Jacob 2:30). Another was the belief that plurality required the suppression of selfishness and possessiveness, demanding the kind of purity of heart and mind necessary to spiritual growth and sanctification. Some female defenders of the right to practice plural marriage, however, likened it to an Abrahamic test—an emotional ordeal from which one hoped for respite in the eternal worlds. The church itself never proffered an official explanation for the practice other than that God commanded it.

What did Latter-day Saint women think about polygamy?

Those who have immersed themselves in the diaries of polygamous wives come away with one striking constant: the majority of women engaged in the practice of plural marriage found living "the principle" an agony rather than a joy. So vocal and widespread was female discontent that Brigham Young repeatedly addressed it in his public sermons. On one occasion, an exasperated Young told the congregation:

> now for my proposition; it is more particularly for my sisters, as it is frequently happening that women say they are unhappy. Men will say, "My wife, though a most excellent woman, has not seen a happy day since I took my second wife," "No, not a happy day for a year," says one; and another has not seen a happy day for five years. . . . I wish . . . all the women of this community . . . [to] determine whether you wish to stay with your husbands or not, and then I am going to set every woman at liberty and say to them, Now go your way, my women with the rest, go your way. Sisters, I am not joking. . . . I know that there is no cessation to the everlasting whining of many of the women in this territory.[1]

Divorce was readily available, and many plural wives did in fact legally separate from their husbands. Another incitement to separate was Young's reported statement that to persist in a plural marriage where attachment was missing was to practice fornication.[2]

Why did so many women submit to a system they found heart-wrenchingly painful? Two principal rationalizations appear in their writings. First, they saw the practice as a higher principle, a refiner's fire. Romania Pratt Penrose, an accomplished physician and plural wife, believed of the practice that "though it be a fiery furnace at some period in our life, it will prove the one thing needful to cleanse and purify our inmost soul of selfishness, jealousy, and other mundane attributes."[3] If marital love survived, it was not the love of Victorian companionate marriage, with two soul mates caught up in a unitary bond to the exclusion of all else. And if romantic love had to die in the process, as it did, it must be because a higher form of love awaited the faithful practitioners of plural marriage. "Their souls will be expanded, and in the place of selfishness, patience and charity will find place in their hearts," insisted one longtime plural wife.[4]

For others, the practice was an Abrahamic test, pure and simple. In the revelation that justified plural marriage, Smith had himself made the analogy to Abraham's willingness to sacrifice his son Isaac, and women frequently saw polygamy in such terms. "In obeying this law it has cost [us] a sacrifice nearly equal to that of Abraham. . . . There is nothing that would induce me to . . . lose my hold upon that crown which awaits all those who have laid their willing but bleeding hearts upon the altar," said one plural wife.[5] Young's second wife, Mary Ann, supposedly concurred: "God will be very cruel if he does not give us poor women adequate compensation for the trials we have endured in polygamy."[6]

Two other justifications appeared occasionally. Some women thought the practice was the LDS version of the "curse of Eve," though this line of thought was inconsistent with the valorization of Eve's decision to eat the forbidden fruit in both the Book of Mormon and the Pearl of Great Price. And others took Young at his word when he characterized plural marriage as requisite to the highest degree of salvation—though he later retreated from this doctrine.

Why did Latter-day Saint women rally in mass support of plural marriage?

Asked by Horace Greeley if the majority of women found the system acceptable, Brigham Young responded: "they could not be more averse to it than I was when it was first revealed."[7] And yet, although women privately recorded their struggles and difficulties with this trial of faith, they rallied publicly in overwhelming support for the principle when politicians and would-be liberators meddled.

In 1856, the Republican Party vowed to eradicate polygamy. The next year, a federal army marched on the Saints' latest place of refuge, in the Salt Lake Valley, and removed Young as territorial governor. Then, in 1869, the House of Representatives passed the Cullom Bill, the third federal legislative effort to punish the Saints for their unusual marriage practice. If approved by the Senate, it threatened to strip polygamists of their citizenship and civil rights.

Days after learning of this development, an LDS Relief Society president presided over a local protest meeting. The women published a resolution, expressing "indignation" at the government's attempts to "uproot every vestige of civil and religious liberty; [and] destroy the rights of conscience."[8] The next week, a larger women's "indignation meeting" was held in the Salt Lake Tabernacle and was attended by several thousand LDS women. They banned all males except members of the press and featured their most talented orators—including a woman widowed in the Missouri persecutions a few decades earlier.

Here we encounter again one of the most striking ironies of LDS history: LDS women, presumably in bondage to a patriarchally imposed system of marriage, holding public protests to maintain the right to a practice that most of them disdained to enter into. The irony is compounded when one learns that in this same era, as the suffrage movement swept the country, Utah led the nation in the number of members of the National American Woman Suffrage Association.

The members of Congress were not averse to allowing LDS women the right to vote, expecting that they would use their franchise to outlaw polygamy. The indignation meeting should have convinced them otherwise; it did not, and Utah women received the vote from the territorial legislature (with congressional approval) later in 1870 becoming the first women in the country to vote in a national election. As if in reproof for Utah women's failure to utilize their new power in accordance with Protestant norms and expectations, their suffrage was revoked in 1887. Polygamy was never an article of faith of the LDS Church, but religious freedom was. As the eleventh such article stated, "we claim the privilege of worshiping Almighty God according to the dictates of our own conscience, and allow all men the same privilege, let them worship how, where, or what they may." That was why LDS women—even committed monogamists—protested the national campaign against polygamy.

How did Latter-day Saint men feel about the practice of plural marriage?

Plural marriage was practiced as a consequence of a felt conviction among Latter-day Saints that God had commanded the practice as part of the "restoration" or "restitution of all things" prophesied by Peter (Acts 3:21) and inaugurated by Joseph Smith. Contrary to sensationalized accounts, plural marriage was not practiced by whim or personal initiative. Those whom Joseph Smith taught the doctrine and enjoined to live it generally did so, if at all, only after struggling with a fiercely ingrained monogamous morality. Brigham Young's famous remark may have been greeted with skepticism by outsiders, but countless diaries and letters of those engaged in "the practice" testify to the genuine anguish and discomfort they experienced. Young wrote: "some of these my brethren know what my feelings were at the time Joseph revealed the doctrine; I was not desirous of shrinking from any duty, nor of failing in the least to do as I was commanded—but it was the first time in my life that I had desired the grave, and I could hardly get over it for a long time. And when I saw a funeral, I felt to envy the corpse its situation."[9] His colleague and fellow apostle John Taylor echoed the feelings of countless others when he initially considered the practice "an appalling thing" which "nothing but . . . the revelations of God . . . could have induced me to embrace."[10] The financial and emotional burdens, not to mention the exposure to contempt and persecution entailed in plural marriage, and the marital politics surrounding jealousy and emotional insecurity seem to have made the practice unsatisfying to most Saints who entered the practice and unappealing to the Saints—a majority—who remained outside it. Certainly there would have been exceptions to pure intent, and the number of men who took much younger plural brides suggests that motives other than the highest spiritual principles were present as well.

Why did polygamy cease, and do Latter-day Saints believe that it will be practiced again here or in heaven?

Joseph Smith and the handful of others who practiced plural marriage in Nauvoo, Illinois, did so in secret. As the martyrdom of Joseph and Hyrum Smith demonstrated, discretion was a matter of personal and institutional survival. In the relative safety of Utah, however, Brigham Young had the apostle Orson Pratt make public announcement of the unorthodox practice, and LDS men and women both wrote and spoke forcefully in defense of their right to engage in it.

As a federal territory, however, Utah was under federal jurisdiction, and lawmakers moved quickly to suppress polygamy. In fact, the party platform of the first Republican convention, meeting in 1856, vowed to eliminate the "twin relics of barbarism," slavery, and polygamy. President Lincoln himself signed the first legislative assault in 1862, the Morrill Anti-Bigamy Act. In exchange for LDS neutrality in the Civil War, however, Lincoln declined to enforce the law. More drastic legislation followed the peace, the most severe of which was the Edmunds-Tucker Act of 1887, upheld in a momentous Supreme Court case in 1890. It disincorporated the church, abolished female LDS suffrage (which had passed in 1870), and required a more stringent voter registration oath.

Under these threats, the church's president, Wilford Woodruff, ordered the practice to cease. Skeptics find his revelation mandating the end of the practice suspiciously convenient, and some hardliners broke with the decision, sowing the seeds of schismatic fundamentalist groups who continue to practice polygamy to this day. Woodruff, however, insisted that the Lord had instructed him to desist, after revealing in a vision the alternative: "the confiscation and loss of all the Temples, and the stopping of all the ordinances therein, both for the living and the dead, and the imprisonment of the First Presidency and Twelve and the heads of families in the church, and the confiscation of personal property of the people (all of which of would put a stop to the practice in any case)."[11]

Initially, many Saints saw polygamy as an eternal principle, necessarily but temporarily suspended. Since the Saints believe that marriages performed while on earth by the appropriate authority will be recognized in heaven, the supposition was that plural wives in this life would expect to be plural wives to their husband in the next. At present, LDS scripture declares that "monogamy is God's standard for marriage" unless otherwise commanded but leaves matters in the world to come indeterminate (D&C Official Declaration 1). At the same time, LDS scripture describes heaven as consisting of "the same sociality which exists among us here, only it will be coupled with eternal glory" (D&C 130:2). In which case, it would appear, most or all heavenly marital relations will be monogamous.

Complicating the issue is the fact that even today, LDS men may be eternally "sealed" serially to more than one wife (after the death of the current spouse), suggesting that in fact the principle of plural marriage continues in force in the world to come. To many faithful LDS women, this is a source of no small pain and anxiety. A woman who loses her husband, by contrast, may marry again, but for "time only," not for "time and eternity." The consequence of all this is that a man may be eternally sealed in his lifetime to more than one wife; a woman in her lifetime can be eternally sealed to only one husband. The only exception is when eternal sealings are being performed vicariously for the dead. In that case, a deceased woman who had more than one husband (after the death of a first) *may* be posthumously sealed to both. Presumably, this is because absent knowledge of her sentiments, she is entitled to make the choice of her eternal companion for herself.

If all this sounds confusing, it is; Saints find some solace in the words of past president Spencer W. Kimball. He counseled a troubled widower in the 1970s by saying that "he did not know exactly how these relationships will be worked out, but he did know that through faithfulness all will be well."[12] A more recent church leader concurred in this sentiment: "we are not concerned about who will be sealed to whom. We simply trust in the Lord's wisdom and love and try to live righteously."[13]

True enough, perhaps. Still, it is clear that the church has not resolved, theologically, the dissonance between its emphatic focus on the reality and centrality of monogamous, heterosexual marriage and family relations as the core of heavenly society, on the one hand, and a stoutly defended polygamous theology of the past, on the other.

4

ORGANIZATION

How is the church organized?

One of the Articles of Faith (6) states: "we believe in the same organization that existed in the primitive church, namely apostles, prophets, pastors [bishops], teachers, evangelists [patriarchs], and so forth." The New Testament reveals only a few bare particulars about early church organization, however, and the modern LDS Church has grown in complexity and evolved according to need. That article of faith refers to a particular framework that is still the critical foundation of the LDS Church: leadership by prophets and apostles who have a God-given authority to preside over an earthly church, receiving inspiration to do so. At the head of the church stands Christ, with the president of the church as his effective mouthpiece and viceroy. That president, more commonly referred to as "the prophet," serves along with two counselors in what is called the First Presidency. They are ordained apostles and serve in the First Presidency until they die or are released, or until the president dies, at which point the First Presidency is dissolved.

Second in authority is the Quorum of Twelve Apostles, who are technically called and sustained by the church membership as "prophets, seers, and revelators." They have lifetime appointments and are presided over by a president of the quorum, who is appointed on the basis of seniority. Following next in the hierarchy are two Quorums of the Seventy, a First and a Second Quorum (which do not necessarily have seventy members; seventy is an office, not a number holding that office). Seventies in the First Quorum serve until age 70, while members of the Second Quorum serve for 3–5 years. A Presidency of the Seventy is a group of seven men chosen from both of these quorums who preside over all the quorums of seventy (eight a present).

Existing outside these quorums is another office, the presiding bishop. Together with his two counselors, the presiding bishop (with no fixed term) is primarily responsible for the temporal aspects of the church, overseeing buildings, commercial enterprises, properties, and the disposition of church tithing funds. All these men abandon their professions or businesses to serve full-time and receive a living allowance, which is not made public but is generally believed to be relatively modest.

All the aforementioned leaders are "General Authorities," meaning their authority is church-wide. Other leaders are appointed with particular geographical jurisdiction. Next in the hierarchy are additional quorums of seventy, composed of "Area Seventies," with stewardship over geographically defined regions of the church. They are directed by Area Presidencies filled by General Authority Seventies from the First and Second Quorums of Seventy. (Fifteen such areas divide up the church outside North America, and eight within.) They travel widely, train and supervise stakes, and administer other church business.

Areas are divided into stakes (equivalent to Catholic dioceses); each stake is presided over by a stake president (along with two counselors). Stakes are made up of local groupings of congregations (similar to Catholic parishes), usually eight to twelve, called wards. In addition to his two counselors, the stake president has a high council, consisting of a dozen men who assist and advise him. Each ward is served by a bishop and two counselors. (In places where member numbers are small, local units called branches have branch presidents.) Wards are generally small enough—generally about 150–200 persons—for their leaders to know their members intimately and for all members to have opportunities for service. Bishops are responsible for all the spiritual as well as temporal needs of the congregation. Bishops supervise welfare programs, preside over the meetings, provide counseling, and appoint (or "call") members to staff the numerous positions in the ward. They typically serve five or six years. Women preside over the women's organization (the Relief Society), the Young Women's Organization, and the youth program (the Primary) at both the stake and ward levels. Women also serve with church-wide authority, though in very limited numbers. At the global church level, they fill three presidencies: the Relief Society, the Young Women's Organization, and the Primary.

Why do the Saints have a lay clergy instead of a paid clergy?

The term "lay clergy" can refer to unordained, or unpaid, clergy. It can also connote nonprofessional or untrained clergy. All LDS leaders are ordained, none are professionally trained, and few are paid. At the highest echelons of church administration, General Authorities—LDS leaders with global jurisdiction and serving full-time—are remunerated at relatively modest levels (given their management of an organization of millions), according to credible estimates, since salaries are not public information. These "General Authorities" include the three members of the First Presidency, the Quorum of the Twelve Apostles, the First and Second Quorums of the Seventy, and the Presiding Bishopric, totaling a little over one hundred leaders in a church of some twelve to fifteen million. The vast majority of leaders serve at the local level as stake presidents and bishops (or pastors of single congregations of 100–600).

A principal advantage of a lay clergy is the elimination of the clergy–laity divide. All (male) members are personally invested in the welfare of the relevant unit because leadership rotates, and responsibilities to fill a term in a bishopric, stake presidency, or high council are abundant over one's lifetime. Members attend and worship with the understanding that almost all will be called on to serve in one capacity or another. In addition, the lay system means that virtually all local leaders come from within the congregations they serve, knowing the people and the local history intimately, rather than being imposed or hired in from outside as strangers.

The drawbacks, from the LDS point of view, are few. No professional clergy means no training in homiletics or theology or pastoral care. The first matters little, as sermonizing is not a principal function of the lay leadership. The second is of disputed value, since Latter-day Saints tend to be suspicious of theology, believing that doctrine is the province of prophets and apostles. And as for pastoral care, Latter-day Saints place their reliance on the spiritual gifts of discernment and inspiration, although few members (or leaders) would doubt that given the extent of counseling responsibilities, pertinent training would often be an asset. The church does have a social services agency, with professional counseling available to supplement that of the lay leaders.

How are Latter-day Saint leaders trained for the ministry?

The LDS Church is a peculiar mix of high church and low church features. Like high church traditions (Catholic and Anglican, for example), the LDS tradition emphasizes clerical authority, saving sacraments, and ritual. However, such ritual is largely confined to temple services. General Sunday worship is very low church, with young boys administering the Lord's Supper, no formal liturgy or readings, and a plain, simple, and unadorned worship environment. Preaching is rather informal, with sermons that are called "talks" and are delivered by men, women, and youth of the congregation.

The LDS Church was established in an age when most Americans were highly suspicious of clerical authority, and anti-Catholicism was widespread. "Priestcraft," or the undue exercise and abuse of clerical authority, was widely decried and condemned. And although the Saints themselves emphasized clerical—or priesthood—authority, that authority was widely disseminated among all males (excepting a post-1852 racial exclusion). As a consequence, there was no clerical class or group of leaders that was singled out or prepared for clerical service. It made no sense to establish schools or seminaries for leaders, if those leaders were believed to be called of God and generally served in temporary capacities.

The top leadership of the church—particularly the apostles and the prophet (longest serving apostle)—are an exception. They serve for life, while members of the First Quorum of Seventy generally serve until age seventy. But following the general rule for church service, they are called without regard for professional background or ministerial training (though the church obviously finds men with business and legal backgrounds useful for managing a multinational church/corporation). Would it not make sense for such a permanent group of leaders to be specially trained for their callings? Probably not. Their principal roles (in the case of the apostles) are to serve as "prophets, seers, and revelators." Personal receptivity to spiritual influences, rather than academic training, is the relevant criterion in that regard. In addition, "continuing revelation" and modern scripture, rather than theological expertise, is the engine behind doctrinal development. Most lifelong members in the church have attended four years of seminary in the sense of a daily course of instruction in scripture and church history undertaken in the high school years. Men (and increasingly women) typically serve a two-year (or eighteen-month) mission, further grounding them in scripture immersion and daily ministering. And with formal sermons unknown in the tradition (twice-yearly General Conference talks being the closest analogy), training in homiletics is deemed unnecessary (though the majority of talks would doubtless benefit from such training). Whatever training LDS leaders receive is generally by way of life experience or in-service training once called to the ministry.

What is a prophet? Is he infallible?

The senior leadership of the church, which includes the president, his (usually) two counselors, and the twelve members of the Quorum of the Twelve Apostles, are all sustained by the general church membership as "prophets, seers, and revelators," but the usual designation for all of them except the president is "apostle." Seership is associated in the Book of Mormon with the gift of bringing "hidden things . . . to light" (Mosiah 8:17), and Latter-day Saints understand revelation as a broad category ranging from inspired writing to actual discourse with heavenly beings. The three terms, in other words, have considerable overlap.

Initially, Joseph Smith was the only leader referred to as "the prophet," in recognition of his unique role in communing with God and angels, translating the Book of Mormon and other ancient texts, and receiving the dozens of revelations that constitute the bulk of the church's Doctrine and Covenants. Gradually, his successors as presidents of the church came to be referred to as "the prophet" during their administrations as well. This was not merely an added honorific; Latter-day Saints believe that an absolutely vital differentiator of their church from other denominations is the reality of continuing revelation, ongoing divine communication, between God and the leader of his church. The apostolic keys empower all holding that title to receive revelation appropriate to their stewardship; however, LDS scripture emphasizes that when it comes to communications that are authoritative for all members, "no one shall be appointed to receive commandments and revelations in this church excepting my servant Joseph Smith, Jun., for he receiveth them even as Moses" (D&C 28:2).

Much as Catholics believe in a papal authority and apostolic succession—the uninterrupted transmission of authority from the original apostles through the popes and bishops who succeed them—so do Latter-day Saints affirm one spiritual head of the church, whose authority derives directly from the original apostles and flows directly to his successors. A quorum of twelve, claiming their authority from Peter, James, and John, is perpetually maintained with the most senior apostle being the president. The comparison to Moses found in the scripture just quoted is apt, but inadequate. In Old Testament usage, the title "prophet" generally designates a spiritual gift associated with a particular vocation, which emphasizes moral instruction, chastisement, and guidance in the role of God's spokesman. The LDS Church's prophets serve in such a capacity, but the vocational designation has been transmuted in LDS usage into a particular office, and one whose paramount import in LDS thought is related to priesthood keys, or ecclesial and sacramental authority with the divine right to direct the affairs of the worldwide church. As LDS scripture states, "unto [the prophet] the kingdom, or in other words, the keys of the church have been given" (D&C 42:69). These keys, first mentioned by the Lord to Peter in Matthew's Gospel, are taken by Latter-day Saints to confer a God-ordained authority to preside over the Lord's church and administer (or supervise the administration of) all the sacraments of salvation. This authority, as it is for Catholics, is believed to be transmitted generationally by the principle of apostolic succession.

The prophet of the LDS Church is revered by the members, and his words carry immense weight and influence. A quip commonly heard among Latter-day Saints is that the Catholics claim that the pope is infallible but no Catholic believes that, and the Saints claim that their prophet is fallible but no Saint believes *that*. There is exaggeration in both parts: Catholics do not believe the pope is in himself infallible, and Latter-day Saints recognize that neither is their prophet. However, the jest reflects an LDS cultural expectation that the prophets seldom or never err. One early LDS prophet's words lend themselves to such an expectation: "the Lord will not permit the prophet to lead his people astray," said Wilford Woodruff.

Why does the church need a prophet today?

The term "prophet" encompasses a variety of roles and connotations, some more relevant to the LDS office than others. In the Old Testament, prophets are God-touched figures who speak under the influence of God's Holy Spirit, testifying, rebuking, warning, preaching, and occasionally predicting. The first section of the Doctrine and Covenants clearly situates prophets of the Church of Jesus Christ in that ancient tradition: "the voice of warning shall be unto all people," and "I the Lord, knowing the calamity which should come upon the inhabitants of the earth, called upon my servant Joseph Smith, Jun., and spake unto him from heaven" (D&C 1:4, 17). To address modern conditions of sin and immorality, in other words, and to prepare the earth for the Second Coming of Jesus Christ, God appoints prophets to call his people to repentance, as did Isaiah or Jeremiah.

The greatest prophet in Jewish history is generally considered to be Moses. He did not merely preach but led the Israelites out of Egypt, through the wilderness of Sinai and into the Promised Land, forging them into the covenant people of ancient Israel in the process. Joseph Smith and Brigham Young fulfilled similar roles, guiding thousands of believers from one place of gathering to another, eventually settling them in the Salt Lake Valley. In the process, Latter-day Saints became more than another Christian denomination: a distinctive, cohesive people that some sociologists liken to a global tribe, a subculture, even—claims the *Harvard Encyclopedia of Ethnic Groups*—a distinct ethnicity.

Finally, Joseph Smith added to those callings the role the New Testament associates with Peter as holder of the keys of the priesthood, standing at the head of the church that Christ himself inaugurated. Latter-day Saints believe that the original institution was lost to heresy, division, and apostasy from the original New Testament church. God reinstituted his church, telling Smith that "unto you the kingdom, or in other words, the keys of the church have been given" (D&C 42:69). So in addition to the responsibility to convey God's words to the human family and to serve as spiritual leader of his disciples, the prophet of the Church of Jesus Christ is "president of the High Priesthood," the person in whom the ultimate authority resides to preside in Christ's stead, to direct the affairs of the church, and to administer (or cause to be administered) all the ordinances (or sacraments) of salvation, being fully authorized by apostolic succession to function in that capacity.

In Joseph Smith's account of his personal quest for religious certainty, he emphasized the insufficiency of the Bible, in contrast to the Protestant doctrine of *sola scriptura*. In his experience, "the teachers of religion of the different sects understood the same passages of scripture so differently as to destroy all confidence in settling the question by an appeal to the Bible" (1:12). From that perspective, the necessity for God to provide continuing direction to inspired modern prophets, tailored to changing circumstances and needs, is evident.

How is the president of the church chosen?

The Church of Jesus Christ of Latter-day Saints is a strongly hierarchical church, very much like the Catholic Church in that regard. Each new head of the church is called and sustained by members as the president of the church and as a prophet, seer, and revelator. Technically, all the apostles are sustained as "prophets, seers, and revelators," although only the church president is referred to as "*the* prophet." When Joseph Smith died, there was no procedure or mechanism in place for an orderly succession. As a consequence, many claimants aspired to be his replacement, and many schisms resulted. The majority of the church accepted the claim of Brigham Young that after the dissolving of the First Presidency of the Church, authority resided with the Quorum of the Twelve Apostles, and the president of that quorum would therefore be the living apostle with the authority to preside. And so Brigham Young did lead the church after Smith's death, as the president of the twelve apostles. Whether from reluctance to assume the title only Smith had held or uncertainty about the need for a perpetuation of the First Presidency, Young waited three years to reorganize that quorum and assume the title of church president, subject to a church-wide sustaining vote. When Young died in 1877, John Taylor was the president of the quorum (the most senior apostle is always president), so he assumed the leadership of the church following the pattern initiated with Young. Taylor, too, waited three years before believing that the Lord had directed him to reorganize a First Presidency, with two counselors, and himself filling the position of president of the church.

When Lorenzo Snow became prophet in 1898, he directed that the Quorum of the Twelve Apostles should move to reorganize a first presidency on the death of the president and not delay, as had been the practice. From that time to the present, the senior surviving apostle moves within a matter of days to reorganize the presidency and receive ordination as president at the hands of his fellow apostles. The definition of "senior apostle" is the apostle with the longest term of service in the quorum (of continuous service, as clarified by Brigham Young). The disadvantage of this system is that presidents of the church are increasingly aged and often subject to both physical and mental impairment in their last years (Gordon B. Hinckley was ninety-seven at his 2008 passing, Thomas S. Monson was ninety when he passed in 2018, and the vigorous Russell M. Nelson was already ninety-three when ordained as president.) The advantages are the smoothness and orderliness of a succession process stripped of any potential politicking and the invaluable experience borne of decades-long service in the highest ranks of leadership.

In recent years, the church began a practice of retiring some general authorities who previously had lifelong appointments—those belonging to the First Quorum of Seventy—at age seventy with emeritus status. It is impossible to predict if such a practice will ever be extended to the First Presidency and the Quorum of the Twelve Apostles.

Why do women not hold the priesthood?

One answer to this question is to look at the origins of the Church of Jesus Christ of Latter-day Saints as a "restorationist" church. In government, in law, and in religion, precedent holds powerful sway as an authoritative grounding for practice. In antebellum America, "primitivists," "seekers," and "restorationists" were designations for persons who anticipated or promoted a return to church organization and practices and teachings of the church described in the New Testament. As Smith himself articulated in two articles of faith, "we believe in the same organization that existed in the primitive church," and "we believe in the gift of tongues, prophecy, revelation, visions, healing, interpretation of tongues, and so forth." Latter-day Saints saw themselves as following the model of the New Testament church, made up of nineteenth- rather than first-century "saints," or disciples. A third article looked to the example of Aaron in the Old Testament and the apostles in the New for a pattern of priesthood authority and ordination in particular. "We believe that a man must be called of God by prophecy and by the laying on of hands by those who are in authority, to preach the gospel and administer in the ordinances thereof." It is not the gender-specific "man" that is influential here but the pattern of looking to scripture for a template of how and to whom priesthood may be extended.

Much like the Catholic Church, the LDS Church believes that Christ established a pattern of formal ordination to a priesthood that was bestowed on males. At the same time, the LDS conception of priesthood transcends ecclesiastical authority and temporal duration. Latter-day Saints believe that God himself operates by priesthood power, and that priesthood will continue into the eternities both as a principle of power and as the ground or matrix by which eternal beings are organized and related in eternal chains of belonging. This dimension of priesthood is most fully evident in LDS temple theology and temple practice, where the "higher" sacraments or ordinances of the gospel are performed, such as "sealing," ceremonies that bind husband and wife in an eternal union, among others. In these priesthood ordinances, women fully engage both as participants and officiators. This is one point of evidence for the view, expressed by such leaders as John Taylor and James Talmage, that women share in, or even hold, the priesthood now, though they do not at present possess all the priesthood "keys" to exercise that priesthood. These points may be too subtle for those who are really asking: "why cannot LDS women exercise a degree of authority comparable to their male counterparts within the institutional church?" And the answer to that would seem to be that the leadership believes that first and foremost the church should be patterned after scriptural precedent. In the temple, women perform priesthood functions; in church administration and sacramental functions outside the temple, only men have the keys to exercise priesthood authority. The church leadership has not provided any more explicit rationale for a male-limited priesthood. In a church predicated on the principle of continuing revelation and living prophets, that policy could change at any time, though few signs exist of such a development.

Why doesn't the composition of the leadership reflect church demographics?

The leadership of the LDS Church is predominantly white and American. Part of the reason for this is historical: missionaries found the majority of their early converts in New York, then Ohio. Soon after the church expanded missionary work abroad, more Latter-day Saints were to be found in Great Britain than in the United States. Relatively isolated after their exodus to Utah, Saints were further cut off from ethnic diversity. The 1852 racial restrictions disallowed evangelizing of blacks, and the persistence of those restrictions into the 1970s precluded any increase in racial diversity, even during years of very high growth.

In 1975, President Spencer W. Kimball called the Native American George P. Lee as a seventy. Since the turn of the twenty-first century, the majority of members hail from Latin American countries, and, increasingly, from Africa. In 1981, Kimball called the first Latin American, Angel Abrea, as a general authority. Many Hispanics have followed: currently there are general authorities from Argentina, Brazil, Chile, Columbia, Mexico, Peru—and a growing list of other countries. The first person of African descent to be called as a general authority (seventy) was the Brazilian Helvecio Martins in 1990. The Kenyan Joseph Sitati followed in 2009 and the Zimbabwean Edward Dube in 2013. In 2019, the first African American was called as a seventy (Peter Johnson).

At the highest levels of leadership, ethnicity is similarly, though slowly, becoming more diverse. Currently the Quorum of Twelve includes a German (Dieter Uchtdorf, called in 2004), a Brazilian (Ulisses Soares, 2018), and an American of Chinese ethnicity (Garrit Gong, 2018).

Is it true that Latter-day Saints take care of their own?

Latter-day Saints are legendary for their intragroup loyalty and cohesion. Much of this cultural feature is institutionally shaped. One key ingredient is the fact that the Saints are virtually alone in the Christian world today in following strict boundary rules. Simply put—you attend a ward whose geographical lines are clearly laid out (like a parish). With rare exceptions, there is no "parish shopping" for better preaching or more compatible cocongregants. So, like a family, members of a ward find themselves part of a unit where they will live and worship and serve together, and it becomes a veritable school of love. In addition, every single member is assigned two "ministers" ("home teachers" in the older nomenclature): two male members who are responsible and accountable for checking up on any needs—spiritual, emotional, or financial—that arise, and personally attending to those or coordinating with those in the leadership who can. Women have their own female ministers in addition to the males, thus getting double coverage as it were.

Weekly leadership meetings presided over by a ward bishop review and assess any reported needs. He has financial resources at his disposal from fast offerings (voluntary contributions associated with a monthly fast) to attend to any financial needs that merit assistance. Members in need are the focus of such relief, but the bishop occasionally provides emergency assistance to non-members in his ward boundaries. Food for those in need is available from a "bishop's storehouse." By 1990, the church held 172,000 acres of farmland, 199 agricultural production projects, fifty-one canneries, and sixty-three grain storage facilities feeding into 113 central, regional, and branch storehouses. This storehouse is well stocked like an effective grocery store and caters to a designated geographical district of the church. The woman's auxiliary president (the Relief Society president), under the bishop's direction, personally oversees such individual assistance, and a truck that typically makes the rounds in that particular region delivers a custom-tailored order for every member receiving assistance.

This welfare program was centralized in 1936, but the practice of organizing by wards, with a bishop taking care of his flock from a bishop's storehouse, goes back to the first days of the church when Edward Partridge was called as bishop of the Saints in Missouri and then Newell Whitney as bishop in Kirtland. To address long-term needs, each stake administers a "self-reliance initiative," working with the un- or underemployed, while the church administers educational programs directed to the same end, including the Perpetual Education Fund, which provides monies for underprivileged members seeking vocational or academic training, and the Pathways program, which offers expansive online college credit. The LDS Church also has its own counseling services that work with families, couples, and individuals.

Do Latter-day Saints only *take care of their own?*

Latter-day Saints are known for taking care of their own, but their charitable acts extend far beyond members of the church. In the closing years of the last century, the church provided aid to 150 countries, including shipment of over 100,000 tons of food, medical and educational supplies, and clothing, valued at a half billion dollars. In that period, the church launched 144 major disaster assistance efforts, helping victims of flooding in Mozambique, Europe, and South America, of famine in Africa, and of war in Afghanistan. Speaking to the National Press Club in 2000, President Gordon B. Hinckley surveyed several examples:

> Today, this very day, as they have been during previous days, two helicopters have been flying rescue and mercy missions over the flood waters of Mozambique and Zimbabwe. When governments in that part of the world said they could do no more, we rented two helicopters at great expense to fly rescue missions. . . . We have dug wells in African villages, fed people, and supplied them with clothing and shelter. We have given aid in the Mexico fire of 1990, in the Bangladesh cyclone of 1991, in the China earthquake of 1991, in the Bosnia civil conflict of 1992, in Rwanda in 1994, in North Korea in 1996–98, in Central America in 1998, and in Kosovo in 1999, and today we are assisting substantially in Venezuela, Mozambique, and Zimbabwe.[1]

Typical of other twenty-first-century LDS responses to world crises was an effort organized in May 2002. Summoned by area leaders, some two hundred humanitarian aid volunteers rallied on Welfare Square in Salt Lake City to assemble 6,750 emergency food boxes for families in drought-stricken Malawi, Zimbabwe, and Madagascar. The church supplemented those packages with 250 tons of cereal grains and substantial clothing shipments. During the Ethiopian drought of 2003, the church responded with ten million pounds of food assistance, much of it in the form of a nourishing porridge called Atmit, produced at the Deseret Dairy powdered products facility at Welfare Square. The first emergency shipment of eighty thousand pounds was flown to Addis Ababa in a church-chartered cargo plane. In 2015, the church had 177 emergency response projects in fifty-six countries and was averaging 40 million dollars in expenditures annually. Those humanitarian efforts are administered without regard to religious affiliation.[2]

In 2018, such efforts expanded to almost three thousand projects in over 140 countries. Since 1985, the church has expended over two billion dollars in aid. One significant development in recent years has been the move to increase coordination with other entities in providing humanitarian support. Also in 2018, Latter-day Saint Charities joined with over nineteen hundred partners to serve millions.[3]

As a more detailed, on-the-ground example of the church's humanitarian commitment, here is a report of work supervised by just one humanitarian missionary couple in just one month of service in Argentina (October 2019):[4]

1. Emergency relief for a flooded area in greater Buenos Aires following the heavy rains the first week of our time here, including delivery of mattresses, blankets, and fresh water
2. Hospital supplies and cribs for children in Neuquen

3. Providing playground and school equipment for a summer camp project for a school that serves underprivileged children in Jujuy
4. An endoscopy equipment sterilization machine for a hospital in Mar del Plata
5. A small medical project to fund the correction of harelip conditions of six children in Mendoza
6. Thirteen pediatric oximeters donated to a hospital in Mendoza
7. School and hygiene kits for refugee children
8. We are preparing to participate in a wheelchair delivery event in mid-November in Paraguay
9. Working with a Catholic group to refurbish a comedor (dining hall for homeless) in Concordia

5

SCRIPTURES

The Book of Mormon

What is the Book of Mormon?

The Book of Mormon, which members of the Church of Jesus Christ accept as scripture alongside the Bible, begins as a clan history, like the patriarchal narratives of Genesis, set close to the year 600 BC. Lehi is the founding patriarch of this saga, and he leads a family group of some two dozen on a voyage to a "land of promise," presumably in the New World. Like the historical books of the Old Testament, the family history develops into a chronicle of peoples and kingdoms that descend from those initial key figures. The clan fractures into two principal groups, the Nephites and the Lamanites, and successive record-keepers narrate their extensive fratricidal wars over the next one thousand years. This book of scripture also includes accounts of a fledgling New World church, its missionaries, and their teachings, like a New World book of Acts, as well as a detailed account of a resurrected Christ's ministry among an indigenous population, rather like a post-Ascension gospel. The Book of Mormon record even includes epistles, though they are written by a prophet to his son rather than an apostle to his scattered congregations.

Nephi is Lehi's son and the initial record-keeper. Nearing his demise, he—like every other record-keeper—entrusts the plates on which he is recording his words to a successor record-keeper. Nephi and subsequent writers maintain two concurrent histories. One is primarily concerned with a political history of the people, recorded on a set of "large plates" and faithfully added to from the exodus of 600 BC until the end of Nephite civilization in the early fifth century. The second chronicle, written on the "small plates," details what Nephi calls "the things of God," matters and teachings and prophetic writings of greater spiritual significance. They cover the period from 600 BC until about 130 BC, after which time only the large plates are maintained, absorbing the function of the small plates into themselves. In the fourth century, the prophet Mormon begins a work of abridgment, condensing almost a millennium of records into a succinct, manageable distillation. Those plates constitute the bulk of the "gold plates" Joseph Smith translates as the Book of Mormon. However, before his death, Mormon entrusts his abridgment to his son Moroni—who appends some of his own writings—adds a separate record of a distinct New World people called the Jaredites, and adjoins the entire collection of the "small plates." In the early fifth century, as the last survivor of his people and facing death, Moroni buries the records.

In September 1823, three years after his First Vision and in response to Smith's prayers seeking to know his standing before God, Moroni—the same man who had sealed up and buried the ancient Nephite plates—appeared to the seventeen-year-old boy as an angelic being. Moroni recounted the story of his people, who had lived in the Americas and left a record of their civilization buried in a stone box inside a hill near Smith's own home, which Smith was directed to retrieve.

Following three annual visits to the site and instruction from the angel, Smith was at last told that the time to receive the plates had come. In company with his wife, Emma, whom he had married months earlier, Smith returned to the hill, which he called Cumorah, and was permitted to secure the plates. Over the next two years, sometimes using a divination device referenced in the Bible and called a Urim and Thummim that was buried with the plates, and sometimes a seer stone in the bottom of a hat, Smith produced a translation of the record, which came off the press in March 1830. With the translation completed, Smith said of the plates that, "according to arrangements, the messenger called for them, I delivered them up to him; and he has them in his charge until this day, being the second day of May, one thousand eight hundred and thirty-eight."[1]

Do Latter-day Saints reject the closed canon of Christianity?

The canon of Christian scripture was finalized in the early fifth century, and few serious challenges to its contents have emerged in subsequent Christian history. Luther demoted the books of the Apocrypha to their own category of dubious standing in 1534, but no candidates for addition have been seriously considered. The Protestant doctrine of *sola scriptura* declared the sufficiency of the Bible as the source of all doctrine. No wonder, then, that LDS acceptance of the Book of Mormon as "the word of God" struck nineteenth-century observers (and many today) as a prima facie instance of "blasphemy!" (the headline of one of the earliest journalistic treatments of that volume).

Some Christians cite Deuteronomy 4:2, with its anathema on any who would "add unto the word which I command you," as proof of the error of additions like the Book of Mormon. Since the entire New Testament was added to the canon centuries after the author of Deuteronomy wrote, Saints believe it is hard to take that injunction as pertaining to more than its original Mosaic referent. Still, the weight of tradition gives pause in the face of what seems the religious audacity of adding not just the Book of Mormon but two other volumes of scripture as well.

Latter-day Saints, however, celebrate an open canon, believing that God "will yet reveal many important things pertaining to the kingdom of God" (Article of Faith 9), and have continued to expand their canon. An entire volume (the Pearl of Great Price) was canonized in 1880, and 101 years later, two revelations were added to the Doctrine and Covenants that had been canonized in 1835 (sections 137 and 138). In one tantalizing prophecy, the Book of Mormon itself foretells that a large portion of the gold plates that Smith did not translate, the "sealed portion," will be revealed to the world "in mine own due time" (Ether 3:27). A veritable flood of scriptural enlightenment may await, given the principle that the Book of Mormon prophet Nephi taught:

> [God] command[s] all men, both in the east and in the west, and in the north, and in the south, and in the islands of the sea, that they shall write the words which I speak unto them; . . . and I shall also speak unto the other tribes of the house of Israel, which I have led away, and they shall write it; and I shall also speak unto all nations of the earth and they shall write it. And it shall come to pass that the Jews shall have the words of the Nephites, and the Nephites shall have the words of the Jews; and the Nephites and the Jews shall have the words of the lost tribes of Israel; and the lost tribes of Israel shall have the words of the Nephites and the Jews. And it shall come to pass that my people, which are of the house of Israel, shall be gathered home unto the lands of their possessions; and my word also shall be gathered in one. (2 Nephi 29:11–14)

Does the Book of Mormon add unique teachings to the Bible or to Christian readings of the Bible?

It may be the case that the Book of Mormon's significance is more a matter of what it represents than what it contains. First and foremost, the Book of Mormon is for Latter-day Saints the most tangible and dramatic evidence that, beginning in the 1800s, God was once again manifesting himself to his people and actively communicating with prophets. The Protestant doctrine of *sola scriptura* holds that everything necessary for human salvation is embodied in the biblical canon and that further scripture or revelation is superfluous, unnecessary, and indeed impossible. Latter-day Saints believe that God's revelation of the plates that were translated as the Book of Mormon is a sign that God is not done revealing truth and light to the earth.

Second, the Book of Mormon illustrates a radically different concept of revelation from that of the Bible. In the Bible, it is rare to find an instance of divine communication with anyone who is not a prophet or patriarch. The Book of Mormon emphatically democratized personal revelation, as it were, teaching that God can reveal his mind and will to any seeking individual, through dreams, visions, inspiration, or direct divine address. In the Book of Mormon, God personally reveals himself to wayward children, worried fathers of missionaries, disciples inquiring about theological principles, and a family in search of food. Smith in fact taught that it was on *this* rock, the rock of individual revelation by means of the Holy Ghost, that Christ established his church. That was his reading of Matthew 16:16–18, wherein, immediately before telling Peter he would build his church "upon this rock," Christ told Peter that his testimony was "revealed" to him by his Father.

A third major innovation is the emphatic denial of the doctrine of original sin, which was virtually universal in the Christian world. This entailed a revision of conventional readings of the Fall. In the Book of Mormon, the decision of Eve and Adam to eat of the fruit was a necessary precursor to the entire plan of salvation. "Adam fell," according to that text, "that men might be. And men are that they might have joy" (2 Nephi 2:25). If they had remained in the garden in a state of innocence, there would have been no children, and the designs of God would have been frustrated. The entire mortal project, in this light, is proceeding according to plan; it is not the aftermath of an Edenic disaster.

A fourth principle follows from this: if there is no original sin, there is no sin or guilt for children to inherit. Children are born innocent, and the baptism of infants is deemed a form of sacrilege.

Other contributions of the Book of Mormon are more a matter of emphasis or clarification than innovation. Human agency is strongly affirmed: "God gave unto man that he should act for himself" (2 Nephi 2:16); therefore "they are free to choose liberty and eternal life . . . or to choose captivity and death" (2 Nephi 2:27). Spiritual gifts, healing, miracles, and other "manifestations of the Spirit . . . never will be done away with" (Moroni 10). Divine justice is clarified as God's respect for human agency. An individual is effectively his "own judge," and is "raised to happiness [or its opposite] according to his desires of happiness [or its opposite]" (Alma 41:5). Those who are in hell or "the gall of bitterness" are simply "in a state contrary to the nature of happiness" (41:11), consequent to their choices.

While valuing the Bible as "the word of God," Latter-day Saints believe the Book of Mormon has particular value, passing as it has through only one stage of transmission and translation between its final composition in the fifth century and its publication in 1830. Smith taught the Saints that a person would get closer to God by following its precepts than the precepts of any other book.

What does the Book of Mormon say about how ancient Americans worshiped Christ before he was born?

One of the more improbable verses in the Book of Mormon, attributed to an ancient American prophet in the sixth century BC, says: "we talk of Christ, we rejoice in Christ, we preach of Christ, we prophesy of Christ, and we write according to our prophecies, that our children may know to what source they may look for a remission of their sins" (2 Nephi 25:26). How did a group of ancient Israelites acquire exact foreknowledge of Jesus when their Jewish contemporaries had, at best, vaguely defined beliefs in some kind of future Messiah? Two second-century Christian authorities, Justin Martyr and Irenaeus, as well as the medieval Book of the Bee and 4 Baruch, cite now unknown passages from Jeremiah that predict details of the Messiah's birth, ministry, and resurrection.[2] Most scholars, however, believe that messianism was in fact a fairly late development in the Jewish world, and was generally lacking in specifics.

The Book of Mormon explains this anachronistic Christianity in two ways. First, the book's authors quote sources (such as Zenos, Neum, Eziah, and Zenock) who were part of an ancient scriptural record the Nephites brought with them in their flight from Jerusalem. These "brass plates" contained an account of creation, "a record of the Jews from the beginning," and "the prophecies of the holy prophets" (1 Nephi 5:11–13). In addition, as if they are aware of the improbable nature of their claimed knowledge, Book of Mormon authors always attribute their witness to special revelations. For instance, Nephi refers to the coming Messiah as Jesus Christ "according to . . . the word of the angel of God" (2 Nephi 25:19). Jacob knows of Christ's scourging and crucifixion because of "the words of the angel who spake it unto me" (2 Nephi 6:9). The name of Christ's mother, Mary, was likewise made known to King Benjamin "by an angel from God" (Mosiah 3:2–8). The high priest Alma the Younger knows the Savior shall be born of Mary in Jerusalem, because "the spirit hath said this much unto me" (Alma 7:9), and so on. Together, these two sources—extrabiblical records and angelic visitation—may be taken to account for what to all appearances is blatant historical anomaly. Another explanation proffered by some LDS believers is that Mormon or Moroni, fourth-to-fifth-century editors of the record, interposed the specifically Christian details into their account.

Did anybody besides Joseph Smith see the gold plates?

The first question often put to Latter-day Saints telling a non-Mormon about the Book of Mormon and its derivation from gold plates is, "where are the plates now?" To which a Latter-day Saint typically responds, half in jest but half in earnest, "in the same place as the stone tablets of Moses."

However, included in each edition from 1830 to the present are the sworn affidavits of eleven men, affirming that they viewed the original plates of gold on which the record was inscribed. Latter-day Saints refer to these individuals as the Three Witnesses and the Eight Witnesses, each group having seen the plates under different circumstances. In their published testimony, the first three witnesses—Oliver Cowdery, Martin Harris, and David Whitmer—describe a visionary encounter that involves heavenly beings. They see the plates "through the grace of God." They know the translation is true, because the voice of God "declared it unto" them. The plates themselves were brought and laid before their eyes by "an angel of God [who] came down from heaven." Although they were close enough to the relics to see "the engravings thereon," as they twice tell us, they neither touched nor handled them for themselves.

The group of eight—Joseph Smith Sr., Hyrum Smith, Samuel H. Smith, Hiram Page, Christian Whitmer, Jacob Whitmer, Peter Whitmer Jr., and John Whitmer—saw the plates under more natural circumstances, and their testimony is lacking in any traces of supernaturalism. Joseph Smith simply showed them the plates, allowing them to make their own examination and draw their own conclusions. Their verdict is thus more compelling even as it is more qualified. The plates, they write, do indeed have "the appearance of gold," the engravings have "the appearance of an ancient work," and as for the translation itself, they mention it without testifying to its truthfulness. As to the plates, "[w]e did handle [them] with our hands," they affirm; "[w]e have seen and hefted, and know of a surety that the said Smith has got the plates of which we have spoken."

Taken together, the two experiences seemed calculated to provide an evidentiary spectrum, satisfying a range of criteria for belief. One group claimed support from a heavenly voice, while the other appealed to ordinary, tactile hands-on experience. Besides these eleven, other persons claimed to have seen or handled the plates as well, through miraculous display by heavenly messenger (Mary Whitmer) or through the loose covering of a smock or cloth (Emma Smith, Katherine Smith, and Lucy Mack Smith).

Did those witnesses who saw and handled the gold plates abandon the church?

Martin Harris was the first witness to be closely associated with Joseph Smith. A well-to-do farmer and neighbor, he heard Smith's account of finding the gold plates and believed his story. Wanting further confirmation for himself that the plates and their translation were not fraudulent, he took a transcription made by Smith of some of the characters from the plates, apparently with their translation as well, to scholars in New York City. According to his account, they were confirmed as authentic. One scholar involved, Charles Anthon, later disputed Harris's report. However, Harris was satisfied enough with what he heard that he returned to assist Smith with the project. Not only did he take dictation as Smith translated from the plates, he financed the costly printing of the first several thousand copies of the finished work. For the next several years, he was entirely supportive of Smith and the growing movement. In 1837, following the collapse of a banking effort Smith had supported, widespread disaffection swept the church. Along with many others, Harris broke with Smith's leadership and was subsequently excommunicated. Five years later, he petitioned for readmission and was rebaptized. Smith was killed in 1844, and the church fragmented under the competing claims of many aspirants to the leadership. For a while, Harris threw in his lot with James Strang, before launching his own short-lived schismatic effort. Throughout all these vicissitudes, however, Harris was known to steadfastly bear witness to his earlier words that he had seen the gold plates and that their translation was the word of God. In 1870, an again repentant Harris expressed a desire to rejoin the Saints, now in Utah. Brigham Young contributed funds to the effort, Harris made the trek, was rebaptized as a sign of renewed commitment, and died firm in his faith.

Oliver Cowdery was the witness most closely involved with the production of the Book of Mormon. A schoolteacher who boarded with Smith's parents, he progressed from curiosity to conviction even before making the trip to meet Joseph, who was by then living in Harmony, Pennsylvania. Smith's translation work had largely stalled by 1829, after his first 116 pages had been stolen, and the demands of his farm and lack of resources afforded little time or energy for the work. Cowdery was young, energetic, and a capable scribe. Work now proceeded at a prodigious rate. As he later recounted, "I wrote with my own pen the entire Book of Mormon (save a few pages) as it fell from the lips of the Prophet Joseph Smith, as he translated it by the gift and power of God, by the means of the Urim and Thummim."[3] A talented, educated believer, Cowdery became Smith's right-hand man. He was named "Second Elder" of the church (Smith was First), was one of six formal founders of the church in 1830, and rose to become assistant president of the church in 1834. A few years later, he, too, fell out with Joseph Smith. In Cowdery's case, the cause was Smith's extramarital practices, which Smith said were sanctioned polygamy and Cowdery saw as adultery. Cowdery also resented what he saw as Smith's claims of authority to dictate in personal and financial matters. Excommunicated in 1838, Cowdery remained in the Midwest and became a successful lawyer and politician. In 1848, he asked for readmission to the church and was rebaptized in Iowa. He died before he could make the journey to Utah to gather with the Saints, but he had consistently maintained his fierce defense of the Book of Mormon.

David Whitmer is the most interesting and controversial of the Three Witnesses. He learned about the Book of Mormon from his friend Oliver Cowdery. He was converted to the cause, and offered his home as a sanctuary where Smith and Cowdery would complete their translation in peace and safety. Like Cowdery, he was highly trusted by Smith and rose to important leadership. By 1834 the church membership was largely split between its original gathering place of Ohio and the new gathering in Missouri, identified as the land of Zion. That June, Whitmer was made president of the church in Missouri. Within a few years, some members came to resent Smith's leadership and backed Whitmer as an alternative. Whitmer showed little interest in putting himself forward as an alternative to Smith. He was excommunicated for dissension in 1838, withdrew from the Saints, and never petitioned for readmission. In 1887 he published a justification for his break with Smith and the Saints. Significantly, he affirmed his belief that Smith had been called as a prophet and that the Book of Mormon was God's word. However, he considered subsequent developments to be evidence that Smith had fallen from his chosen position: this was evident, he wrote, in the practice of polygamy and the publication of additional scriptures besides the Book of Mormon.

How did Smith translate the Book of Mormon?

Regarding the manner of Smith's translation of the Book of Mormon, we know some details but not others. Several witnesses to the actual process agree that Smith dictated streams of words unprompted by notes or texts. Manuscript evidence also attests to an orally produced text taken down by a scribe. His wife, Emma, told an interviewer years later: "when my husband was translating the Book of Mormon, I wrote a part of it, as he dictated each sentence, word for word, and when he came to proper names he could not pronounce, or long words, he spelled them out. . . . When he stopped for any purpose at any time he would, when he commenced again, begin where he left off without any hesitation." Oliver Cowdery, who took the vast majority of Smith's dictation, affirmed that he "wrote with [his] own pen the entire Book of Mormon (save a few pages) as it fell from the lips of the prophet."[4]

John H. Gilbert, the principal compositor at E. B. Grandin's shop, where the book was first printed, described the first twenty-four pages of manuscript delivered by Smith's brother Hyrum as "closely written and legible, but not a punctuation mark from beginning to end."[5] In what manner or form those words came to Smith is unclear. In the first phase of translation, he employed the Urim and Thummim, also called "interpreters," two clear stones set in rims, that he had received on the same night as the plates. At some point in the two months Harris wrote for him, from mid-April to mid-June, Smith apparently took to using a seer stone interchangeably with the interpreters. Several witnesses described the stone as egg-shaped, but flatter, and dark brown. Smith would place it in the bottom of a hat and place his face in the hat, so as to exclude outside light, and then dictate. The plates themselves were, in the later stages particularly, not even immediately present to Smith but often safely ensconced in another part of the room or house. In other words, his "translation" was actually an oral text he channeled or produced virtually spontaneously.

Of all those closely involved with the process, Martin Harris gave the most specific information about Smith's translation method: "by aid of the seer stone, sentences would appear and were read by the Prophet and written by Martin, and when finished he would say, 'Written,' and if correctly written, that sentence would disappear and another appear in its place, but if not written correctly it remained until corrected." Smith himself was reluctant to say much about the process of translation. In response to a question from his own brother Hyrum, Joseph said in an October 1831 conference of the church "that it was not intended to tell the world all the particulars of the coming forth of the Book of Mormon; and also said that it was not expedient for him to relate these things."[6] After several stops and starts and lost pages of translation, Cowdery began scribing for Smith in earnest in April 1829. Given interruptions caused by the need to seek occasional employment to buy necessities, Smith's ongoing family responsibilities, and the need to address doctrinal questions that arose, Smith and Cowdery managed a truly prodigious rate of translation during the months of April and May—over 3,500 original words a day essentially set down indelibly as they were spoken (or about fourteen double-spaced pages of 250 words per page).

Do you have to believe the Book of Mormon to be a Latter-day Saint?

Most Latter-day Saints believe the Book of Mormon is an actual, historical account of peoples who inhabited lands somewhere in the Western Hemisphere, arriving here centuries before Christ. They consider it scripture, on a par with the Bible. Joseph Smith called the book "the keystone of Mormonism." A keystone is the center stone in an arch, which sustains the integrity of the structure. The Book of Mormon is not foundational; it does not contain the majority of the faith's distinctive tenets or core teachings. However, it is the essential link connecting the person Joseph Smith to the sources of divine authority and revelation to which he laid claim. Smith declared that the final author/editor of the Book of Mormon, Moroni, appeared to him as a resurrected being, led him to the gold plates, and charged him with their translation. If the Book of Mormon is not the genuine ancient record it purports to be, and if the gold plates were simple fantasy or of his own making, then Smith's story about ancient artifacts, angelic messengers, and the authority they bequeathed him would be mere fables, and the claims of the church to be an authorized restoration of Christianity impossible to sustain. By comparison, the stories of Adam and Eve, or Noah and the flood, could be myths or inspired fiction without undermining the Christian religion, because the authority of Christianity is not tied to the historicity of those accounts. Joseph Smith, on the other hand, did emphatically tie his own authority as a prophet and apostle to the reality of ancient records transmitted to him by an angelic being who was himself a character in that narrative. If you pull the thread named Moroni and it comes loose, the entire garment unravels: his reality as an ancient writer, the authenticity of the gold plates, Joseph Smith's claims to angelic visitations and the power of seership, and the priesthood authority he claimed to receive from other messengers following in the wake of Moroni.

At the same time, formal assent to the historicity of the Book of Mormon is nowhere explicitly required in the conversion process or to qualify for admission to the temple, the metric of full and total investment in the LDS faith. And indeed, a significant number of Latter-day Saints have expressed in private and in public an indifference to, or outright rejection of, the historical reality of Moroni and the entire cast of Book of Mormon characters and their civilization. As is true in many denominations, some adherents find a comfortable and enriching existence in the faith community without embracing the totality of its religious claims.

How like the Bible is the Book of Mormon?

To those familiar with the Bible, the Book of Mormon will present a mix of the new and the known. It suggests a number of familiar themes, only to recast them with enough novelty to make of them a new scripture. For example, it opens with a scene steeped in the trappings of biblical prophets and prophecy at the time of Jeremiah but elaborates repeated interactions of God with individuals who are neither prophets nor kings, redefining revelation as literal, egalitarian, and indicative of an entirely accessible, personal God. The beginning is set in Jerusalem (another portion commences at Babel), but the account quickly moves to the New World, in a location never precisely specified. The Book of Mormon quotes extensively from the prophecies of Isaiah, even as it introduces scriptural texts from never-before-heard-of Old World prophets—Zenock, Neum, and Zenos—as well as a panoply of New World voices. Portions of Christ's Sermon on the Mount are repeated virtually verbatim in King James English, as are some of the phrases we hear in Paul. They appear side by side with entirely new parables, sermons, and allegories.

Christ is a central figure in the Book of Mormon, as he is in the New Testament. The Book of Mormon documents his Palestinian birth and life, crucifixion, and resurrection but then explodes their historical uniqueness by narrating a postresurrection ministry of Christ in this New World setting and indicating there were other venues for Christ's ministry besides. The book affirms Jehovah's special covenants with Israel (although indicating that Jehovah of the Old Testament is in fact Jesus Christ), even as it specifies America as a separate "land of promise," and then chronicles a whole series of portable Zions founded and abandoned by covenant peoples in successive waves. The Book of Mormon affirms the Bible's status as scripture, even as it qualifies it. For while it testifies to "the gospel of Jesus Christ" and predicts its modern-day restoration in purity, the Book of Mormon demolishes the Bible's monopoly as scripture. It makes the Bible one in a series of God's textual revelations to humankind. In these ways and others, the Book of Mormon occupies the unusual position of invoking and affirming biblical concepts and motifs even as it rewrites them in fairly dramatic ways. The book has thus unavoidably been seen by readers past and present as emulating Christian scripture in innumerable ways, even as it subverts Christian ideas about the closed nature of the Christian scriptural canon.

What is the evidence for the Book of Mormon?

The reception history of the Book of Mormon is really two distinct, parallel histories. It is the story of a group of people who were attracted to and galvanized by the report of a new scripture with its claim to be a sign of God's renewed contact with the world. That story tells of a pervasive hunger among nineteenth-century religious seekers, and others since, for signs of God's present workings, of widespread expectations for restoration of and return to primitive Christian forms, of a populist passion for universal access to miracles, spiritual gifts, and personal revelation—and how the Book of Mormon met those yearnings. That history is about the spiritual evidence believers find in the fruits of the life the Book of Mormon invites one to lead, and the Christ that for some is revealed there.

But there is also the story of a protracted debate about the logical plausibility of a book laying claim not just to spiritual value but to actual historical foundations in an ancient American setting, with Israelite characters who have seemed wildly out of place and a Christian religion that has seemed wildly out of its proper time frame. This story, like the first, continues into the new millennium with unabated fervor. Nobody claims that any archaeological evidence in direct support of the Book of Mormon has been found in the New World (although stone altars with a Book of Mormon place name have been found in Yemen, at the spot where the Book of Mormon describes the path of its principal characters' exodus). So LDS scholarship in support of the Book of Mormon has turned largely to internal, or textual, evidence that supports its alleged Near Eastern origins. As Hugh Nibley, the twentieth-century church's most erudite apologist, framed the challenge in the 1940s, "does it correctly reflect 'the cultural horizon and religious and social ideas and practices of the time'? Does it have authentic historical and geographical background? . . . Is its local color correct, and are its proper names convincing?"[7]

Critics point to perceived anachronisms (horses, chariots) and doctrinal debates common to the nineteenth century (universalism, infant baptism). On the other hand, Nibley and numerous LDS scholars cite internal evidence, such as pervasive use of Hebrew constructions and poetic forms, including chiasmus (the poetic form of reverse parallelism, common in Semitic languages); coronation rituals; rites of execution; Egyptian etymologies; olive horticulture; and dozens of other elements with Middle Eastern resonances. As even one skeptic of such claims acknowledges, Latter-day Saints have pointed out "striking coincidences between elements in the Book of Mormon and the ancient world, and some notable matters of Book of Mormon style."[8] Two evangelical scholars wrote in a much cited paper that "in recent years the sophistication and erudition of LDS apologetics has risen considerably . . . [and] is clearly seen in their approach to the Book of Mormon. . . . LDS academicians are producing serious research which desperately needs to be critically examined."[9]

After almost two centuries in the ring, it is unlikely that either side in the debates will land a knock-out blow. From an LDS perspective, the words of Austin Farrer are the point: "though argument does not create conviction, lack of it destroys belief. What seems to be proved may not be embraced; but what no one shows the ability to defend is quickly abandoned. Rational argument does not create belief, but it maintains a climate in which belief may flourish."[10] For LDS believers, sufficient evidence of Book of Mormon antiquity exists to make their faith in it as God's word seem reasonable.

What does DNA evidence say about the Book of Mormon?

The bearing of DNA evidence on the Book of Mormon is one of the most hotly contested subjects in LDS apologetics. It is undisputed that most Native Americans are carriers of Asian DNA, whereas the Book of Mormon alleges a Middle Eastern origin for the people that the record describes. If the Book of

Mormon claimed a single set of Middle Eastern progenitors for the entire Native American population, the contradiction would be devastating to belief in the historicity of the Book of Mormon. Most Saints long operated on that assumption; for a time, an editorial introduction referred to the Book of Mormon "Lamanites" as "the principal ancestors of the American Indians." However, more cautious statements, going back to Smith himself, have always acknowledged that the Book of Mormon nowhere indicates that Lehi's people occupied an otherwise uninhabited continent, and since 2007 the introduction has referred to the Lamanites as "among the ancestors" of the Native American population. Recently LDS scholars have shown convincing textual evidence that the Book of Mormon peoples describe their territory as the size of Palestine, not a continent, let alone a hemisphere.

A molecular biologist and member of a scientific review panel for the National Science Foundation has pointed out that numerous factors make DNA evidence irrelevant to the question of Book of Mormon historicity. The particular genetic makeup of the founding pool of the supposed Book of Mormon peoples is unknown, and its inevitable genetic contamination during one thousand years of Book of Mormon history and the fifteen centuries since would render modern analysis meaningless. What geneticists call "the founder effect," "population bottleneck," and "genetic drift"—these and kindred technical obstacles exist to the application of DNA analysis to the Book of Mormon. The church's cultural assumptions about the origin of modern-day Native Americans have undoubtedly undergone a significant transformation, but for most members such changes do not impugn the credibility of the sacred text itself.

Where did the events in the Book of Mormon take place?

One prominent religious scholar, not of the LDS faith, has insisted that the Church of Jesus Christ of Latter-day Saints can flourish in the age of increasing secularism and liberalism only if it learns to mythologize its scriptures. The chances of that happening as an institutional development are nil. Smith's insistence on real angelic visitations delivering actual ancient records he claimed to translate leaves little room for mythologizing or "spiritualizing" the Book of Mormon. Although the church has no official position on Book of Mormon geography, most LDS scholars who embrace the scripture's historicity have adopted the position of John Sorenson, an anthropologist who has insisted that "the Book of Mormon account actually did take place *some*where."

Initially, Smith believed that the volume recorded the history of the Native Americans as traceable from two migrations to the New World, the first at the time of the fall of the Tower of Babel, and a second, more enduring settlement in the early sixth century BCE. Smith and early Saints seem to have assumed that after their arrival the migrants spread throughout the hemisphere and that the mounds scattered throughout the Mississippi River Valley were evidence of their habitation. In 1841, Smith acquired a copy of John Lloyd Stephens's *Incidents of Travel in Central America, Chiapas, and Yucatan*, the first English-language account of the Mayan civilization and an immediate bestseller. The lavish illustrations of highly complex ruins revealed a level of sophisticated culture that was previously unknown, and Smith and others began to associate Book of Mormon geography with areas southward. "Even the most credulous cannot doubt," the editor of the church's *Times and Seasons* wrote. "These wonderful ruins of *Palenque* are among the mighty works of the Nephites—and the mystery is solved."[11] By 1879, the Book of Mormon was even annotated to correlate Lehi's landing with the coast of Chile, although the editor identified other Book of Mormon places with sites from the Gulf of California to Lake Ontario. By 1920, the church had adopted a more cautious attitude and removed all geographical identifications. In 1986, John Sorenson published an extended defense of a "limited geography" model that confined Book of Mormon civilization to a Mesoamerican area three hundred by six hundred miles. He also defended the "two Cumorahs" thesis, arguing that the hill of that name in New York where Smith found the plates is no more the site of the final, cataclysmic battle described in the final pages of the Book of Mormon than Ithaca, New York, is the home of the Greek hero Odysseus. In both cases, an original place-name is only echoed in a later one by way of commemoration or borrowing.

The church has no official position on Book of Mormon geography; however, publications of the church owned and administered Maxwell Institute for Religious Scholarship (FARMS, or the Foundation for Ancient Research and Mormon Studies in an earlier incarnation) have favored the Sorenson model. Some dissident voices have urged a return to a "heartland model" or other conjectures, but Sorenson has pointed to what he has seen as the three nonnegotiable requirements for a Book of Mormon geography that are only met by the Mesoamerican hypothesis: the map internally constructed by Mormon, principal editor of the plates, did not exceed the aforementioned dimensions; the Book of Mormon described advanced civilizations with cities; and, most crucially, the Book of Mormon peoples had a writing system, a practice known at that time only in Mesoamerica. For these reasons, those Latter-day Saints who accept the book as both scripture and ancient history typically accept Sorenson's conclusions.

Pearl of Great Price

What is the Pearl of Great Price?

In addition to the Bible, the Book of Mormon, and the Doctrine and Covenants, members of the Church of Jesus Christ accept a fourth book of scripture—the Pearl of Great Price. Franklin D. Richards, an apostle and mission president in Great Britain, produced a pamphlet of that name, consisting largely of writings of Joseph Smith, for missionaries and new members in 1851. He explained his purposes in a preface to the first published edition: to demonstrate that the "doctrine and ordinances" of Mormonism were "the same as were revealed to Adam for his salvation after his expulsion from the garden" and that those doctrines and ordinances were "the only means appointed of God by which the generations of men may regain his presence." In other words, he believed that a principal claim of the LDS Church, not clearly evident in its other scriptures, was the antiquity of Christianity. According to a narrative that according to Smith was missing from Genesis, Adam and Eve were taught the gospel, including the future coming of a savior, and they received baptism and the gift of the Holy Ghost. This narrative, coming out of Smith's project to retranslate the Bible, was called the Book of Moses.

In addition, Richards included portions of a "Book of Abraham" that Smith had produced from Egyptian papyri he purchased in 1835. First published in the church's newspaper, these texts added details to the life of Abraham and recounted a "Divine Assembly" at which he and other human spirits were present before the creation of the world. The narrative also includes an account of creation closely paralleling the Genesis version but involving a council of "Gods."

Believing that an authoritative summary of the church's origins and teachings would be invaluable, Richards included in his pamphlet Joseph Smith's own recitation of his First Vision of God and Christ and the events surrounding Smith's reception, translation, and publication of the Book of Mormon. Richards appended Smith's selective summation of church teachings, the Thirteen Articles of Faith. Finally, Richards included a few of Smith's revelations, his revision of Matthew 24, and a poem. Over the ensuing years, leaders quoted freely from the collection, and in 1880 the decision was made to include the volume, with some modifications, in the corpus of LDS scripture.

What are the doctrinal contributions of the Pearl of Great Price?

Few of the church's distinctive doctrines are found in the Book of Mormon. It is actually in the Pearl of Great Price that the religion's unique doctrines first appear. It is there, in the Book of Moses, that one finds Adam and Eve being taught the gospel and receiving baptism. What other Christians call the New Covenant, here the New and Everlasting Covenant, is traced to the Garden of Eden rather than Christ's earthly appearing. The same book alludes to the premortal creation of humans (preexistence receives more detailed discussion in the Book of Abraham). Human participation in a heavenly council, wherein all spirits learn of the plan of earthly probation and progress toward godhood, is described. In such a context, the Fall emerges as part of God's plan, the necessary immersion of humankind in a world of trial and tribulation. The Book of Moses describes Eve as celebrating rather than lamenting the consequences of the fall. Human life for all God's spirit children is only possible because Eve and Adam willfully chose mortality and temporary separation from God. The Book of Moses also provides an early reference to humans progressing to become like God, inheriting his "throne," in Enoch's language. The "prophecy of Enoch," part of the Book of Moses, depicted God the Father immersed in sorrow over the misery of his children. Three times, the prophet Enoch enquires into the baffling phenomenon of this weeping God.

The Book of Abraham adds another radical doctrine to the corpus of LDS belief when it rewrites the creation narrative as involving not a triune God but a group of Gods. Latter-day Saints reject the doctrine of the Trinity as a late and unbiblical innovation. The scriptural seeds of LDS "social Trinitarianism," wherein God and Christ are separate, distinct, embodied beings, are here in the Book of Abraham.

A teaching absolutely central to the church of the nineteenth century was that of gathering. The Book of Moses recounts the story of Enoch, whose people achieved such a degree of unity and righteousness that they were taken into heaven. Smith immediately began to shape the church accordingly, aspiring to gather the people into tightly knit communities, share all things in common, and fashion a new world Zion. With regard to both doctrine and social practice, the Pearl of Great Price constitutes a foundational set of texts.

What is the Book of Abraham?

In the early nineteenth century, prompted in part by Napoleon's acquisition of Egyptian artifacts and the translation of the Rosetta Stone (1822), "Egyptomania" reached a fever pitch in America. Members of the Church of Jesus Christ had additional motivation to be deeply interested in things Egyptian: the Book of Mormon had allegedly been written in "reformed Egyptian," it made reference to additional ancient texts that would come forth in the latter-days, and it indicated that Joseph Smith himself was a descendent of Joseph of Egypt. In 1835, Michael Chandler, a traveling antiquities dealer, entered the town of Kirtland, Ohio, offering for sale four mummies and papyrus scrolls and fragments. Smith was interested. He examined the papyri and announced that they were sacred writings of the patriarch Abraham when he was in Egypt and also of Joseph of the many-colored coat. Smith purchased the papyri and the mummies for $2,400 (about $67,000 in today's terms).

Through a process about which little is known, Smith labored for some months to translate the records, returning to the project in 1842, and published some of the results in that year. The narrative was to play an important role in Smith's theology, which was reaching its fullest exposition in the last years of his life, and centered on the role of the temple and its ordinances. Employing concepts derived from the Book of Abraham, Smith now conceived of the gospel as a "new and everlasting covenant" that originated in premortal, heavenly councils. Other LDS scriptures refer to the human soul as having its origin before the earth's creation. However, the Book of Abraham gives the fullest account of the setting in which that creation was planned, councils in which humans participated. Abraham sees in vision "the intelligences that were organized before the world was" and God's design to send those spirits into mortality "to see if they will do all things whatsoever the Lord their God shall command them" (Abraham 3:22–25). He sees God's intention to add glory upon the heads of the faithful, and he sees both the selection of Christ as the earth's redeemer and the rejection and subsequent rebellion of Satan and those who follow him. God's grand project, in this conception, was to fully integrate the human family into an eternal chain of belonging through rites solemnized in the temple.

Smith reinterpreted the Abrahamic covenant accordingly. What is promised to Abraham is the right and responsibility, pertaining to him and his posterity, to "bear this ministry and this priesthood" to the inhabitants of the earth. And the hint is given that his "seed" will persist beyond the time frame of mortality (Abraham 2). In LDS thought, this will develop into the understanding that the fullness of the gospel was known to Abraham (and even to Father Adam). And that Abraham and his descendants will be the purveyors of the gospel of salvation, with the consequent blessing of an eternal posterity hereafter. This amounts to a complete reworking of Christian covenant theology, which typically sees an Adamic covenant based on works, which Adam and Eve fail to live up to, and a replacement covenant of grace, inaugurated by Christ and fulfilled in his sacrifice. For Latter-day Saints, there is essentially one covenant, which, it is implied, is associated with a "Council in Heaven," where Abraham and an assembly of premortal spirits are present. The covenant is reaffirmed to him in mortality and portends the salvation of the entire human family, made possible by Christ's foreordained mediation. And that salvation goes beyond mere personal return to God's presence to include endless family lines. This is the root of the LDS conception of eternal marriage and eternal families as the warp and woof of eternal life. Smith's institution of these sacraments (the temple "endowment") and his 1842 work on the Book of Abraham were therefore mutually reinforcing and deeply interconnected.

Why do Latter-day Saints believe the Book of Abraham is scripture if Egyptologists call it a fraud?

In 1835 Joseph Smith acquired four Egyptian mummies, along with a quantity of papyrus. Over the next few years, he labored to understand the Egyptian language, which had only begun to be deciphered the previous decade with the translation of the Rosetta Stone. Smith and his colleagues worked to construct a grammar of the Egyptian language relying on a mix of amateur scholarship and prophetic inspiration, either after or in concert with Smith's own inspired production—which he called a translation—of the text he called "the Book of Abraham." He published extracts in the church newspaper but never designated it as scripture or claimed the same authority for its translation that he did for the Book of Mormon, the Book of Moses, or his scores of revelations. Nevertheless, decades after his death it was canonized in 1880 as part of the Pearl of Great Price and is embraced as scripture today by church members.

Many of the papyri in Smith's possession disappeared or were destroyed in the Chicago Fire of 1871, but several remain and have been translated by Egyptologists, who have identified them as pertaining to an Egyptian Book of the Dead—a funerary text that includes Egyptian beliefs about death and the afterlife. Those same scholars point out that the existing texts from which the translation of Smith seems to have been made do not correspond to the narrative published by Smith. Some Latter-day Saints have been shaken by these revelations and lost their faith in the church. For most Saints, however, these developments are not determinative, for two reasons in particular.

First, LDS scholar Hugh Nibley and others have demonstrated impressive parallels between the Book of Abraham and a number of ancient Egyptian texts and traditions. These and the Book of the Dead itself in fact detail many of the themes that are treated in the Book of Abraham but not included in the biblical story of Abraham. In other words, even if the papyri were not precisely what Smith thought them to be, the text he produced has the hallmarks of ancient Egyptian authenticity. Nibley alone, one of the most revered intellectuals in the LDS tradition and competent in Egyptian, wrote literally thousands of pages exploring such connections, including themes of human sacrifice, altar descriptions, the teaching of astronomy to Pharaoh's court, a heavenly council, premortal existence, a cosmic map, and so forth.

Second, it is abundantly clear that Smith used the word "translate" very loosely. He referred to his work on the Bible as a "new translation," even though he did not employ any original manuscripts or ancient languages and only redacted, or edited, his version of the King James Bible, adding interpolations as the inspiration struck him. The same was true with the plates from which he produced the Book of Mormon; he called himself translator in that instance as well but did not actually work with the plates; he left them covered nearby while he channeled the words that a scribe wrote down. So, too, with the Egyptian papyri, LDS scholars suggest, Smith's revelatory imagination was fueled by the physical artifacts, but they served as catalyst rather than literal source. So, the argument goes, even if Smith incorrectly believed he was deciphering the hieroglyphics before him, the texts he produced were inspired scripture. The mechanisms by which LDS scriptures were produced tend to be secondary to the value believers find in them.

Doctrine and Covenants

What is the Doctrine and Covenants?

The Book of Mormon may be the keystone of Mormonism—a sign of Joseph Smith's prophetic authority and the sign to the faithful of Latter-day gathering and Christ's imminent return—but that prophetic authority found expression in numerous revelations and visitations Smith received over the course of a quarter century. "Revelation" as the word is used by Latter-day Saints is best understood as a spectrum that ranges from a verbatim transcription of heavenly communication to utterance that is authoritative by virtue of the speaker's status alone. Smith recorded as revelation some words that he claimed to hear from the mouths of angels or even from Deity. At other times, he saw and heard things in a kind of trance, while others present in the room felt and saw nothing. The majority of his revelations were apparently pronouncements he dictated while feeling himself under the influence of spiritual guidance but in the absence of supernatural manifestations of any kind.

In most instances, the words he channeled took the form of divine address: "thus sayeth the Lord" typically prefaces an admonition, directive, or commandment. But some of his revelations took the form of epistles (127, 128), "items of instruction" (130), and even a "declaration of belief regarding Governments and Laws" (134). Initially, Smith circulated texts of some revelations at church conferences, beginning with the organizational meeting of April 1830. Within three months of the church's founding, Smith and John Whitmer began to collect and arrange the revelations Smith had received. At a conference in Hiram, Ohio, in November 1831, a decision was made to compile and publish the "many revelations . . . received from the Lord prior to this time" (D&C 1, heading). The next year, a selection of revelations went to press in Independence, Missouri. Before they could be published, a mob destroyed the press and scattered the printed sheets. A few hundred salvaged copies containing some sixty-five revelations to the prophet were bound as *The Book of Commandments.* More revelations were added to a subsequent edition newly titled the *Doctrine and Covenants* in 1835. Those revelations were referred to as "commandments." The "Doctrine" part of the collection referred to a set of "lectures on theology." Smith approved these essays on faith as a primer in LDS doctrine. Not all of his revelations were incorporated into LDS scriptures. At least forty known revelations have never been included.[12] Additional revelations were again incorporated into a new edition of the *Doctrine and Covenants* in 1876, and a "Manifesto" of Wilford Woodruff was included from 1908 on; in 1921, Joseph's "Lectures on Faith," which had been included since 1835, were removed.[13] In 1976, two revelations received in 1836 and 1918 were added to another collection of scripture, the Pearl of Great Price. In 1981, they were transferred to the *Doctrine and Covenants*, along with an "Official Declaration" on the Priesthood. Smith obviously meant it when he wrote to John Wentworth that "we believe all that God has revealed, all that He does now reveal, and we believe that He will yet reveal many great and important things pertaining to the Kingdom of God" (Article of Faith 9).

What are the more significant revelations of Joseph Smith?

Though not as well known outside LDS circles (and not as well studied within them) as the Book of Mormon, the Doctrine and Covenants has been more influential in grounding LDS doctrines. Section 89, known to the Saints as the revelation on the Word of Wisdom, provides members with their famous code of health, "showing forth the order and will of God in the temporal salvation of all saints," and section 119 establishes tithing as the economic law of the church. The magnificent epiphany of the three degrees of glory recorded in section 76 was so celebrated in Joseph's day that it was known simply as "The Vision," a title that most Saints would today associate with the original visitation of the Father and Son to the boy prophet.

Smith had felt impressed in his work on the Bible that "if God rewarded every one according to the deeds done in the body, the term 'Heaven,' as intended for the Saints' eternal home, must include more kingdoms than one" (D&C 76, heading). Pondering the reference to resurrection in John 5:29, Smith and his companion Sidney Rigdon both experienced a detailed vision of three distinct spheres of heaven, named by them in descending order as the celestial, terrestrial, and telestial kingdoms. The LDS understanding of a graded salvation, and one that is nearly universal, derives from this section.

Section 20 lays out the principles of church organization and government and, along with section 107, discusses the priesthood and defines the duties pertaining to its several offices. Section 130 canonizes the LDS doctrine of a corporeal God, and section 132 is the prophet's official pronouncement on both plural and eternal marriage. Other notable sections include his 1832 prophecy that a civil war would erupt, beginning in South Carolina (87); his "Olive Leaf" revelation, which defines the Light of Christ as both the power that enlightens the human mind and "the light which is in all things, which giveth life to all things" (88), and Smith's plaintive plea to the Lord for succor while incarcerated in Liberty Jail, Missouri: "O God, where art thou? And where is the pavilion of thy hiding place?" (121); as well as the Lord's gentle rebuke: "the Son of man hath descended below them all. Art thou greater than he? . . . Thy days are known, and thy years shall not be numbered less; therefore, fear not what man can do, for God is with thee forever and ever."

The most recent addition to the scriptural volume, section 138, is a 1918 vision that one of Smith's successors, Joseph F. Smith, had of the postmortal spirit world. In that vision, prompted by Peter's words that "the gospel [is] preached also to them that are dead" (1 Peter 4:6), Smith saw the work of evangelizing taking place among the spirits of the departed. Learning that faithful missionaries continue their labors after death and witnessing the joyful reception of the gospel on the other side of death lent greater urgency and meaning to the work of Latter-day Saints in researching family history and participating in temple work that includes baptisms and other ordinances for those who accept the gospel postmortem.

The Bible

Do Latter-day Saints read the Bible differently from other Christians?

Latter-day Saints "believe the Bible to be the word of God as far as it is translated correctly" (Article of Faith 8). Virtually every denomination finds a basis for at least some of their distinctive doctrines in their particular interpretation of key passages. Catholics find a biblical basis for good works and sacramentalism, Protestants for salvation by grace alone, and charismatic groups for speaking in tongues. Latter-day Saints are no exception in this regard. The following are a few examples that illustrate how Latter-day Saints find biblical support for some of the church's more unconventional beliefs and practices.

Vicarious Salvation

Several New Testament scriptures are invoked by Latter-day Saints to support their unique practice of performing saving sacraments, like baptism for the dead, on behalf of those who have passed out of life without embracing the gospel. In the epistles of Peter, the author writes that "Christ also hath once suffered for sins, the just for the unjust, that he might bring us to God, being put to death in the flesh, but quickened by the Spirit: By which also he went and preached unto the spirits in prison; Which sometime were disobedient, when once the longsuffering of God waited in the days of Noah" (1 Peter 3:18–20). A few verses later, he adds the detail that "for this cause was the gospel preached also to them that are dead, that they might be judged according to men in the flesh, but live according to God in the spirit" (1 Peter 4:6). Accordingly, Latter-day Saints believe that those who have lacked exposure to the gospel of Jesus Christ in their mortal life will be evangelized in the hereafter. And believing, as Catholics and other Christians do, that baptism is God's designated portal into salvation, they extend the opportunity for baptism to those deceased who have accepted the gospel in the afterlife. Paul, they believe, was referring to just such a practice in his letter to the Corinthians when he asked, in reference to the Resurrection: "else what shall they do which are baptized for the dead, if the dead rise not at all? why are they then baptized for the dead?" (1 Corinthians 15:29).

An Expanded Canon

The Old Testament prophet Ezekiel, prophesying of the last days, describes God's instruction to "take thee one stick, and write upon it, For Judah, and for the children of Israel his companions: then take another stick, and write upon it, For Joseph, the stick of Ephraim, and for all the house of Israel his companions: And join them one to another into one stick; and they shall become one in thine hand" (Ezekiel 37:16–17). The reference to a record of Judah that will at some point be joined to a record of Ephraim is read by many Latter-day Saints as referring to the Jewish scriptures, the basis of the Bible, finding a companion volume in the last days when it is joined to a record of another offshoot of the House of Israel, that is, a branch of Joseph that migrated to the New World and produced the Book of Mormon. Isaiah, the Saints believe, also saw that event unfold when he prophesied of Israelites who "shalt be brought down, and shalt speak out of the ground, and thy speech shall be low out of the dust, and thy voice shall be, as of one that hath a familiar spirit, out of the ground, and thy speech shall whisper out of the dust" (Isaiah 29:4). Finally, in the Book of Mormon itself, Jesus interprets his reference to the "other sheep" he would visit, which he mentioned in connection with his death (John 10:16), as referring to those same Israelite descendants whom he visited subsequent to his resurrection, as described in 3 Nephi 15.

Preexistence and postmortal theosis, or deification

While Latter-day Saints base their doctrine of premortal existence on nineteenth-century revelations, they find traces of the idea in the biblical record. The idea was current among the Jewish people, as the apostles' query to Jesus indicates. In reference to a blind man, they ask if a premortal sin was the cause of his being "born blind" (John 9:2). And the prophet Jeremiah, Latter-day Saints note, was told that he was ordained as a prophet before he was "formed in the belly" (1:5). While such language might be read as referring to foreordination in the mind of God only, the Saints take it literally. Finally, Job hears the Lord refer to a time before the earth's creation when "all the sons of God shouted for joy" (38:7). While most Christians would find in these words a reference to angelic hosts, the Latter-day Saints associate that scene with jubilation at the unfolding of God's plan for humankind's spiritual descent into mortality.

At the other end of the human spirit's eternal saga, Latter-day Saints do not hesitate to read literally the words of Jesus, when he quotes a psalm to emphasize humankind's exalted potential (in support of his own claims to divinity): "is it not written in your law, I said, Ye are gods?" (John 10:34, quoting Psalm 82:6). Or, as Paul writes, we are "heirs of God, and joint-heirs with Christ" (Romans 8:17).

Does some Latter-day Saint doctrine conflict with the Bible?

The havoc wrought in Christendom by the Reformation was the result of the mass dissemination of the Bible and the varying interpretations new waves of readers brought to the text. One Christian's interpretation is seldom another's. Nevertheless, some biblical passages do seem flatly at variance with LDS teachings. The LDS response to these discrepancies takes two forms. Sometimes, the Saints have appealed to missing contexts that would alter the meaning of the text; sometimes, Joseph Smith simply declared the biblical text to be in error.

An example of the first response pertains to Matthew's Gospel, when Jesus is queried about which husband, of seven, will be a woman's spouse in the life to come. Jesus responds: "in the resurrection they neither marry, nor are given in marriage, but are as the angels of God in heaven" (Matthew 22:30). Most Christians would not be averse to the continuation of loving relationships into the heavenly sphere, but the common ceremonial words "till death do you part" offer a semiofficial endorsement of the view suggested in Matthew. This view of marriage is in stark contrast with the LDS belief—and there are few as pivotal—in the eternity of the marriage bond, when properly administered and lived up to. How to reconcile the LDS doctrine of eternal marriage with its nonexistence in the biblical Resurrection? Latter-day Saints leaders have suggested that the words of Jesus do not preclude marriage itself but the giving in marriage. In other words, marriage, like baptism, is a sacred sacrament that must be performed on earth—either by those so joined or by others performing the ritual vicariously on their behalf. Those who do not receive the sacrament will live singly in the eternities, as ministering angels.

Other instances of scriptural conflict are more resistant to context-based shifts in meaning. The Westminster Confession affirms belief in a God "without body, parts, or passions." Latter-day Saints, by contrast, affirm that God possesses all three. The Saints' scripture is emphatic that "the Father has a body of flesh and bones as tangible as man's; the Son also" (D&C 130:22). Those words are inconsistent with both Old and New Testament texts. It is at this juncture that, in LDS practice, Joseph Smith's revelations trump a biblical text from which "many plain and precious parts" have been excised or distorted, according to the Book of Mormon. Smith insisted that "many things in the bible do not, as they now stand, accord with the revelation of the Holy Ghost to me."[14] He believed himself called to make revisions and corrections to the Bible as part of his prophetic remit. Thus, the words of Jesus to the Samaritan woman, "God is a Spirit," become revised as "unto [true worshipers] hath God promised his spirit."[15] By the same token, the statement in Exodus that "thou canst not see my face; for there shall no man see me, and live" becomes "neither shall there be any *sinful* man at any time that shall see my face and live [emphasis added]."[16] John's "no man hath seen God at any time" gains the caveat "except he hath borne record of the Son."[17] Such instances of recasting the language of the Bible to comport with Smith's teachings are relatively few.

Do Latter-day Saints read the Bible literally?

LDS attitudes toward biblical interpretation vary. The only official declaration on the subject appears in one of the Articles of Faith, stating that "we believe the Bible to be the word of God," with the significant caveat *"as far as it is translated correctly."* "*Translated* correctly" is often taken to mean the more open-ended "*transmitted* correctly." As a rule, Latter-day Saints tend to fall between biblical fundamentalists and liberal Protestants in their approach to interpretation. Joseph Smith—and the Book of Mormon—emphatically criticize the Bible as missing many "plain and precious things" and as being in "many" cases out of harmony with Smith's revelations. His clear assertion that the Book of Mormon is the "most perfect" of books effectively gives it more authority than the Bible in the LDS faith. Smith in fact spent years working on his own translation of the Bible. Not knowing New Testament Greek or ancient Hebrew, he relied on inspiration to produce what was in reality an edited, revised version. His edits included interpolations (several chapters in some cases), deletions, and rewordings. Hence, by precedent and clear example, Latter-day Saints are not bound to the Bible as an unerring guide. This cautious attitude is understandable given that the church's very origins could be said to be rooted in Smith's personal experience of the failure of *sola scriptura*, or the doctrine of the Bible as the sole and sufficient basis of religious authority. In recounting the background to his own First Vision, Smith described a scene of religious contention and verbal violence, priest contending against priest and convert against convert. He became convinced, he wrote, that humans were manifestly incapable of resolving religious controversies "by an appeal to the Bible."[18]

On the other hand, Latter-day Saints do consider the common Bible (the King James version in the US), not the Joseph Smith Translation, as one of their "Standard Works" and use it in both mission work and in worship and study. None of the leaders receives training in seminaries or theology departments, and developments in biblical scholarship, from "higher criticism" to the "documentary hypothesis," have made little inroads in the LDS mind; consequently, biblical interpretation has tended to be very conservative. No official decrees mandate acceptance of a literal flood, for example, but past leaders have veered toward literalism often enough to make such literal readings commonplace among the laity (this, even though Brigham Young expressed skepticism about the Bible's "baby stories").

Do Latter-day Saints have their own version of the Bible?

Shortly after publishing the Book of Mormon in 1830, Smith came to believe that he was called by God to retranslate the Bible. (He never worked with the original languages, so it was actually a redaction rather than a translation.) He believed this assignment was so important that he referred to it as a "branch" of his calling as prophet. The most important outcome of the project was his production of what he called the "Book of Moses," a narrative that provided significant additional details about Adam and Eve. Most striking was the description of Adam and Eve being taught the gospel and receiving baptism, the gift of the Holy Ghost, and angelic instruction about the Atonement of Jesus Christ. This account occasioned an utter reconstruction of the covenant theology so central to the Christian tradition, a theology in which the failed covenant of works made with Adam is replaced with the later covenant of grace. The New Testament (which depicts the "new covenant") is almost universally believed in Christendom to be a remedy for the failure of Adam (and in supersessionist thinking, the Jews) to maintain their original obligations outlined in the Old Testament (which narrates the "old covenant"). Smith synthesized those two versions of the covenant into one "Everlasting Covenant," originating before the world was formed. Testifying to the antiquity of this one eternal covenant, Smith's revisions also refer to the spiritual creation of humans before the world's formation and the plan for a Savior that was in place long before Adam.

Except for these chapters that Smith interpolated into the book of Genesis, most of his revisions were relatively minor but doctrinally significant. They erased much of the harshness of a Calvinist-leaning depiction of God (he emended verses where God was said to harden hearts or predispose individuals to wickedness) and depicted the Mosaic law as a regression from, rather than simple preparation for, a gospel fullness (which fullness, in Smith's telling, the first set of stone tablets given to Moses by God contained.) Original sin is portrayed as a false doctrine (children are born in innocence), and God is more overtly anthropomorphic (humans are created in the image of his *body*).

It may seem strange that Smith's revision was never published by the LDS Church (though it was by an offshoot, the Reorganized Church of Jesus Christ of Latter Day Saints, now Community of Christ). The manuscripts of the retranslation were retained by Emma, Joseph Smith's widow, who broke with the church under the leadership of Brigham Young. Relations between the rival organization (the Reorganized Church) and the Utah church were poor, and Young showed no interest in petitioning for access to the manuscripts. Perhaps more important, a church with its own idiosyncratic rendering of the Bible would be handicapped in efforts to evangelize a Christian world (the church's primary goal then, as now) using a version not recognized by other Christians.

Why do Latter-day Saints employ the King James Version of the Bible?

Although Smith made his own "translation" of the Bible, it never became the LDS standard version, for reasons of access to Smith's manuscripts and the imperatives of evangelizing other Christians. Published in 1611, the King James Version grew in use until it was virtually unchallenged as the Bible of the English-speaking Protestant world. Today, the New International Version is more popular with evangelicals, and biblical scholars give the Revised Standard Version higher marks for accuracy. However, the King James Version has done more to shape and inspire the English tongue than any other volume in history. Its language and rhythms have become part of the unconscious cultural grammar of the English-speaking world. This fact and the unparalleled beauty and lyricism of the text explain only in part why it continues to be the most read Bible among the LDS population.

Latter-day Saints have another reason, unique to their faith, for their fidelity to the King James Version. When Smith translated the Book of Mormon, he did so employing the language of the Bible version then in universal use. The Book of Mormon abounds in "thees" and "thous" and in Hebraic constructions ("plates of brass" and "rod of iron," never "brass plates" or "iron rod"; "dreamed a dream," "build buildings," and "judge judgment"— not "had a dream," "construct buildings," or "render judgment"). Steeped in the Book of Mormon as they are, and commonly practicing daily scripture study, Latter-day Saints are probably more steeped in the language of the 1611 Bible than any other group of Christian readers. In addition, the Book of Mormon contains many passages that parallel, even replicate verbatim, passages from the New Testament. Employing a different Bible version would impede or obfuscate the symmetry and intertextuality that is otherwise so readily detectable. And given the fact that the Book of Mormon was translated "by the gift and power of God," as the Latter-day Saints believe, it is virtually unthinkable that Smith's translation will be recast—at least in any church-sanctioned effort—in a more modern idiom. Permanently interrelated with the King Jamesian Book of Mormon, the King James Version seems likely to endure indefinitely as the officially approved version of the English Bible in the LDS church.

6

BELIEFS

What are the most distinctive beliefs of Latter-day Saints?

One unique teaching of the Latter-day Saints is belief in God as a divine being who exists in eternal relationship with a "Heavenly Mother." The Church of Jesus Christ has little to say about this divine figure other than that she is a counterpart to God the Father. In some sacred, real sense, they are the parents of the family of human spirits. Unlike the God of the creeds, "without body, parts, or passions," the LDS God possesses all three. He is embodied, and he fully shares in and is susceptible to human suffering. Christian theology has been defined as "the whole complex of the Divine dispensation from the fall of Adam to the Redemption through Christ."[1] The Church of Jesus Christ, however, posits a premortal world before the Fall in which humans lived as spirit children of heavenly parents. Saints hold the spirit to be eternal, though it was given its form by God. What Christians call the Fall the LDS consider more in the nature of an ascent. Eve led the way in subjecting herself and her posterity to the painful but educative processes of mortal incarnation. So Latter-day Saints reject original sin and the Fall as a catastrophe. Life is necessary to acquire a physical body like God (which body will be perfected at the Resurrection) and to learn by experience to prize the good and choose holiness and virtue.

Another peculiarity of LDS doctrine is belief in the evangelization of humankind's ancestors. Since the Saints believe that a just God would extend the same opportunities for salvation to all people, those deprived of the opportunity in this life must receive the message of the gospel in the "spirit world" to which the departed go. Those "ordinances" or sacraments, such as baptism, that they did not undergo while alive they can receive vicariously. That is, living individuals can be baptized on their behalf—hence the practice of "baptism for the dead" that has stirred controversy from time to time. Such ordinances have efficacy, Latter-day Saints believe, only if the deceased candidates choose to accept the sacrament and the associated covenants they entail.

Salvation itself has a different character in the Church of Jesus Christ. The greatest joys in life are those experienced in relationship with loved ones. The Saints believe that the "same sociality which exists among us here will exist among us there, only it will be coupled with eternal glory" (D&C 130:2). At the heart of that sociality are family relationships and marital love; the LDS preach that marriage vows properly administered and honored can have eternal efficacy. In some manner or form that is not doctrinally articulated, men and women in the Celestial Kingdom will continue the process of adopting or producing and nurturing "the souls of men." In sum, Latter-day Saints preach an embodied male and female Deity, an eternal existence of the human soul, life as a planned education in the costs and consequences of free will, and heaven as a sociable, dynamic, progressive community of celestialized persons—to which all persons, living and dead, may eventually be shepherded.

What do Latter-day Saints mean by "apostasy" and "Restoration"?

Recurrently in Christian history, individuals have felt that the church had at some point diverged or apostatized from its original, God-ordained trajectory. In the West, the Protestant Reformation was but the first effort to effect substantial course corrections of doctrine and organization that resulted in entirely new, thriving denominations. For some figures, reform was insufficient, and a complete reinauguration of Christianity was thought necessary. Some of these Christians became known as "seekers," and in the nineteenth century some constituted part of the "restorationist" tradition (descendants of which include the Disciples of Christ, among others). They believed that God would effectively start over, by inspiring or calling individuals to restore a faith in strict harmony with New Testament Christianity.

The Church of Jesus Christ of Latter-day Saints, by its very name, identifies itself in just such "restorationist" terms. The name harks back to the church Christ instituted with apostles, teachers, pastors, and so on (see for instance Ephesians 4:11) and identifies the current incarnation as a "latter-day" counterpart to the original. The Church of Jesus Christ differs from typical restorationist projects in some essential regards. First, the Latter-day Saints did not begin by stripping away historical accretions, following the "back to the Bible" mantra of others. Restorationists, like the Puritans before them, worked largely by subtraction. Much to the contrary, the Saints expanded the concept of revelation and of the canon itself as they sought to reconstitute a gospel fullness greater even than that described in the New Testament, or circumscribed by the covers of the Bible. To this end, they incorporated key doctrines not explicitly or clearly fleshed out biblically.

Most fundamental in this regard was the conception of human premortality as a sphere in which the human family lived as spirit children of heavenly parents. Life, in this view, was an ascent toward godliness, requiring embodiment, spiritual education, and the goal of consolidation into an eternal family extending horizontally to family and kin as well as vertically to God. What Latter-day Saints mean by "apostasy" was the loss of two things in particular: first, the essential blueprint of human origins, purpose, and destiny, and second, a priesthood authority to administer the kingdom of God on earth and perform those sacramental rites that fully integrate individuals into a divine family.

Here we find a second major difference between the Church of Jesus Christ and other restorationist projects—and indeed all Protestant churches. Latter-day Saints believe that certain sacraments are the indispensable means ordained by God to effect the salvation of the human family, under the authority of an ordained Priesthood. Hence, Restoration for Saints includes the twin ideas of a restored cosmic narrative that gives true understanding of humankind's place in the cosmos and the literal reordination of apostles and prophets by God's messengers. The first was largely brought about by the Book of Moses, the Book of Abraham, and the Book of Mormon, together with numerous revelations canonized as the Doctrine and Covenants. The second occurred when angelic beings—including resurrected biblical figures from Elijah to John the Baptist and Peter, James, and John—appeared to Smith and conferred on him keys and authority.

Does the Latter-day Saint concept of apostasy mean that no one else has the truth?

Joseph Smith's understanding of the Great Apostasy was largely based on his reading of Revelation 12, wherein a woman (generally read by Protestants as symbolizing the church) is threatened by a dragon (read here Satan, or the forces of evil). It would appear to be significant in Smith's thinking that the woman "fled into the wilderness, where she hath a place prepared of God" (12:6). He apparently took this to mean that many gospel elements were hidden, obscured, or in retreat from the orthodox tradition but not erased entirely. Smith recurrently described the Restoration as the bringing of the church "out of the wilderness." To that end, he frequently drew on outside teachings and writings that he felt were divinely inspired and incorporated them into his ongoing project of Restoration. He found allusions to baptism for the dead and to eternal progression in apocryphal sources and in the work of the contemporary Scottish thinker Thomas Dick. He detected usable elements of temple ritual in Masonic ceremonies. Some of the language and illustrations of contemporary Universalists made their way into his revelations as well. Mainstream Christianity was also a source of crucial truths. He was quite explicit about this, in fact, once telling an audience: "have the Presbyterians any truth? Embrace that. Have the Baptists, Methodists, and so forth? Embrace that. Get all the good in the world, and you will come out a pure Mormon."[2] Elsewhere he said: "we don't ask any people to throw away any good they have got. We only ask them to come and get more."[3] The editor of the church newspaper, Thomas Ward, found in Catholicism inspired understanding of the influence the living could have on the disposition of the dead: "we believe, that fallen as the Roman church may be, she has traces of many glorious principles that were once in the church of Christ."[4] One of Smith's successors, John Taylor, also acknowledged important elements of truth and beauty in the Roman Catholic tradition: "there were [people] in those dark ages who could commune with God. And who, by the power of faith, could draw aside the curtain of eternity and gaze upon the invisible world. There were those who could gaze upon the face of God, have the ministering of angels, and unfold the future destinies of the world. If those were dark ages I pray God to give me a little darkness."[5]

Secular learning too constituted part of the gospel in Smith's view. He dictated revelations in which the Saints were commanded to "teach one another words of wisdom; yea, seek ye out of the best books words of wisdom; seek learning, even by study and also by faith" (D&C 88:118). In sum, Smith was far from believing that only Latter-day Saints possessed or had access to the truth. A cosmic narrative beginning in a human pre-existence and a divinely transmitted priesthood authority set the Latter-day Saints apart from their peers. Divine truth emanates from the Holy Spirit, "which is the gift of God unto all those who diligently seek him," in the prophet Nephi's words (1 Nephi 10:17).

Is the Church of Jesus Christ of Latter-day Saints "the only true church"?

Latter-day scripture declares the Church of Jesus Christ of Latter-day Saints to be "the only true and living church upon the face of the whole earth." The apostle Henry Eyring explained his understanding of the phrase: "this is the true Church, the only true Church, because in it are the keys of the priesthood," that is, God-given authority, and also because "through the Church and the ordinances which are in it . . . the blessings of the sealing power reach into the spirit world."[6] The Church of Jesus Christ is the institutional form of that body of leaders and believers who have the sacred stewardship to disseminate the gospel as far and widely as possible, and to provide the sacraments for the living and the dead that bind them to God and to each other.

Latter-day Saints may be alone in believing that the world's unevangelized billions are taught the gospel after death in the spirit world. And those ordinances (or sacraments) that incorporate them into a heavenly family are performed vicariously for them in LDS temples. As they live the precepts of the gospel in the spirit world and grow in truth and light, they continue to progress toward salvation, as do Christ's disciples living on the earth. Salvation is defined by Latter-day Saints as a heavenly existence in eternal, loving relationship with God and other humans, in a sanctified and glorified condition. And God intends for all his children, in and outside his institutional church, living and deceased, to find their way home. In this view, the Church of Jesus Christ of Latter-day Saints is a portal of salvation, not the reservoir of the righteous or the domain of the saved. Progress will be continual, here and hereafter, for virtually everyone.

Will only Latter-day Saints be saved?

In a public sermon Smith preached that "all who would follow the precepts of the Bible, whether Mormon or not, would assuredly be saved."[7] A Latter-day Saint scripture corroborates this teaching: "whosoever repenteth and cometh unto me, the same is my church" (D&C 10:67). Latter-day Saints are confident that, with rare exceptions, the vast sea of humanity will come to embrace the Savior's teachings and offering—either here or in the spirit world after death. God's invitation for his spirit children to become like him, and join with him in eternal life, was extended to the entire human family. To navigate through the educative but hazardous labyrinths of mortality, the resources and power of correct understanding, covenantal reinforcement, and specific, essential salvific ordinances were necessary. However, an institutional church preaching the fullness of gospel understanding has been available to limited numbers of people in limited times and places. Far more have and will always pass through life in ignorance of or disregard for the cosmic background and moral precepts that guide humankind into eternal life. Yet, if they are all to be made participants in this scheme whose original conception, Smith taught, they witnessed and assented to in premortal realms, provision must be made for the gospel and its sealing sacraments to encompass the entire range of humanity, living and dead, including those who lived and passed before, outside, and unknowing of the Savior's mission.

Membership in the church is no guarantee of salvation, and a position outside the church is no absolute bar. The church is simply the steward over the fullest exposition of the human saga from premortal existence to eternal life, and over the temple sacraments that can bind together the entire human family in an unbroken chain.

What is the church's relationship to Christianity?

The Church of Jesus Christ has had a vexed relationship to mainstream Christianity.

When people say "Christian," they typically have one of two things in mind. One meaning pertains to a religious tradition that is defined by a series of historic creeds codified by church councils in the fourth century, whose primary purpose was to define the nature of the Christian God. The result of their deliberations is known as Trinitarianism—the belief that Christ is "consubstantial with the Father," that there are three persons in the Trinity, the Father, Son, and Holy Spirit, "but not three Gods but one God." In the opening years of the twenty-first century, the Methodist, Presbyterian, Southern Baptist, and Catholic churches all declared that, in the language of the Methodists, the Church of Jesus Christ of Latter-day Saints "does not fit within the bounds of the historic, apostolic tradition of Christian faith."[8] The LDS rejection of Trinitarianism is often cited as the principal disqualifier, along with belief in extrabiblical scripture (like the Book of Mormon), for inclusion in the Christian fold.

Latter-day Saints readily agree that many of their doctrines are out of harmony with the official creeds of historic Christianity. Asserting an embodied God, separate and distinct from Jesus Christ, places them squarely outside the three-in-one and one-in-three Trinitarianism. Another distinctive LDS belief that is little discussed but deeply held is that "God" can be understood as a name for a Heavenly Father and Heavenly Mother in eternal relationship. As for scripture—the Saints profess the Bible "to be the word of God, as far as it is translated correctly." They also believe the Book of Mormon to be God's word, along with a collection of revelations received by Joseph Smith (the Doctrine and Covenants) and a collection of various other writings by Smith and his interpolations to the Bible (the Pearl of Great Price). Catholics accept only the Bible as scripture, and Protestants elevate the Bible even higher, making it the only source of authority and doctrine alike—the doctrine called *sola scriptura*. The Latter-day Saints utterly reject the idea of a closed canon, believing that God continues now and in diverse times and places in the past to reveal his word to prophets. A Bible "with the cover torn off" is a highly destabilizing idea and runs counter to the general Christian consensus of a fixed body of doctrine, an "original deposit of faith" that is whole and sufficient, subject only to gradual and careful development under the influence of the Holy Spirit.

Another way of understanding the term "Christian," however, might be as the name for any individual who believes that Jesus was the promised Messiah, or Christ, that he was born of a virgin, healed the sick and afflicted, was crucified for the sins of the world, and rose on the third day. A Christian in this sense would believe that her own resurrection and return to the Father—or "salvation"—comes through faith in and devotion to Christ and his teachings, and in no other way. In this sense the Latter-day Saints can certainly be classed as Christian. Their first of thirteen articles of faith stipulates belief in "God the Eternal Father, and in his Son, Jesus Christ, and in the Holy Ghost." The third asserts that "through the atonement of Christ, all mankind may be saved, by obedience to the laws and ordinances of the gospel." One Book of Mormon verse captures the place of Christ in the Latter-day Saint faith: "and we talk of Christ, we rejoice in Christ, we preach of Christ, we prophesy of Christ, and we write according to our prophecies, that our children may know to what source they may look for a remission of their sins" (2 Nephi 25:26).

How do the Latter-day Saints understand sin and salvation?

The LDS religion does not affirm a catastrophe in Eden, an inherited condition of original sin, or the need for redemption or salvation from that condition. The Saints do, however, believe in sin and salvation. They believe that in a primeval beginning before the Creation, heavenly parents invited the human family (who existed as unembodied souls) to continue the process of becoming like them. In the Lectures on Faith overseen by Smith, salvation was defined in uniquely restorationist language:

> Where shall we find a prototype into whose likeness we may be assimilated, in order that we may be made partakers of life and salvation? or in other words, where shall we find a *saved being*? for if we can find a saved being, we may ascertain, without much difficulty, what all others must be, in order to be saved—they must be like that individual or they cannot be saved: . . . whatever constitutes the salvation of one, will constitute the salvation of every creature which will be saved: . . . We ask, then, where is the prototype? or where is the saved being? . . . it is Christ: all will agree in this that he is the prototype or standard of salvation, or in other words, that he is a saved being. . . . How it is that he is saved? . . . because he is a just and holy being; and if he were anything different from what he is he would not be saved; for his salvation depends on his being precisely what he is and nothing else; . . . Thus says John, in his first epistle, Behold, now we are the sons of God, and it doth not appear what we shall be; but we know, that when he shall appear we shall be like him; for we shall see him as he is. And any man that has this hope in him purifies himself, even as he is pure.—Why purify himself as he is pure? because, if they do not they cannot be like him.[9]

In other words, for members of the Church of Jesus Christ, becoming a saint, or being sanctified, is a process of aligning the self with eternal principles—a process made possible and facilitated by Christ's example and selfless offering but not possible through his righteousness alone. Salvation is a natural consequence of one's chosen compliance with eternal laws that relate cause to effect, just as God's own standing as God is the natural and inevitable consequence of his perfect compliance with eternal laws. In this scheme, sin is the violation of those principles that define and constitute the nature of happiness and thus the nature of God (Alma 41). Those principles are articulated as moral laws. The natural fruit of obeying those laws is happiness and peace; the fruit of disobedience (or sin) is pain, suffering, and alienation from God and those one loves. No one is capable of living in perfect harmony with those principles, and humans willfully make sinful choices along the way. Christ's perfect love, manifest in his atoning sacrifice, provides the means for healing and renewed efforts until one reaches the perfect day. In that sense, he is our Savior and Redeemer, our Healer and facilitator of salvation.

Are there Latter-day Saint theologians?

The relationship of the Church of Jesus Christ to theology is complicated. Joseph Smith was himself a dynamic, speculative, adventuresome thinker. As a contemporary theologian has commented, the scope of his theological innovations led to "realms of doctrine unimagined in traditional Christian theology."[10] "By proving contrarieties truth is made manifest," Smith said on one occasion, suggesting a key to his modus operandi. He produced a number of dictated revelations and translations, but he also expressed his desire to be untrammeled in giving his opinion freely without his words being taken as dogma. He supervised a series of "Lectures on Theology" given at the School of the Prophets, which he organized. Brigham Young was similarly an original religious innovator, although many of his innovations later died or were repudiated, including a doctrine of Adam as God, Atonement by the shedding of human blood, and polygamy as essential to eternal life. With the passing of Young, the church leadership increasingly came to associate the project of theology with apostate Christendom. In the early twentieth century, a group of vibrant and highly educated leaders were charged with developing church doctrine and manuals: James Talmage, B. H. Roberts, and John Widtsoe produced a number of influential works of systematic and speculative theology. Following a failed experiment in sending church educators to the University of Chicago Divinity School in the 1930s (some were converted to progressive, liberal Protestant ideas), the church entered a period of retrenchment and doctrinal consolidation. From that time on, the notion that "theology is what happens when revelation fails" has been the common sensibility.

The LDS scriptural canon alternately enjoins both doctrinal exceptionalism and intellectual openness. "Ye are not sent forth to be taught, but to teach the children of men the things which I have put into your hands by the power of my Spirit" (D&C 43:15) reads one revelation. This explains a general LDS reluctance to look to wider Christendom for inspired doctrine. At the same time, Smith himself taught: "if the Presbyterians have any truth, embrace that. If the Baptists and Methodists have truth, embrace that too. Get all the good in the world if you want to come out a pure Mormon."[11] In his personal library, he had books by Calvinist preachers, lectures on Universalism, a Catholic prayer book, and meditations by the Anglican clergyman James Hervey.

Ultimately, theology will always have a subordinate—or nonexistent—role in the institutional LDS Church, for the compelling reason that the members of the First Presidency and the Quorum of the Twelve Apostles are all sustained as "prophets, seers, and revelators." The church is founded on the belief in the reality of a divine inspiration that preempts scholarly avenues to doctrine. The Saints are not oblivious of the merits of academic training, but they are in accord with Kierkegaard's views on the apostolic calling: "to honor one's father because he is exceptionally intelligent is impiety," in his famous formulation. As he explains, "when God appoints a specific human being to have divine authority. . . . The person called in this way does not, in the relation between persons, relate himself qua human being . . . (as a genius, an exceptionally gifted person, etc)."[12] In other words, the authority of that individual, and his or her claim on humanity ("with regard to what God had entrusted to him"), is independent of any qualities or qualifications of that person judged on his or her own merits.

In recent years, the academic subdiscipline of "Mormon studies" has grown at a prodigious rate. Utah State University, Claremont Graduate University, and the University of Virginia all have chairs or programs in Mormon studies. Inevitably, many works (and even a journal) devoted to LDS theology have appeared. However, such works and the figures behind them have no official and little unofficial impact on the course of LDS doctrinal teachings.

Do Latter-day Saints worship Joseph Smith?

Latter-day Saints categorically deny that they worship Joseph Smith; however, they send out confusing signals that explain such a perception. His autobiographical writings have been canonized, the LDS hymnbook includes anthems that praise him, and an LDS scripture asserts that he "has done more, save Jesus only, for the salvation of men in this world, than any other man that ever lived in it" (D&C 135:3). Other denominations, such as Methodism and Lutheranism, managed to develop their traditions without attributing such high status to their founders, Wesley and Luther, respectively. The case of the Latter-day Saints is different. Protestant groups assert that the real authority behind their churches resides in the Bible. Founding figures can therefore fade into the background without detriment to the doctrinal foundations of those traditions. Young Joseph Smith found the Bible inadequate to the task of establishing religious truth—as witnessed by the fracturing and fragmentation in Christendom. He claimed that direct apostolic authority was necessary. The original apostolic succession beginning with Jesus's twelve ordained apostles had, he believed, been interrupted in the first century AD. Only heavenly messengers could relaunch the chain of succession. Smith said that Peter, James, and John, in resurrected form, personally appeared to him and his associate Oliver Cowdery and conferred on them apostolic authority.

The entire authority of the church Smith founded, in other words, depends not on a particular interpretation of scripture but on his claim to have been personally the recipient of Heaven's authorizing acts. His personal narrative about such experiences is integral to the very viability of the church. The church canonized his account—"The Joseph Smith History"—in 1880 and continues to treat it as foundational to a "testimony" of the church he founded, the scriptures he produced, and the doctrines he taught. The result is an emphasis on Joseph Smith that finds a closer parallel in Mohammed's place in Islam than to any Christian figure's role in Christian history.

Smith was himself emphatic that he was just a man, an instrument in restoring the fullness of the gospel. He refers to himself as one of "the weak things of the earth" (D&C 124:1), and there are canonized revelations in which God reproves him for lapses in obedience and faithfulness.

Do Latter-day Saints believe in hell?

Latter-day Saints believe that spirits, on dying, pass into the spirit world, entering either a condition known as paradise or spirit prison, depending on the choices made in this mortal life. Christ on the cross promised the penitent thief crucified next to him that on that very day of his death he would be in Paradise. The Saints do not interpret this as a final state but believe that all those who live lives of virtue do immediately after death find themselves in a blessed condition. Those who were never taught the gospel—or may have rejected it as mortals—will be taught in that realm and progress accordingly.

The term "prison" comes from Peter's reference to the "spirits in prison" whom Christ evangelizes after death, who "sometime were disobedient" to the moral law (1 Peter 3:20). The spirit's postmortem condition appears to be more a function of self-selection than assignment, and more a state of soul than location. An LDS scripture says: "where the [wicked] were darkness reigned, but among the righteous there was peace" (D&C 138:22). Hell is but a name for the pained condition of those who have cut themselves off from the spirit of God. Another LDS scripture indicates that the pains of the hell that await can be extrapolated from what "even in the least degree you have tasted at the time I withdrew my Spirit" (D&C 19:20). The terrors described biblically are real. In the world to come, "woes shall go forth, weeping, wailing and gnashing of teeth, yea, to those who are found on my left hand." However, Latter-day Saints do not believe such pains are inflicted by a vengeful God.

The Book of Mormon teaches that we humans *choose* our pain. When we "transgress," we "withdraw [our]selves from the Spirit of the Lord, that it may have no place in [us]" (Mosiah 2:36). Another Book of Mormon prophet elaborates that those who choose "iniquity" choose to be "without God in the world, and they have gone contrary to the nature of God; therefore, they are in a state contrary to the nature of happiness" (Alma 41:11). In other words, according to what the Book of Mormon calls the law of Restoration, one becomes the kind of person, in the kind of relationship with God and others, that one has willfully chosen. And the nature and quality of one's eventual character and relationships determine the level of happiness or sorrow, joy or misery, that one inhabits.

As for who inherits hell, Latter-day Saints believe that it will eventually have very few—if any—occupants (figuratively speaking). In what may have been Smith's most remarkable vision, he saw a multitiered heaven—all of the tiers kingdoms of glory. Those "who are thrust down to hell" will be redeemed and find themselves in the "telestial" kingdom of heaven, the lowest of three kingdoms of glory (D&C 76:84). Although some scripture seems to suggest that punishment is unending, Smith recorded the Lord's explanation that "it is not written that there shall be no end to this torment, but it is written endless torment. . . . Again, it is written eternal damnation; . . . For, behold, I am endless, and the punishment which is given from my hand is endless punishment, for Endless is my name. Wherefore—Eternal punishment is God's punishment. Endless punishment is God's punishment" (D&C 19:6–12). On another occasion, Smith says that God intends to "ferret out and save . . . every spirit in the eternal world" who does not resist his efforts.[13]

Is there a final judgment?

The LDS scriptures are emphatic that virtually every man, woman, and child shall be redeemed in a kingdom of heaven. The process may be more protracted and painful for those who resist the entreaties of the Spirit and who procrastinate repentance and reformation. Not because God punishes the rebellious but because such individuals are living "contrary to the nature of happiness" (Alma 41:11). Joseph Smith taught that God will "ferret out" every soul that can be saved. Only two questions remain for Latter-day Saints. First, will anyone remain in hell forever? And for those who progress into one of the three degrees of glory, will their progress be limited to that kingdom?

The LDS scripture is cryptic on the subject of eternal damnation. One category of souls is referred to as "sons of perdition," those who, with full understanding and an uncompromised will, persist in choosing to reject God's love and compliance with the eternal laws through which alone sanctification and happiness are achieved. A minuscule segment of humanity appear to be beyond forgiveness, for the simple reason that they have put themselves beyond repentance. However, even in their case, "the end thereof . . . no man knoweth" (D&C 76:45).

Of more concern to Latter-day Saints is the question of "eternal progression." That term is a staple of LDS culture, but there is disagreement as to whether such unending development is available to all the redeemed, or only to those who find themselves in the highest—or celestial—kingdom. Joseph Smith and most of his successors apparently taught that progression *through* the kingdoms as well as *within* each was assured to all. Final judgment, in this reading, is final in the sense a final exam is final. It represents an assessment, an evaluation, and a process of self-diagnosis and self-recognition at the end of one crucial stage and before movement to the next (we are all our "own judges"; Alma 41:7). Leaders and thinkers like Hyrum Smith, B. H. Roberts, James Talmage, and J. Reuben Clark were emphatic on this point. For them, the Book of Mormon's insistence on this life as "the time to prepare to meet God" meant that conditions are now optimal for repentance, and today is always the best day to choose discipleship over worldliness—not that it was the *only* time for repentance. Around the middle of the twentieth century, a few powerful voices declared such liberality heresy, and the earlier, more generous interpretations largely disappeared from LDS consciousness. At present, the official position of the leadership is that there *is no* official position on the question of eternal progression for all.

For many if not most in the church, however, heaven hardly qualifies as heaven if it includes permanent separation from loved ones who strayed, affords no second chances, and is behind permanently closed doors. A longer timetable for the slow in spirit, with no final buzzer, is an idea embraced by growing numbers of Latter-day Saints.

Are Latter-day Saints saved by grace or by works?

As is so often the case with interfaith dialogue, the same word can mean very different things to people operating in different religious traditions—and a simple answer to this question in particular can muddy more than it clarifies. Latter-day Saints understand the terms "salvation" and "grace" in ways

Protestants may not. Latter-day Saints believe that salvation is a condition one attains through thoroughgoing imitation of Christ. Joseph Smith taught salvation in these terms: "where is the prototype? or where is the saved being? . . . it is Christ: all will agree in this that he is the prototype or standard of salvation . . . because he is a just and holy being; and no being can possess [salvation] but himself or one like him." Salvation, the fullest form of which the Saints call exaltation or eternal life, consists not merely in a life everlasting but a destiny modeled on the existence, character, and nature of God himself. According to LDS scripture, "eternal" is one of God's names; eternal life is therefore the life God lives.

For Latter-day Saints, salvation is not a reward dispensed to those who comply with a set of requirements imposed by God—through either faith *or* works. Salvation is a state of being to which one aspires, aided and guided by Christ. Mortality is an important educative phase in humanity's ascent toward godliness. Agency, or the power to willfully choose between competing, appealing options, is essential to this process. Contrary to some Protestant teachings, Latter-day Saints do not believe that humans can borrow, be judged by, or have imputed to us Christ's righteousness. To become like Christ, one must learn by experience to live and love as he does. In the crucible of mortal training, one inevitably sins and errs along the way. Christ's sacrificial offering of himself, his Atonement, in a way not fully understood, provides the means, the motivation, and the power by which one finds forgiveness and healing for the harm of every sort one does to oneself and others. But until one learns, through remorse and rechoosing (repentance), to embrace principles of righteousness and live in harmony with them, one cannot be fully and successfully responsive to God's shaping influence in one's life. A revelation to Smith clarifies the doctrine: "that which breaketh a law . . . cannot be sanctified by law, neither by mercy" (D&C 88:35). Or as the Book of Mormon states, one cannot be "saved in [one's] sins" (Alma 11:37). Only by compliance with the law of chastity may one become chaste. Only by the practice of love does one become loving. Christ may strengthen and empower one in one's efforts, but he cannot impute to one his chastity or his charity. Or as Brigham Young put the case, "it being the will and design of the Father, Son, and Holy Ghost . . . that you should be a Saint, [God] will not make you one, contrary to your own choice."[14] In *that* sense, one cannot be saved by his grace. However, the very possibility of rechoosing after initial sin and failure, freed from the prison of one's own worst choices and inclinations, is only made available by his atoning sacrifice. The grace of Christ, in *this* context, refers to his unmerited, free offering of himself, to make humans' repentance, forgiveness, sanctification, and resurrection possible. His grace is both the precondition and the empowering force on which their salvation ultimately depends.

At the same time, his grace does not impinge on one's own freedom to choose. It can only make the choice to emulate him a live option for one. The incomparable gift of love that the Saints call grace is the most powerfully transformative force in the universe. So one is not saved by grace alone, but one cannot be saved without it. Neither is salvation a reward meted out for good works. Salvation is the process by which, enabled and empowered by his love, one gradually comes to acquire his divine nature. Gift, freedom, and willing submission to his guiding will all work in harmony.

What do Latter-day Saints understand by the Atonement of Christ?

The Atonement, or vicarious sacrifice, of Jesus Christ has always been at the heart of the Christian gospel, but its meaning has been a contested and shifting doctrine over the centuries. Latter-day Saints believe that Christ's willing death on the cross was but the culmination of his agony that reached its acme earlier in Gethsemane, when it caused him "to bleed at every pore, and to suffer both body and spirit—and would that [he] might not drink the bitter cup, and shrink" (D&C 19:18). LDS doctrine stops short of articulating either why, exactly, his pain and death were necessary or what the mechanism or source of pain was. The Book of Mormon refers to his suffering "the pains of every living creature" (1 Nephi 9:21), assuming "their infirmities" (Alma 7:12), as well as their sins, suggesting that his suffering was not by way of divine retribution but by way of infinite empathy and solidarity. The implication is that all actions have consequences, and Christ's Atonement in some manner mitigates or heals the consequences of sin—personal sin, not original sin. At the same time, the Book of Mormon emphasizes that the power and efficacy of the Atonement is in its power to draw one in love and move one to repentance. He suffers and dies that he "may draw all men unto him," in the words of one prophet (2 Nephi 26:24). His Atonement provides the compelling catalyst, or "bringeth about means unto men that they may have faith unto repentance," in the words of another (Alma 34:15).

The effects of the Atonement, in LDS understanding, are twofold. One consequence is universal. Every man, woman, and child will be resurrected through Christ's conquest of death. The Book of Mormon prophet Lehi taught that "because of the intercession for all, all men come unto God; wherefore, they [again] stand in the presence of him" (2 Nephi 2:10). Such a rescue from death is not an improvised solution to Adam's transgression. In LDS thought, one's continued progression toward godliness requires an immersion in the crucible of life. Embodiment is part of that progression (since immortal beings are embodied), which birth provides. However, death is necessary as a point of termination for this "state of probation" and transition into one's next estate. In some manner unknown to humans, Christ's death and resurrection make a similar passage from corruption into incorruption possible for them.

The other consequence is conditional: those who exercise faith in Christ as Savior, and conform their lives to be more in harmony with divine principles, break free of the cycle of sin and suffering, for "God . . . suffered these things for all, that they might not suffer if they would repent" (D&C 19:16). The Atonement provides the empowerment and motivation for humans to overcome their fractured selves and alienation from God and each other. In this way it effectually provides its power of "at-one-ment." Humans' actions frequently reverberate for ill, to themselves and others, in ways they can neither fully anticipate nor rectify. Christ's infinite capacity to empathize and to heal is integral to his indispensable role as Savior and Healer.

Whether Christ's pain, which he intimated was the result of the withdrawal of the Father's spirit, was inevitably felt through his infinite capacity for empathy or experienced as his willing subjection to such pain in some substitutionary sense is not clear. What is clear is that his grace-filled decision to drink to the full that "bitter cup" was the indispensable precondition for humans' own ascent into immortality and eternal life.

Why do some people consider Mormonism a cult?

"Cult" is one of those words that at one time had a clearly defined meaning useful in the sociology of religion. Sadly, as religion scholar Martin Marty once said, it has come to mean "a religious group I don't like," and now has mostly pejorative connotations that stifle understanding rather than open up conversation. The same concerns that lead some Christians to conclude that Latter-day Saints do not belong in their fellowship led the most extreme critics to label Latter-day Saints members of a cult. In addition to espousing a non-Trinitarian God and extrabiblical scripture, they believe in highly unconventional doctrines such as a Heavenly Mother, a human preexistence, and marriage for eternity. Latter-day Saints are so cohesive as a religious group that sociologists have referred to them as a people, a global tribe, a subculture, or even an ethnicity. They set themselves apart from the world by a strict health code, a strict law of chastity, and fervent, self-funded missionary work. Perhaps most significant for the cult label, some allege that Latter-day Saints are unduly obedient to a central authority figure, inviting comparison with extremist groups whose members are unquestioning in their loyalty to a charismatic leader.

However, Latter-day Saints now constitute a global community of millions that has survived and flourished well beyond the death of its original, charismatic leader. They are fully integrated into the communities and societies in which they live, and they teach and practice loyalty to the laws and governments under which they reside. They do, no doubt, exhibit a degree of cohesiveness as a people seldom paralleled. Some scholars have suggested that one way to reconcile these divergent attitudes about the Church of Jesus Christ's status would be to consider it a new religious tradition, having a relationship to Christianity not entirely unlike Christianity's relationship to Judaism. That would, in many ways, be an optimum solution. For Latter-day Saints do indeed reconceptualize Christian history and see themselves as true inheritors of the apostolic teachings and authority, just as Christianity reinterprets the Hebrew Bible and covenant theology and sees itself as emerging out of Mosaic foreshadowing and preparations. They inhabit a paradoxical position: Latter-day Saints worship and adore Jesus Christ; yet they diverge substantially from Christian doctrine and teachings as they developed from the fourth-century church councils and creeds onwards.

How do Latter-day Saints understand revelation to their prophets?

An early revelation to Joseph Smith stipulated that "no one shall be appointed to receive commandments and revelations in this church excepting my servant Joseph Smith, Jun., for he receiveth them even as Moses" (D&C 28:2). In the Bible, when God revealed himself to Moses on Mount Sinai, he said, "you cannot see my face, for man shall not see me and live" but that he would allow Moses to see his back (Exodus 33:19–23). This passage is generally interpreted symbolically in mainstream Christianity. Latter-day Saints, however, take very literally the notion of God as an embodied being who can appear to his people and speak in articulate human speech. Smith was emphatic, from his earliest days, that he had experienced, albeit in vision, a literal visitation of God the Father and Jesus Christ. Subsequently, he would assert that he had been visited by other angelic beings, at times feeling the weight of their hands on his head as they ordained him to various offices, callings, or duties. On such occasions, it was common for Smith to report the words that had been spoken to him by God or his agents.

Such visitations were not the normal context in which Smith received his "revelations." Far more often, his prophetic mode was a matter of inspiration working on his own mind as he sought to express what he felt was God's mind and will. Smith himself recorded what he learned from God about the form revelation would take: "I will tell you in your mind and in your heart, by the Holy Ghost, which shall come upon you" (D&C 8:2). The vast majority of Smith's canonized revelations are not represented as direct speech emanating from God. In fact, Smith enlisted a team of colleagues to work with him on revising, refining, and amending his published revelations—clearly with the understanding that he was attempting to find, through his own language and conceptual vocabulary, words adequate to convey what he felt as inspirations rather than words uttered directly by God.

Latter-day Saints believe that this is how revelation has always worked, with prophets like Isaiah and Jeremiah, with a prophet such as Joseph Smith, and with individuals who seek and receive the gift of prophecy and revelation. Theophanies are the rare exception; inspired writings given under the Spirit's influence are the rule. For Latter-day Saints, what constitutes the role of the prophet is not the dramatic rending of the heavens, or any personal spiritual gifts he brings to the task, but the authority vested in that position. The nature of this authority is captured by Smith in the word "keys." The term appears almost sixty times in Smith's revelations and is taken to mean essentially what the term means to Catholics as used by Christ in his bestowal of "the keys of the kingdom" on Peter (Matt. 16:19): a divinely bestowed authority by which an individual is commissioned to act in God's name as pertaining to the saving sacraments and the administration of his church.

For a Latter-day Saint, the keys delivered to Joseph Smith continue to be held, in their fullness, by his successors in the position of "prophet, seer, and revelator." The current prophet, or church president, has the authority to direct the church in Christ's stead, to direct others in the execution of their priesthood responsibilities, and to be custodian of all of the ordinances or sacraments of salvation. At the same time, as "revelator," the prophet has the authority to pronounce God's word and will, whether received by heavenly manifestation or by the more subtle workings of the Spirit on his heart and mind.

Do Latter-day Saints accept the creeds?

Following are four of the most influential creeds in Christendom, and their relation to Latter-day Saint thought.

The Apostles' Creed

> I believe in God the Father Almighty; Maker of heaven and earth. And in Jesus Christ his only (begotten) Son our Lord; who was conceived by the Holy Ghost, born of the Virgin Mary; suffered under Pontius Pilate, was crucified, dead, and buried; he descended into hell [Hades, spirit-world]; the third day he rose from the dead; he ascended into heaven; and sitteth at the right hand of God the Father Almighty; from thence he shall come to judge the quick and the dead. I believe in the Holy Ghost; the holy catholic Church; the communion of saints; the

forgiveness of sins; the resurrection of the body [flesh]; and the life everlasting. Amen.[15]

This is the most widely accepted statement of the fundamentals of Christian belief, originating in the first Christian centuries. Surprisingly to many, perhaps, Latter-day Saints embrace the principles here outlined. (The meaning of "catholic," here and in following creeds, means the universal or Christian faith.)

The Nicene Creed (excerpt)

I believe in one God the Father Almighty; Maker of heaven and earth, and of all things visible and invisible. And in one Lord Jesus Christ, the only-begotten Son of God, begotten of the Father before all worlds [God of God], Light of Light, very God of very God, begotten, not made, being of one substance [essence] with the Father, by whom all things were made.

First formulated at the Council of Nicaea in 325, this influential creed sorted out the controversies of the era regarding the nature of God and of Jesus Christ. Contrary to the theologically contentious concept of "one essence" (homoousion), Latter-day Saints assert that the Father and Son are separate and distinct persons; the unity of godhead is in purpose only, not in substance. They invoke not only Joseph Smith's experiences and teachings but those of early Christian Fathers. As one Catholic scholar writes, "divine embodiment would have been part of the theological mainstream prior to Origen and Augustine."[16]

The Athanasian Creed (excerpt)

Whosoever will be saved: before all things it is necessary that he hold the Catholic Faith. . . . We worship one God in Trinity, and Trinity in Unity; neither confounding the Persons: nor dividing the Substance [essence]. For there

> is one Person of the Father: another of the Son: another of the Holy Ghost. But the Godhead of the father, of the Son, and of the Holy Ghost, is all one. . . . The Father incomprehensible: the Son incomprehensible: and the Holy Ghost incomprehensible. . . . And yet there are not three eternals: but one eternal. . . . So the Father is God: the Son is God: and the Holy Ghost is God. And yet there are not three Gods: but one God. . . . And in this Trinity none is afore, or after another: none is greater, or less than another. . . . But the whole three Persons are coeternal, and coequal.

Originally ascribed to Athanasius (fourth century), now believed to have been written between the fourth and eighth centuries, this creed is a hugely influential statement of Trinitarian thought. Not only, as I have shown, do Latter-day Saints accept the distinct personhood of the Father and Son, but also they consider the Father to have clear precedence in the heavenly hierarchy. The designation of Christ as the "firstborn of every creature" (Colossians 1:15) has reference, Saints believe, not just to his resurrection (as Colossians 1:18 suggests) but to his precedence among God's spirit progeny. In addition, while Latter-day Saints do not believe they can fully comprehend the three members of the godhead, they emphasize humans' connection as children of God, made in his literal image, rather than an almost infinite gulf separating the Creator from the creature.

The Westminster Confession (excerpts)

> The Holy Scriptures [are] most necessary; those former ways of God's revealing his will unto his people being now ceased . . . unto which nothing at any time is to be added . . . by new revelations.
>
> There is but one only living and true God, who is infinite in being and perfection, a most pure spirit, invisible, without body, parts, or passions.

> He is the alone foundation of all being.
>
> God from all eternity did, by the most wise and holy counsel of his own will, freely and unchangeably ordain whatsoever comes to pass.
>
> By the decree of God, for the manifestation of his glory, some men and angels are predestinated unto everlasting life, and others foreordained to everlasting death.
>
> By this sin [our first parents] fell from their original righteousness and communion, with God, and so became dead in sin, and wholly defiled in all the parts and faculties of soul and body. They being the root of all mankind, the guilt of this sin was imputed; and the same death in sin, and corrupted nature, conveyed to all their posterity descending from them by ordinary generation.

Approved by the English Parliament in 1648, this document establishes the basis of Reformed theology (of Calvinist or Zwinglian descent), which was embraced by the Anglicans and by the Puritans in England and the American colonies, as well as by the Presbyterians. It also served as basis for the Baptist creeds and, with minor modifications, was adopted by the Congregationalists and later the Methodists.

With this creedal development, the future gulf between the Latter-day Saints and other Christian branches is magnified enormously. In some cases, by this Confession new emphases in creedal Christianity are brought to the fore; in other cases, new doctrinal developments are even further removed from what will be LDS doctrines. There are six reasons for this situation. First, Latter-day Saints espouse an open, rather than closed, canon, along with the principle of continuing revelation. Second, Latter-day Saints embrace a God of body, parts, and—most emphatically—passions, that is, the capacity to be moved to grief by the pain of another. Third, Latter-day Saints reject the idea of creation ex nihilo, believing that God organized preexisting matter rather than serving as the source of all existence. Fourth, they deny that God has ordained or orchestrated all events, historical and personal, that have unfolded in human history. Human agency and human choice are the primary engines of the ills humans suffer. Fifth, Latter-day Saints emphatically reject the doctrines of predestination as they pertain to human destinies. Humans are "free forever . . . "free to choose liberty and eternal life . . . or to choose captivity and death" (2 Nephi 2:26–27). Sixth, they believe humankind does not inherit the sin or guilt of Adam and is not inherently good or evil but rather innocent (D&C 93:38). Though humans all inhabit a bodily condition with its earthly desires and propensities, total depravity and deadness to all good are not accurate characterizations of human nature.

Do Latter-day Saints have their own creed?

Like many Protestants of the nineteenth century, the Latter-day Saints were suspicious of creeds, and Smith was particularly hostile toward them. He called it "the first and fundamental principle of our holy religion" to be free "to embrace all, and every item of truth, without limitation or without being circumscribed or prohibited by the creeds or superstitious notions of men, or by the dominations of one another."[17] Nevertheless, the first revelation to be canonized by the LDS Church was an effectual creed, summarizing the essential core of Restoration doctrine. Now part of section 20 of the Doctrine and Covenants, the relevant passage reads in part:

> we know that there is a God in heaven, who is infinite and eternal, from everlasting to everlasting the same unchangeable God, the framer of heaven and earth, and all things which are in them; And that he created man, male and female, after his own image and in his own likeness, created he them. . . . Wherefore, the Almighty God gave his Only Begotten Son. . . . He was crucified, died, and rose again the third day; And ascended into heaven, to

> sit down on the right hand of the Father, to reign with almighty power according to the will of the Father; That as many as would believe and be baptized in his holy name, and endure in faith to the end, should be saved—Not only those who believed after he came in the meridian of time, in the flesh, but all those from the beginning, even as many as were before he came, who believed in the words of the holy prophets . . . should have eternal life.[18]

Except for the hint of a more universally accessible salvation, the passage was largely indistinguishable from other Christian creeds.

An evangelizing church, however, could not escape the task of formulating a brief summation of its more distinctive beliefs. In 1842, a Chicago newspaper editor asked Joseph Smith to provide him with a summary of LDS history and doctrine. Smith responded with a list of thirteen "Articles of Faith" (see the appendix).

The articles are a curious blend of careful conservatism and pointed iconoclasm. In the first, espousal of belief in God, Christ, and the Holy Ghost avoids the fact that Latter-day Saints consider them to be three separate and distinct entities. In the second, denial of the idea of original sin is clear and emphatic. The third, which predicates salvation on obedience (as well as on Christ's Atonement), distances Latter-day Saints from the *sola gratia* (by grace alone) of most Protestants, while the fourth's embrace of faith, repentance, baptism, and the gift of the Holy Ghost by the laying on of hands situates the church with other restorationist movements. So also do the sixth and seventh, which refer to the primitive church's organization and spiritual gifts, respectively. A fifth article on authority for the ministry hints at an apostolic priesthood similar to that of the Catholic Church, while the Book of Mormon is emphatically elevated to the same scriptural status as the Bible in article 8. In a similar vein, article 9 espouses ongoing revelation and confidence in scripture yet to be revealed. Many nineteenth-century Christians were millennialists, and the tenth article of faith lays out belief in Christ's return, an American New Jerusalem, and the gathering of the ten lost tribes of Israel. The three final articles round out the summary, reassuring anxious Americans of LDS belief in religious freedom, civic loyalty, and the pursuit of Christian virtues.

Some of the most distinctive LDS doctrines are missing from this brief exposition. One finds no mention of a God of body, parts, and passion, or of human preexistence; no elements of vicarious sacraments or temple theology, no collapse of old and new covenants into one. The cosmic scope of the gospel, its antiquity in premortal councils, its culmination in the theosis of humans and their integration into a heavenly family; the universal reach of God's plan for the human race extending across time, culture, and death's barrier, and in which light the Fall was an ordained path rather than cosmic catastrophe; life cast as an educative process of ascent rather than punitive exile—this panoramic sweep was not even attempted. What Smith mostly expounded in these articles of faith was ecclesiology—how the church was organized and what its ordinances, scriptures, and spiritual practices entailed—touching only those theological points shared with many or most in the Christian fold, along with a few distinctives.

Why do Latter-day Saints believe in human preexistence?

The premortal existence of human beings appears in many ancient traditions, in Jewish texts and Greek thought, and is suggested by the incident in John 9, where the disciples ask Jesus if a man was born blind because of his own sin or that of his parents. Many early Christian writers believed and taught of human preexistence, including Clement of Alexandria, Origen, Evagrius, and others. Early in his career, Augustine, one of the principal founders of the Christian tradition, was a firm believer as well. The teaching was not condemned until the end of the fourth century, and then again and more definitely by the emperor Justinian in the sixth century. The idea had become increasingly associated with Origen, whose other teachings were controversial; it was also associated with the Gnostics, considered a heretical group. The doctrine of creation *ex nihilo* was gaining supremacy, requiring that no person or thing compete with God's unique, primal existence. Preexistence was closely associated with another doctrine that was falling under suspicion: theosis, or the belief that as humans originated in heaven, they would inevitably return to take their place there as divine beings.

The idea of preexistence emerges in the Church of Jesus Christ in a number of early texts. The Book of Mormon had hints (as when the premortal Christ appears to the Brother of Jared, in Ether 3). Then Smith's revision of the Bible spoke of a creation of "all things spiritually before they were naturally upon the face of the earth." Finally, an 1830 revelation, "The Prophecy of Enoch," clearly stated that God "made the world, and men before they were in the flesh" (Moses 6:51). Smith fleshed out the idea in subsequent revelations, making preexistence not just an incidental curiosity but a way of reframing the whole cosmic narrative.

Congruent with many ancient traditions, Smith described a premortal heavenly council in which the creation of the earth and mortal incarnation were proposed, as an educative stage through which all spirits could pass en route to a continuing ascent toward full participation in the divine nature and life. A third of the spirits refused (in line with the biblical reference to a third of heaven's stars falling [Revelation 12:4]), and followed the lead dissenter, known scripturally as Lucifer ("Light bearer" [Isaiah 14:12]). John Milton's *Paradise Lost* probably offers the fullest account of this premortal "War in Heaven," which was long a part of Christian tradition but is now largely forgotten. (Probably few students at the University of Oxford know that their Michaelmas term is named for the Archangel Michael's victory in the heavenly war.)

The LDS scripture indicates that Jesus was, in those premortal councils, anointed as the Christ, because the mortal probation would involve suffering and sin in need of healing. Belief in preexistence, for Latter-day Saints, means that humans have an eternal identity and are not contingent beings and that we were coparticipants in the plan that brings us into a world fraught with both beauty and danger.

Along with the author of the epistle to the Hebrews, Latter-day Saints believe that "it is given unto man once to die" (Hebrews 9:27). Hence, preexistence is different from and unrelated to Eastern traditions of reincarnation. Human existence is a three-act play (preexistence, mortality, postmortality), not an endless cycle of dramas wherein one assumes different roles.

What are Latter-day Saints' beliefs regarding the body?

Latter-day Saints believe that God the Father is an embodied being, having "a body of flesh and bones as tangible as man's" (D&C 130:2). Spirit is not a higher form of existence and the body is not a relic of a fallen condition. This is a teaching at odds with much of the mainstream Christian tradition (as well as classical philosophy), which has often emphasized the inherent inferiority of matter to spirit. On the contrary, Latter-day Saints believe that individuals grow more like their heavenly parents by coming to earth and receiving physical bodies. The opportunity to progress to mortal embodiment was presented as part of the Father's plan in premortal councils. Lucifer and his followers who rejected that plan were denied the privilege of such embodiment and persist as unembodied spirits. An LDS scripture declares that only "spirit and element, inseparably connected, receive a fulness of joy" (D&C 93:33).

This appraisal of the body as a constituent element in divine beings helps explain LDS attitudes toward the body, its treatment, and sexuality. One revelation celebrates the pure sensual delight we should enjoy in a physical creation apprehended through bodily senses "made for the benefit and the use of man, both to please the eye and to gladden the heart; Yea, for food and for raiment, for taste and for smell, to strengthen the body and to enliven the soul. And it pleaseth God that he hath given all these things unto man; for unto this end were they made to be used" (D&C 59:18–20). The LDS health code (the Word of Wisdom) is one way Saints show reverence for the body, treating it with respect as a sacred tabernacle of the spirit. It also explains why they consider sexuality and sexual relations inherently sacred, since the body and its creative powers mirror aspects of the Divine.

Like most other Christians, Latter-day Saints anticipate a bodily resurrection. Just as Jesus Christ rose in a body that was immortalized and glorified, so do they believe they will awaken in like form. The Book of Mormon teaches: "the spirit and the body shall be reunited again in its perfect form. . . . Now, this restoration shall come to all, both old and young, both bond and free, both male and female, both the wicked and the righteous; and even there shall not so much as a hair of their heads be lost; but every thing shall be restored to its perfect frame" (Alma 11:43–44). And the pleasures of physicality will be enjoyed there as well as here. According to early LDS theologian Parley Pratt, "in the resurrection, and the life to come, men that are prepared will actually possess a material inheritance on the earth. . . . They will eat, drink, converse, think, walk, taste, smell and enjoy."[19]

Do Latter-day Saints believe in original sin?

In the traditional Christian narrative, one historian of theology writes, "God's purpose and goal in redemption is to reverse the sin, corruption and death introduced into humanity by Adam."[20] Or, as a Catholic theologian summarizes it, "the story immediately unfolds with a catastrophe. . . . Evil follows evil like an avalanche."[21] Consequently, the personal history of every human being begins in deficit, with loss, sin, corruption, alienation. God's plan is thwarted, and justice demands payment.

In the Church of Jesus Christ, this narrative arc is emphatically rejected. For Latter-day Saints, the Fall is part of an original blueprint, not a divergence from it. Mortality is designed as an educative ascent from premortality, and the couple Eve and Adam's decision to eat the fruit is needful and entirely to God's purposes. The strict injunction not to partake of the Tree of Knowledge is tempered in Smith's rewrite of Genesis 3: "nevertheless thou mayest choose for thyself, for it is given thee," the Lord says. As a consequence of Eve's (then Adam's) decision, the Garden is revealed as prologue, not permanent home, and abundant life rather than death is the immediate consequence: "[Human beings] were *born* into the world by the fall" is how Smith's revision characterizes the aftermath in the 1851 edition of Moses 6:59.[22] In sum, an early LDS catechism says, the Saints see "the Fall of our first parents as one of the great steps to eternal exaltation and happiness, and one ordered by God in his infinite wisdom." Eve, in this telling, is closer to heroine than villainess in making possible—at great cost—the grand designs of life and mortality for all those premortal souls willing to embark on the second phase of their eternal existence. Presumably, though this is never clarified dogmatically in LDS teachings, the pain and risks incurred in the crucible of life necessitated an emphatic, willful decision on the part of Adam and Eve as the race's spiritual heads, God's caution notwithstanding. Hence the phrase "*if* you eat, *then* you will die," which Smith taught was more fatherly warning than stern prohibition.

The Church of Jesus Christ recasts Adam and Eve's expulsion from the Garden and denial of access to the Tree of Life not as punishment but rather as an act of mercy, allowing growth, repentance, and learning to precede their immortal transformation. In this restructuring of the cosmic narrative, life is an intended arena of spiritual education, pain and suffering are the collateral damage incurred throughout a process that allows for no gentler way to the divine nature, and whatever sins are committed en route are held to the account of those who commit them.

Do Latter-day Saints believe in a God the Mother?

Preexilic Israel is now widely regarded as having worshiped a female deity called Asherah. Her worship was tolerated until the reforming kings of the seventh century, but eventually Hebrew monotheism was purged of competing gods as well as putative consorts. A female God has never been a part of orthodox Christian belief, though there have been gestures in that direction by isolated Quakers, the sect of the Shakers, the influential Unitarian Theodore Parker (who prayed in public to the "Heavenly Father and Mother"), and others. The flowering of feminist theologies in recent decades has produced several strategies to redress the historical exclusion or subordination of the feminine from divine constructions; some reinterpret God and Christology alike with more room for feminine aspects, while some promote a language and a theology that move beyond gender altogether.

Latter-day Saints go further than these efforts by positing, alongside a literal, anthropomorphic God the Father, a separate and distinct God the Mother. The LDS idea of the Heavenly Mother first appears in print in a letter of W. W. Phelps, wherein he exclaims: "O Mormonism! Thy father is God, thy mother is the Queen of heaven." That Phelps's reference to a Mother in heaven is literal is clear in the tableau that follows, describing Jesus Christ's premortal designation as Savior: "he was anointed with holy oil in heaven, and crowned in the midst of brothers and sisters, while his mother stood with approving virtue and smiled upon a Son that kept the faith as the heir of all things."[23] While "Queen of Heaven" had a long history as a Catholic term for Mary, the Latter-day Saints conceived of the Heavenly Mother as a different, fully divine counterpart to God the Father.

The idea's most popular and enduring formulation in the LDS tradition was poetic: Eliza R. Snow—one of Smith's plural wives—wrote a poem in late 1845 she titled "My Father in Heaven," though it became known as "O my Father." Snow expounded the teaching as an intuitive truth:

> I had learn'd to call thee Father,
> Through thy Spirit from on high,
> But, until the key of knowledge
> Was restor'd, I knew not why.
> In the heav'ns are parents single?
> No, the thought makes reason stare!
> Truth is reason—truth eternal
> Tells me I've a mother there.

In 1885, apostle Erastus Snow (no relation) wrote: "it is not said in so many words in the Scriptures, that we have a Mother in heaven as well as a Father. It is left for us to infer this from what we see and know of all living things. . . . 'What,' says one, 'do you mean we should understand that Deity consists of man and woman?' Most certainly I do. . . . There never was a God, and there never will be in all eternities, except they are made of these two component parts; a man and a woman; the male and the female."[24]

The church has officially endorsed the reality of a Mother in Heaven in a number of statements. The church website now affirms that "men and women cannot be exalted without each other. Just as we have a Father in Heaven, we have a Mother in Heaven. As Elder Dallin H. Oaks of the Quorum of the Twelve Apostles has said, 'Our theology begins with heavenly parents. Our highest aspiration is to be like them.'"[25] At the same time, acknowledgment of a Heavenly Mother stops firmly short of endorsing her worship. Latter-day Saints are directed to follow the New Testament model of praying to a Heavenly Father only.

Do Latter-day Saints believe they can become gods?

If by adding the Book of Mormon to the canon of scripture Latter-day Saints seem to flirt with blasphemy, the LDS doctrine of theosis seems well across the line. Theosis, also called deification ("exaltation" by members of the church), actually has a long history in Christian thought. Paul referred to "joint-heirship" with Christ (Romans 8:17), the epistle of Peter promises participation "in the divine nature" (2 Peter 1:4), and Jesus himself (John 10:34) quotes the words of the Psalmist, that "ye are gods" (Psalm 82:6). Early Christian writers often invoked this theme, with statements such as "he was made man that we might be made God" (Athanasius) or "the Word of God became man, that thou mayest learn from man how man may become God" (Clement).[26] Some church fathers seemed even more emphatic. Basil the Great wrote that "those who have become perfect . . . are called by the appellation of gods, being destined to sit on thrones with the other gods that have been first put in their places by the Saviour," and Gregory Nazianzen celebrated the prospect not just of "being made like to God" but "highest of all, the being made God."[27]

The definition of theosis given by the sixth-century theologian pseudo-Dionysius clarifies where the LDS teaching differs from mainline Christianity. "Deification (theosis) is the attaining of likeness to God and union with him *so far as is possible*" (my emphasis).[28] Most Christians have believed "so far as is possible" to be a very limited or imputed divinity; that is, as "partakers of the divine nature" humans remain very much finite creatures forevermore, separated from the Creator by an infinite, qualitative divide.

Latter-day Saints believe that in whatever exalted state humans attain, they will remain forevermore subordinate to and worshipful of God the Father and Jesus Christ. At the same time, they believe, as the early apostle Parley Pratt wrote, that "God, angels, and humans" are all "of one species,"[29] and that in a very real way humans are eternal beings and offspring of heavenly parents. In the fullest LDS scriptural exposition of what participation in the divine nature might look like, in a visionary encounter the prophet Enoch ascends to the presence of God and beholds him weeping on behalf of humankind. Subsequently, "the Lord . . . told Enoch all the doings of the children of men; wherefore Enoch knew, and looked upon their wickedness, and their misery, and wept and stretched forth his arms, and his heart swelled wide as eternity; and his bowels yearned; and all eternity shook" (Moses 7:41). Through this mentoring in the cosmic perspective, the divine potential of humans and the divine nature of God are shown to be the same. Godliness turns out to be more about infinite empathy than infinite power; the divine nature constitutes infinite capacity for pain as well as for joy. Humans can become partakers of the divine nature through full integration into God's Heavenly Family, but that implies a love that has its wrenching costs as well as supernal blisses.

As for creating and presiding over one's own worlds—Brigham Young and some of his contemporaries speculated in such terms, but those ideas are not found in LDS scripture or official pronouncements. The same is true of Joseph Smith's teaching that God was himself once a man. The idea never made its way into LDS scripture and has received little to no emphasis in past decades, though it was commonly invoked in earlier generations.

Do Latter-day Saints believe in the Second Coming?

The Church of Jesus Christ was birthed in an era of fervent millennialism. Much of the energy that drove the Second Great Awakening of the early nineteenth century was the eager anticipation (or anxious dread) of an imminent return of Christ. The very name of the church as constituted of "latter-day saints" draws attention to this dispensation as a *latter-day* epoch, the final era before the end times predicted in biblical scripture. In the events surrounding the Restoration, Latter-day Saints see the long-anticipated "signs of the times." They see Paul's words about a "falling away" and Peter's allusion to a time of "restitution" as predicting the general apostasy of the Christian world and the restoration of gospel truth and authority by way of Joseph Smith (2 Thessalonians 2:3; Acts 3:21). Ezekiel's words of a "stick of Joseph" that would be joined to a "stick of Judah" and of a voice that would speak "out of the dust" are seen by many Saints to have specific reference to the coming forth of the Book of Mormon (Ezekiel 37:16–17; Isaiah 29:4). The gathering and restoration of Israel is a frequent theme of the Old Testament prophets. The Saints believe such prophecies began their literal fulfillment as the literal descendants of Ephraim (one of the Twelve Tribes of Israel) and others accepted the restored gospel and gathered with the Saints.

Members of the church believed that the establishment of Zion, the founding of a community of believers who would live, like the early Christians depicted in Acts 4, in perfect harmony, sharing all things in common and practicing principles of love and holiness, was one of the final steps to be taken as an immediate prelude to Christ's return. Expectations were further heightened when Smith identified the place of Zion (a settlement in Missouri), led his people there, began to institute communitarian principles, and planned for a temple. In 1832, conflict with old settlers led to these members' forcible expulsion from the country. Smith launched a paramilitary expedition, "Zion's Camp," to reclaim what they saw as their rightful spiritual inheritance, but it failed.

Smith told the disappointed Saints that the Lord had told him that the time for Zion's redemption was postponed. Throughout the nineteenth century, after exodus from Missouri and then Illinois, Latter-day Saints kept alive the hope that they would yet live to see their Zion repossessed and Christ return to initiate the millennium. Today, for Latter-day Saints, the Second Coming remains an important element of their faith, but they more readily acknowledge that "no man knoweth the hour."

What is the Latter-day Saint conception of sacraments?

"Whoever wishes to be saved, needs above all to hold the catholic faith," as the Athanasian Creed put forth.[30] For centuries this was thought to be the case because the Fall of Adam immersed his posterity in a blanket condemnation from which no one could escape through his or her own merits. The saving grace of Christ was administered through ordained channels or sacraments, performed by a group of men authorized to act as ministers on Christ's behalf. Protestants by and large denied both the special authority of an ordained class of clergy and the necessity of sacraments for salvation. They were held to be "instituted for the nourishing of faith," potent assists or "signs of grace," but not indispensable conduits.

Latter-day Saints are closer to the Catholic position. They believe in a priesthood passed on through apostolic succession, traceable to Christ through Peter. Rather than tracing its descent through history as the Catholics do, however, the Saints claim that a resurrected Peter, in company with James and John, appeared to Smith and bestowed priesthood authority on him. And the Saints do believe that certain sacraments—which they call ordinances—are essential to salvation. Key differences exist, however, in the Saints' conception of both salvation and the meaning of these sacraments. For them, salvation is essentially a matter of relation: heaven is conceived of as an endless chain of belonging, or what Smith called a "sociality . . . coupled with eternal glory" (D&C 130:2). Sacraments have the principal function of creating, reinforcing, and concretizing those relationships—to God and to other human beings. Therefore, the LDS sacraments are not the channels of grace or signs of grace but the materials out of which heaven itself is constituted.

This, at least, is the case with those sacraments that are sometimes called "saving ordinances" and that include baptism (adoption into Christ's family), temple marriage (eternal "sealing" to one's spouse), and the endowment (incorporating covenantal obligations that evidence one's total commitment to God). Other nonsaving sacraments have a function more like the Protestant "nourishing of faith" role: naming and blessing of children, blessing the sick, partaking of the Lord's Supper, and others.

Why do some Latter-day Saints refer to outsiders as "Gentiles"?

God's covenant with Abraham is generally taken as the origin of the Jews as a people "set apart" with special privileges and promises. From the perspective of biblical writers, the world is thenceforth divided between Israel and Gentile or, by New Testament times, Jew and Gentile. The Book of Mormon spans both the Old and New Testament eras, and its writers employ the term in a similar way. Book of Mormon prophets refer to the "Gentile" nations and predict that in the latter days, the gospel will be established among them (particularly in the Western Hemisphere). From the Book of Mormon perspective, the church was restored among "Gentiles."

In the Book of Mormon the clear ethnic distinction between literal Israel and non-Israel Gentiles breaks down when the prophet Nephi asserts that those Gentiles who repent "are [also] the covenant people of the Lord" (2 Nephi 30:2). Thus is set in place an ambiguous template that informs LDS discourse to the present day. Latter-day Saints who have the habit of referring to non-LDS people—even Jews—as Gentiles are using the label as a signifier of nonbelief or, more specifically, nonparticipation in a covenant they believe Joseph Smith reintroduced. In LDS thinking this covenant makes assent to the gospel as taught by Smith the sign of membership in the house of Israel, of status as Abraham's seed. Orson Whitney offered the explanation that "the name Gentile is not with us a term of reproach. It comes from Gentilis, meaning, of a nation, a family or a people not of Israel—that is all. 'Mormon' is a nickname for Latter-day Saint, but 'Gentile' is not a nickname. It simply means, with us, one who does not belong to the Church."[31]

The Book of Mormon further complicates the issue with a prophecy that Smith took to refer to himself. The Lord promised the Old Testament patriarch Jacob's son Joseph that a "choice seer" would come "out of the fruit of [his] loins" who would perform a powerful ministry among "a branch which was to be broken off" of the house of Israel (2 Nephi 3:5–6). Smith took this to mean that although he was of a Gentile nation, he was personally descended from an Israelite. And the belief developed that those who accepted the gospel were most likely literal descendants of the house of Israel as well—generally of Ephraim or others of the ten tribes. Early Latter-day Saints believed that the modern work of "gathering" that was prophetically foretold was not a figurative but a literal searching out of the lost tribes of Israel. The American Indians were also thought to constitute one segment of Israel—an offshoot of Manasseh.

Today, the distinction between literal Israelites and adopted Israelites has all but disappeared in LDS thought. Similarly, referring to people who do not belong to the church as Gentiles is largely a relic of another era.

What do Latter-day Saints believe about the Creation?

Most Christians hold that God created the earth out of nothingness (*ex nihilo* creation); for those inclined toward Protestant fundamentalism, the process lasted six literal days, and all of this transpired about six thousand years ago. The Church of Jesus Christ did not align itself behind any of those three propositions.

Latter-day Saints reject the idea of *ex nihilo* creation outright. Joseph Smith taught as early as 1833 that "the elements are eternal" (D&C 93:3). How long the six creative periods or "days" lasted was not a matter of definitive official statement. However, the Book of Abraham, produced by Smith in 1835, introduced indeterminate "times" into the creation story rather than "days" (Abraham 4:5–31). And as for the dating of creation itself, Smith's close associate W. W. Phelps recognized that Smith's teachings in this regard conformed to, rather than conflicted with, the new science of geology. Writing to William Smith, Phelps noted that Joseph had learned from his work on the papyri that "eternity, agreeably to the records found in the catacombs of Egypt, has been going on in this system . . . millions of years: and to know at the same time, that deists, geologists and others are trying to prove that matter must have existed hundreds of thousands of years;—it almost tempts the flesh to fly to God, or muster faith like Enoch to be translated."[32]

What do Latter-day Saints believe about evolution?

Response to the theory of evolution has been mixed. After the 1859 publication of Charles Darwin's book *On the Origin of Species*, Darwin and his theories were seldom mentioned by name from the LDS pulpit; when they were mentioned by Orson Pratt or Erastus Snow, it was with caution or mild dismissal, and Brigham Young University (BYU) was resistant to teaching human evolution in the first years of the twentieth century. By 1931 the church was more cautious, with the First Presidency declaring: "[the idea that] 'there were not pre-Adamites upon the earth' is not a doctrine of the Church. Neither side of the [pre-Adamite] controversy has been accepted as a doctrine at all. . . . Leave [scientific research to] geology, biology, archaeology and anthropology."[33]

Some outspoken dissenters attempted to force an official opposition to Darwin; the apostle Joseph Fielding Smith, in his book *Man, His Origin and Destiny,* published in 1954, openly opposed much of modern science, including evolution. However, the book was quickly withdrawn as a text in the church's educational system, and the author's pulpit condemnations of evolution were countered by the equally influential apostles James Talmage and John Widtsoe and the scientist Henry Eyring, all of whom spoke in support of a more nuanced approach to scientific understanding. Notwithstanding vociferous attacks by the apostle Bruce R. McConkie, the church never officially proclaimed or endorsed an antievolution position. As a church website states, "the Church has no official position on the theory of evolution."[34]

At present, BYU teaches evolution in a manner consistent with modern scientific understanding. In 1972 the university's president, future apostle Dallin Oaks, noted with self-conscious irony: "the bones are there and cannot really be ignored by a major university that is almost literally sitting on top of them."[35] To reconcile human evolution with the narrative of the Creation, many Saints adopt the position that life developed on earth according to evolutionary principles; at the appropriate stage, perhaps at that moment when humans were sufficiently developed to house a spirit or to enter into covenantal relationship with God, he endowed a human couple with their premortal souls and called them Eve and Adam.

Do Latter-day Saints believe in angels?

The founding of the Church of Jesus Christ is inextricably bound up with angelic visitations. Smith's first vision, in 1820, was of God the Father and Jesus Christ. Significantly, however, he dated the start of his role as a prophet to 1827, when a messenger who identified himself as the angel Moroni appeared to him for the fifth time (1823 being the first) and directed him to the place where a set of gold plates was buried (the future Book of Mormon). Over the ensuing years, Smith said that he was visited by numerous angelic beings—most commonly figures from the Old and New Testaments, who conveyed "keys" to him, that is, priesthood authority, like the "keys" Jesus mentioned giving to Peter in Matthew's gospel. Smith recorded visitations by Peter, James, John, Moses, Elijah, John the Baptist, and many others.

Smith divided angels into two categories: he appears to have interacted most often with resurrected beings, having bodies of flesh and bone. But angels could also include "the spirits of just men made perfect" (D&C 129:3), in other words, personages who lived on earth and have not yet been resurrected in physical form yet serve as messengers of God.

The church has no official position on the reality of "guardian angels." The term was frequently invoked in the early years of the church, but in the twentieth century the leadership concluded that the notion was largely rooted in folklore and would be superfluous given the reality of the Holy Ghost as a constant companion. Nevertheless, they continue to affirm the reality of angelic ministrations that may occur in a time of spiritual or temporal need.

A further category of angelic being would be those commonly known as "fallen angels." In LDS understanding these are spirit siblings of the human family. When the plan for a mortal probation was propounded in premortal councils, one-third of the heavenly family rejected the plan—presumably because of the high cost of pain and suffering incident to the mortal state. Those spirits progressed from rejection to rebellion and hostility to God's purposes. They now constitute the evil spirits known throughout history as demons, devils, and kindred names.

Does Latter-day Saint baptism differ from other Christian baptism?

Following New Testament precedent, Latter-day Saints practice baptism "for the remission of sins." Because repentance and remission of sins are associated with faith and a change of heart, this remission is a process rather than an instantaneous event. Baptism is nonetheless more than a sign or symbol; it is the divinely ordained means, administered through a divinely authorized authority, through which the Atonement is to effect on the repentant sinner its first work of purification, subject to the candidate's genuine repentance.

In the larger scheme of things, however, the ordinance signifies a shift in eternal status that moves far beyond simple forgiveness of sin. Consistent with New Testament usage, Latter-day Saints have emphasized that by taking Christ's name on themselves through baptism, they are adopted by him. This adoption fully qualifies one to be "son" or "daughter" of God. Such had been the position of the Anglican divine John Bradford, who called baptism "initiation . . . wherewith we be enrolled, as it were, into the household and family of God."[36] The LDS embraced this same logic but with radically literalized meaning. The Saints see all ordinances as the constituting of the human race into a celestial family—a principal purpose of mortality itself—and the church as the instrument through which those relations are to be ordered. Baptism is the sacrament by which an individual begins the process of initiation, of reincorporation—after one's descent into the world and personal transgression—into heirship with heavenly parents, with Christ as spiritual father. Taking upon oneself the name of Christ, in this context, meant a legally valid process of adoption—parallel to an earthly incorporation into a family with new parents. It represents the first step of one's inauguration into what Latter-day Saints call the New and Everlasting Covenant.

A passage from the Book of Mormon enumerates implicit covenantal obligations that candidates for baptism undertake. By accepting baptism they agree that they "are willing to bear one another's burdens, that they may be light; Yea, and are willing to mourn with those that mourn; yea, and comfort those that stand in need of comfort" (Mosiah 18:8–9). New members pledge themselves to become coparticipants with Christ in his work of bearing burdens, mourning with sufferers, and comforting those in need. Their baptism is an ordinance that brings them into covenantal relationship with God and with the community at the same time. For Latter-day Saints, religion does not exist on any other terms. Because the Saints believe that children begin to be morally accountable agents around age eight, that is the minimum age for baptism. Infant baptism is entirely rejected, since LDS scripture affirms the innocence of children, asserting that no taint of original guilt inheres in any human.

The mode of baptism is fully immersive, on the New Testament model. For Latter-day Saints, only being "buried" in the water can effect the symbolism of the death of the old person and rebirth as a new person, with a new identity in Christ. At the same time, of course, rising from the font with a new identity evokes the physical rebirth from the grave that it foreshadows.

Two aspects of baptismal theology align Latter-day Saints more closely with Catholics than Protestants. First, they believe that God instituted certain sacraments as essential elements of humans' heavenward progression. Those sacraments, of which baptism is the first, condition, strengthen, and concretize one's connection to the Divine and give one access to his salvific powers. And since these sacraments were commanded of believers, they are indispensable conduits, necessary for one's salvation. Second, the Saints believe that God's house "is a house of order," and as such, authority to administer his sacraments (or ordinances) is bestowed through apostolic descent. For the Saints, an apostolic line was reinitiated when the resurrected Peter, James, and John appeared to Joseph Smith as angelic beings and conveyed to him that apostolic authority. The specific authority to baptize was given to Smith by a resurrected John the Baptist.

Who can receive the Holy Ghost?

Latter-day Saints believe that all members of the human family have access to divine inspiration. The "Light of Christ" is a universal endowment, inborn, that serves as what many would call conscience. It is the basic moral awareness of right and wrong. It also functions in a way analogous to what some Christians call "prevenient grace"; that is, it is a gift from God that enables one to recognize and accept even greater truth and light.

In addition, all people may receive guidance or inspiration from that member of the godhead called the Holy Ghost or Holy Spirit. (God and Christ are physical beings in LDS teaching; the Holy Ghost, by contrast, is a divine "personage of Spirit.") The Book of Mormon teaches that the Holy Ghost is "the gift of God unto *all* those who diligently seek him" (1 Nephi 10:17). Any individual, regardless of church affiliation or ordinances received, is eligible to receive light and knowledge from God, through this intermediary. And indeed, Latter-day Saints believe that God has been generous in dispensing such light and knowledge liberally across time and culture.

Following baptism in the Church of Jesus Christ, a convert or young member receives the ordinance of confirmation. This sacrament is the process by which one receives the "gift of the Holy Ghost." In contradistinction to a general access to the influence of the Holy Ghost, the "gift" entails a promise of constant companionship, conditional on the recipient's living in harmony with gospel principles and standards. The bottom line is that worthiness and sincerity trump mere forms. A devout and humble truth-seeker of any persuasion will be more liable to access the powers of heaven than a confirmed member of the Church of Jesus Christ who neglects to live up to his or her covenants.

Do Latter-day Saints believe in transubstantiation?

Like Catholics and unlike Protestants, Latter-day Saints are sacramentalists—in other words, their view of the sacraments (which they call ordinances) is that some ordinances are indispensable to salvation. Such ordinances include baptism, confirmation, sealing (including temple marriage), and others associated with temple worship. However, some ordinances are viewed more in the way Protestants see them, as signs or supports that strengthen faith. This is true, for example, of what other Christians call the Eucharist, or Communion, or the Lord's Supper, which Latter-day Saints call simply "*the* sacrament."

Catholics are taught the doctrine of the "real presence," that the priest effects the transformation of the wine and wafer into the actual blood and body of Christ. Latter-day Saints, like many Protestants, believe that when Christ said "this is my body" in reference to the bread of the Last Supper, he was speaking metaphorically. Latter-day Saints pray that God will "bless and sanctify" the emblems (called the "elements" in a Catholic service) as a token of covenant between congregants and God. They bear witness that they will take upon themselves Christ's name, keep his commandments, and always remember him. In return, they are promised the companionship of the Holy Spirit.

Though LDS worship lacks the liturgical richness of high-church services, "the sacrament," as it is called, is the central purpose of the weekly worship, and in fact the weekly worship service is called "sacrament meeting." The administration of the sacrament is understood as a time for self-reflection and meditation on the sacrifice of Christ, which it commemorates. Originally, people gave sermons or read scriptures during the administration of the sacrament. In 1946, the First Presidency decreed "absolute quiet during the passing of the sacrament" as "the ideal condition." Originally, the Saints used wine to represent the blood of Christ. A revelation instructed Smith not to purchase wine but to use wine of the Saints' own making, or anything else: the particular choice "mattereth not" (D&C 27:2). Water is now the standard employed throughout the church. Young men who are ordained as priests in their sixteenth year generally pray over the emblems; deacons, generally boys aged eleven to thirteen, carry the trays of bread and water to the congregation.

7

PRACTICE

Why did Latter-day Saints practice communalism?

From a variety of secular and religious motivations, in the nineteenth century many individuals experimented with communalist societies—Latter-day Saints included. Some Christians looked to the book of Acts for authorization and inspiration, for Luke describes the first Christians as having "all things [in] common" (2:44). Latter-day Saints' enthusiasm for the practice kicked into high gear with Joseph Smith's production of the "prophecy of Enoch," purporting to be an ancient text that gave a fuller account of the life and ministry of the Old Testament prophet. The few pertinent words in Genesis refer to a man who "walked with God" until one day "he was not; for God took him" (Genesis 5:24). Ancient Jewish legends refer to his ascension together with thousands of followers. In Smith's version, which he published in 1832, Enoch founded a city that was called "Zion" by the Lord, "because they were of one heart and one mind, and dwelt in righteousness; and there was no poor among them" (Moses 7:18). Consequently, the entire city "was taken up into heaven" (7:21).

Smith quickly came to see himself as a modern-day Enoch, trying to similarly create a righteous people united in temporal as well as spiritual matters. Hence, he inaugurated what was initially called "the law of Enoch." This was the most ambitious moral law Smith would ever propound. It required members, in order to eliminate inequality and deprivation, to "consecrate of [their] properties for their support . . . with a deed and a covenant" (D&C 42:30). In other words, the Saints were being asked—commanded actually—to contribute their goods to a common pool that would be distributed according to need. The experiment met with limited success over the next seven years. Economic selflessness is hard to cultivate in the best of times. In these years, the Saints were experiencing repeated displacements and exiles, destruction and appropriation of their properties, and a continual influx of new—often poor—converts. In 1838, the law of Enoch, or Law of Consecration as it came to be known, was effectively replaced with the law of tithing, which required 10 percent of one's "increase" rather than the deeding over of property.

Once the Saints arrived in Utah, a number of communities attempted to return to the Law of Consecration. The most successful of these was Orderville, established at Brigham Young's behest in 1878 specifically to live the "united order." There, the practice in which no one owned private property lasted a decade. Today, the Law of Consecration takes the form of a temple covenant made by all those who receive their temple ordinances (sacraments in which Saints participate ritualistically in their temples). The Law is understood as an effective dedication of all one's means, resources, and talents to the building of God's kingdom. No formal deeding of property is involved.

Are Latter-day Saints as happy and successful as they are said to be?

Latter-day Saints do have a reputation for being an uncommonly happy people. And they do tend to have higher than average levels of education and professional achievement. In part, the LDS psyche may be a product of a theology that is itself profoundly optimistic. The church has from its inception utterly rejected the doctrine of a catastrophic fall, inherited sin, and human depravity. Seeing mortality as a necessary educative stage of humans' eternal development gives meaning and context to the trials and travails of life. The language of hell and damnation is lacking in LDS discourse as well. Smith taught that with the fewest of exceptions, all humans will inherit a kingdom of glory and immortality. Individuals are taught from their earliest years that they are literally children of heavenly parents and can be part of an eternal family. The eventual destiny that awaits the faithful is to participate fully in the divine nature, becoming gods. The quest for perfection is thus hardwired into the religion and is evident at all levels. The upside is a culture that emphasizes perpetual striving, improvement, and the power of individual agency. This can have its downside; LDS women in particular often suffer the consequences of unrealistic expectations and a virtual mania for perfection.

Crucial aspects of the lived experience of Latter-day Saints are doubtless relevant as well. The family-centeredness of the religion is legendary. Divorce rates among committed Latter-day Saints are well below the national average. And any number of sociological studies have affirmed the connection between marital satisfaction and stable families on the one hand and life satisfaction on the other.

Studies of "blue zones," geographic regions around the world of abnormal longevity, have consistently revealed that the single most important factor in health and well-being is the strength and prevalence of close social bonds. The family unity so central to LDS striving finds an extended form in the close-knit LDS community. Originally, Latter-day Saints congregated geographically in places of "gathering," in Ohio, Missouri, Illinois, and eventually Utah. Shared faith and shared persecution, and then the shared challenge of taming a desolate wilderness, all worked to foment particularly intense intragroup loyalty and cohesion. Although gathering ceased in the twentieth century, organizing congregations geographically and implementing programs of reciprocal ministering effectively reproduce the experience of nineteenth-century solidarity. Active Latter-day Saints are thoroughly insinuated into a network of reliable social bonds that far transcend Sunday interactions. Presumably these are some of the most relevant factors behind President Spencer W. Kimball's declaration to the church that "we should be the happiest of all people."[1]

How does the church mark the stages of a member's life?

A member of the Church of Jesus Christ is first recognized sacramentally by the ordinance called the naming and blessing. In the New Testament, Jesus took children up in his arms "and blessed them" (Mark 10:16). And so Latter-day Saints bring their new children, usually a few days or weeks after birth, before the church congregation to formally give them a name and a blessing, which follows no prescribed form. The sacrament is generally performed by the father and is usually done on the first Sunday of the month. If the father does not hold the priesthood, he or the mother (if a single parent) may designate someone else to perform the blessing.

At the age of eight, judged to be the age of "accountability" (D&C 29:47; 68:25), the child is eligible for baptism. The practice is to have an interview with the bishop to ensure that the child is familiar with the basic principles of the gospel, recognizes the significance of the sacrament, and desires to have it done. As with the infant blessing, the father usually performs this ordinance. However, anyone holding the office of priest or any man holding any office in the Melchizedek priesthood (discussed later in this chapter) can do the baptism. Sometimes, an older brother or grandfather performs the ordinance.

In the New Testament, the gift of the Holy Ghost is associated with the "laying on of hands." Following this pattern, and subsequent to baptism (sometimes immediately and sometimes in the next sacrament meeting), a Melchizedek priesthood holder (elder or high priest) places his hands on the candidate's head, confirms the person as a member of the Church of Jesus Christ of Latter-day Saints, and pronounces the words "receive the Holy Ghost." Generally, the priesthood holder then pronounces some words of blessing as he feels inspired to do.

On entering their twelfth year, boys are ordained to the Aaronic priesthood, while young women at the same age progress from the children's primary organization to the Young Women's organization. At this age, young women and young men alike become eligible to participate in the temple ordinance of "baptism for the dead."

At age eighteen, young men are eligible to be ordained elders in the Melchizedek priesthood, receive their temple "endowment," and serve as full-time missionaries. Women leave the Young Women's program at age eighteen to enter the Relief Society, the church's auxiliary (recently redesignated an "organization") for all LDS women. At age nineteen, they are eligible for missions and may receive their endowment at that time (or earlier if getting married). In both cases, men and women who do not choose to serve missions generally do not receive their temple endowment until marriage or at a time later in life that they determine in consultation with their bishop.

Postmission, the next major life event in the life of a Latter-day Saint is temple marriage. Technically, the ordinance is a "sealing," or eternal binding, of a couple who have been wed, either as part of the sealing ceremony or in a previous civil ceremony. For most Latter-day Saints, such temple marriage is the culmination of that series of formal and sacramental milestones that began with their blessing as infants—and is often the fulfillment of hopes and promises made at that time. Men and women may receive many subsequent callings, and some of them (for men) may involve substantial ecclesiastical authority. However, nothing subsequent to temple sealing to a spouse represents any further progress or necessary step in the path toward eternal life.

How does the lay priesthood work?

Generally it is in their twelfth year that LDS boys are eligible to receive the Aaronic priesthood and be ordained to the office of deacon. The principal duty associated with this office in the modern church is to administer the sacrament by passing the trays of bread and water to the members of the congregation in sacrament meetings.

In their fourteenth year the young men progress to the office of teacher (who can participate in the ministering program and help in the preparation of the sacramental bread and water), and in their sixteenth year to the office of priest (who can pronounce the sacramental prayers and perform baptisms). Those constitute the three offices of the Aaronic, or preparatory, priesthood, through which young males progress. At each stage, they belong to a quorum of their peers holding that office. Rights and privileges in the priesthood are cumulative, so at every office, the priesthood holder has the authority pertaining to that and every previous office. For example, a priest can baptize and can also pass the sacrament.

At age eighteen, young men can be ordained as elders in the Melchizedek priesthood—the second and higher order of priesthood in the LDS Church. At this time, they leave the Young Men's program to join the elders quorum and are encouraged to serve their two-year missions. As part of their mission preparation, they also become eligible to make special temple covenants, a power referred to as the "endowment." From that point on, they also wear the "special garments," a principal purpose of which is to keep them mindful of these sacred covenants.

Having reached the office of elder, and being thereby qualified to make temple covenants, a male Latter-day Saint has attained all those powers and privileges that the Saints believe are necessary for him to find his way forward to sanctification and exaltation (or salvation). If he is subsequently called to serve in a bishopric, or in a stake or mission presidency, he will first be ordained to the office of high priest.

How does one become a Latter-day Saint?

Every year, some hundreds of thousands of converts make their way into the faith (between 200,000 and 300,000 annually in most recent years). How does that happen, and what does the process entail? The primary drivers of new convert growth are (1) missionaries and (2) missionary-minded members. With over sixty thousand full-time missionaries in the field, many thousands are found by missionaries going door to door. More effective by far are the efforts of members who invite friends to church or share the Book of Mormon. An often-repeated mantra is "every member a missionary," and members are constantly urged to share the gospel with friends, coworkers, and neighbors. Ward units generally have a "mission leader" assigned to supervise members' missionary efforts and coordinate with the full-time missionaries assigned to that ward. In either case, prospective members listen to a set of "discussions," really more a set of lessons that cover such topics as "the plan of salvation," "the commandments," and "the message of the Restoration." At each stage, those studying the church are encouraged to attend LDS Church services, study the Book of Mormon, and pray for spiritual confirmation of what they are hearing.

If the candidate accepts the invitation to be baptized, an interview follows to ascertain whether the person understands the nature of the obligations involved and is committed to observe them. Those commitments encompass both belief and practice. The major tenets that require assent are belief in God the Eternal Father and in Jesus Christ as Savior and Redeemer and belief that Joseph Smith restored the gospel, meaning that he recuperated both the true teachings of Jesus Christ and the authority to act in his name. Finally, one must recognize the current church president as the prophetic successor to Joseph Smith.

The Great Commission of the New Testament ("Teach all nations, baptizing them in the name of the Father, and of the Son, and of the Holy Ghost; Matthew 28:19) and teachings of the New Testament apostles always connected baptism to personal repentance. And so the interview will also ascertain whether the candidate has repented of past sins and is committed to observe God's commandments. Four of those commandments are singled out for particular attention: the law of sexual chastity, which limits sexual activity to marriage between a man and a woman; the law of tithing, whereby one commits 10 percent of one's income to the church; the Word of Wisdom, the health code prohibiting coffee, tea, alcohol, and tobacco and enjoining a healthy diet; and observance of the Sabbath day.

Though they are not articulated, three covenants from the Book of Mormon are often associated in the LDS mind with a baptismal commitment: to bear one another's burdens, to mourn with those who mourn, and to comfort those in need of comfort (Mosiah 18:8–10). If one is prepared and approved for baptism, the sacrament is administered by a priest in the Aaronic priesthood (generally aged sixteen and older) or any man holding the Melchizedek priesthood and is performed by full immersion. Unlike the mainstream Christian denominations, including Catholicism, the Saints do not recognize the validity of prior baptism in another faith tradition. (At the same time, Catholics and Protestants alike do not recognize the validity of LDS baptism.) The ordinance is followed by the sacrament of confirmation, whereby one receives the gift of the Holy Ghost and is formally accepted as a new member of the church.

What is eternal marriage?

Latter-day Saints are known for their family-centeredness. More than one sociologist has pointed to this as a key ingredient in the appeal of the Church of Jesus Christ as a faith tradition, especially in an age characterized by family fragmentation, single parenthood, and rampant divorce. The church's focus on family is both institutional and theological. In the first instance, programs like Family Home Evening are designed to set aside a regular, weekly designated time for family instruction and family nurturing. The family takes priority in all church programs and planning and practice. Theologically, the faith undergirds such programs and practices with an explicit doctrine of the eternal nature of the family. Latter-day Saints do not believe that the family is a sociologically or culturally derived institution or one that God ordained merely for the sanctifying of sex and the peopling of the planet. On the contrary, the Saints believe that God effectively wedded Adam and Eve in the Garden and are prone to point out that the marriage was performed at a time when death had not yet entered the world. Hence, the first marriage was, by design and by way of template, a forever marriage.

While many Christians intuitively hope—or believe—that they will be reunited with loved ones in the hereafter, Latter-day Saints ratify such hope with sacramental practice. The temple marriage for which young Saints are taught to prepare from the earliest age is considered a crowning achievement of devotion to gospel living. The marriage ceremony promises the wedded couple that their union will extend into the eternities, as will their "seed," that is, posterity. It is not clearly stated anywhere in LDS doctrine what the mechanism of such progeny will be; Latter-day Saints simply believe that in some way or fashion, the production and nurturing of earthly families is a foretaste of a heavenly future. Since only those members with "special recommends" to enter the temple may attend such ceremonies, the practice has kept many nonmember relatives of the betrothed out of the most important day of their lives. Recently, the church adopted a policy of allowing couples in America to marry in a civil ceremony open to all, followed immediately by a temple "sealing." Previously, only members living in countries that did not recognize religious ceremonies had that option; American Saints had to wait a full year for a sealing if they did not avail themselves of the temple option for the marriage ceremony.

It has been common in Christian thinking about heaven to see earthly relations as pointing humans toward, or preparing them for, the all-consuming love and adoration they will one day experience in the divine presence. This "theocentric" heaven is challenged in LDS thought by the concept of eternal relationships that extend vertically but also horizontally. In other words, the Saints believe in a sociable heaven. Smith himself, in words that were canonized, taught that "the same sociality that exists here will exist there, but it will be coupled with eternal glory" (D&C 130:2). In this view, God himself does not exist in a self-sufficient holy solitude, nor does the mystery of the Trinity serve as a kind of divine surrogate for interpersonal connectedness. God himself, taught one LDS apostle, actually has reference to an eternally united, exalted male and female. God's kingdom is in reality, the Saints believe, a "kin-dom," and eternally wedded Latter-day Saints both mirror and extend God's own eternal relationality.

With such a theological background, it is no wonder that Latter-day Saints have a higher marriage rate, a lower marital age, and higher birth rate than the national average in the United States. And those who marry in LDS temples have a significantly lower divorce rate than their counterparts.

How do Latter-day Saints observe the Sabbath?

In the Old Testament (or Hebrew Bible), God set apart the seventh day—Saturday—as a day of rest. The early Christians did not so much change the Sabbath to Sunday as reinvent the concept. The Sabbath had been described largely in terms of what was precluded on that day: work. The Christians honored the new Sabbath (Sunday) in terms of what it commemorated: Christ's resurrection. At various times and in various

Christian practices, the two ideas have merged: believers worship God and abstain from work. In the modern Christian world, however, the prohibitions tend to receive a great deal less emphasis than in times past. Latter-day Saints have defied this trend. Observant Saints tend to be rather scrupulous about not working themselves and avoiding all commerce that would require others to work. No shopping or eating out is the general rule for Sundays. Similarly, you are not likely to find members of the church heading to the lake or movie theaters or soccer stadiums—at least not to the same degree as their neighbors. When the demands of their employment or sports teams require Sabbath participation, they will often put pragmatism ahead of strict adherence; however, the strictest in the faith will find other work and miss the game or stop playing the sport.

So how do Latter-day Saints fill their Sundays? In the modern era, meetings tended to occupy much of the Sabbath. Men and boys had early priesthood meeting. Then they retrieved wives and children and returned for Sunday school. After a break of a few hours, they returned again for an evening worship service ("sacrament meeting"). Beginning in 1980, the church moved to a "consolidated meeting schedule," in which all three meetings were held consecutively in a three-hour block. The contemplation of this move arose from the energy crisis of the early 1970s. When the shift took place, the stated purpose was to afford families more time together and to allow all members to engage in personal gospel service, family activities, and meaningful service.

The new schedule was enthusiastically embraced, since it generally meant only a morning or afternoon was expended in meetings, leaving an unprecedented amount of time free for the family to use as they wished. More than a generation later, a weekly three-hour sequence of meetings challenged the endurance of many whose basis of comparison was not the LDS past but their contemporary Christian neighbors who could fulfill their worship obligations in an hour-long mass or worship service. Three hours was especially taxing for parents of small children (and the children themselves and the teachers responsible for the two hours of care and instruction pertaining to little ones). Considering also a need for parents and individuals and parents to assume greater responsibility over their own gospel instruction, the leadership announced an abbreviated two-hour block effective 2019. This new dispensation was gratefully received. Members have been encouraged to take advantage of the additional free time to spend time as a family together or as individuals in gospel study, in particular employing the self-guided course named the "Come, Follow Me" program.

Why do Latter-day Saints fast?

Fasting has historically been practiced in most religious traditions. Depriving the body of necessary sustenance and the satisfaction of natural cravings—whether for food, sleep, or pleasure—has been seen as an effective means of disciplining and subordinating the stubborn flesh to the higher aspirations and preoccupations of the spirit. One can also see fasting as itself a kind of sacrifice. Believers offer a sacrifice of their own bodily wants and satisfactions.

The Israelites fasted to incur God's favor and allay his wrath, as well as to demonstrate sorrow. David fasted to add power and efficacy to his prayers, as when he petitioned God for the healing of his child (2 Samuel 12), and Ezra fasted to obtain spiritual guidance on the return to Jerusalem (Ezra 8:23). The use of fasting to acquire and invoke greater spiritual power is both modeled and encouraged by Jesus in the New Testament; he fasts in the wilderness to acquire strength for his ministry (Matthew 4) and admonishes his disciples to fast for greater influence over demonic forces (Matthew 17).

The (now mostly obsolete) Christian practice of fasting before feast days suggests an intention to heighten the joy of abundance by the experience of scarcity. Such a logic appears in the first LDS scriptural reference to fasting, an 1831 revelation that enjoins the preparation of food in such a frame of mind "that thy fasting may be perfect, or in other words, that thy joy may be full" (D&C 59:13). The Book of Mormon mentions fasting several times, always in conjunction with prayer (Alma 6:6; 17:3; 28:6, etc.). Early in the history of the Church of Jesus Christ, fasting acquired an additional function that it maintains to this day. As Brigham Young expressed the principle in the 1840s, "we have kept the poor by having fast meeting and giving to the poor—if we can sustain our poor by fasting one day in four weeks—it is a cheap tax—it makes them glad and we are all as one mind."[2]

Like the Old Testament prohibition against gleaning one's own fields (leaving the grain leftover from the harvest to the poor), fasting became a communal form of social welfare. The deliberate experience of deprivation was meant to elicit solidarity with the needy, and the resources saved by that self-deprivation could be redirected to alleviate the hunger of the needy. Spiritual and pragmatic benefits were merged. Brigham Young designated the first Thursday of every month as a day of fasting, and in 1896 the day was moved to the first Sunday of every month, which remains the current practice. Adult Latter-day Saints are encouraged to forego food and drink for twenty-four hours, donating the equivalent worth of those meals (or several times their value) as a free will offering to the poor, with the funds administered locally by the bishop to those in need. In addition, as Young frequently urged the Saints to individually "fast and pray until they get the spirit of God," so is fasting encouraged today as an aspect of private devotion and discipleship, and at times of special need or spiritual questing.

What is a typical week like for a Latter-day Saint?

To maximize the utility of meetinghouses, two and sometimes three or more congregations (wards) will usually share one chapel (the name Saints give to both the sanctuary and the building itself) with staggered schedules. Sunday therefore begins for most Latter-day Saints with a worship service commencing at 9:00, 11:00, or 1:00, but almost any time between 8:00 and 4:00 is possible. (In some areas of the world, members of the church observe the Sabbath on a different day: Friday in some Islamic countries, Saturday in Israel, and any day of the seven in Hong Kong, where many domestic workers only have one day a week off.) If the household has a mother or father in a leadership position, that parent may well be at the chapel for a meeting or meetings hours before the worship service begins. It is not at all unusual for LDS men (and some women) to begin the day with a meeting at 6:00. As of 2019, the first general meeting is the Sacrament Meeting, consisting of hymns, prayers, the passing of the sacrament (or Lord's Supper), and two or three sermons ("talks") (or sharing of "testimonies" in lieu of talks on the first, "fast" Sunday).

After a closing prayer followed by a ten-minute break, children under age eleven or twelve go to "Primary" or "nursery," and young adults go to their Sunday school or, on alternating Sundays, their Young Women or Young Men classes. Adults attend a Gospel Doctrine Sunday school class; on alternating Sundays they attend a Priesthood Meeting (for men eighteen and older) or Relief Society meeting (for women eighteen and older).

After church services, members of the local bishopric remain to process tithes, and youth leaders may meet briefly with the bishop to plan activities and events. Returning home, members are encouraged to devote at least some of the day to personal gospel study—an activity that has received renewed emphasis in light of the shortened meeting schedule. The rest of the day is generally given over to quiet activities. Sunday is often the day members use to do their "ministering," which was called "home teaching" until 2018—visiting assigned individuals or families to check on their spiritual and temporal welfare.

Monday morning ideally begins with family (or personal) scripture study. The practice is not universal, but many Latter-day Saints remember the morning ritual of being prodded from their beds for the reading of verses—usually from the Book of Mormon—as a devotional start to the day, followed by family prayer. If there are high-school-age teens in the home, they most likely soon head off for "seminary," an hour-long gospel class generally held before school, five days a week. The curriculum rotates among Old Testament, New Testament, Book of Mormon, and Church History/Doctrine and Covenants. Outside Utah, the classes are held either in the member-teacher's home or in the ward chapel. In Utah, seminary is generally held during school hours and on school property, in a "release time" program. (This is a point of tension between the hordes of sleep-deprived LDS youth who diligently arise daily in time for their 6:00 travel for the class and their Utah peers who stroll into a classroom at 2:00 for the same purpose.)

Monday evening is generally observed as "Family Home Evening." The program is a semi-formalized hour or so filled with a hymn, prayer, brief lesson, activity, and refreshments, with every member of the family playing a part. In some areas of the church, singles are assigned to family home evening groups, as are "empty nesters." Latter-day Saint leaders never schedule other meetings or activities on Mondays, holding the day sacrosanct for that purpose.

Wednesday nights are generally reserved for the Young Women's and Young Men's programs, held at the chapel. Most weeks involve a lesson, with a monthly activity that can be recreational or service oriented. Saturdays are often occupied with church basketball (in season), or whatever sport prevails in that particular region of the church. Two or three families in the church will typically spend part of Saturday cleaning the chapel, as that service opportunity rotates among all able members of the ward.

No two families experience their religious lives according to the exact same template, but the foregoing description is roughly typical. Variations exist according to the density of the LDS population, the circumstances of the individuals, and the constraints that vary geographically.

How do Latter-day Saints worship?

Unlike the highly formalized rituals of temple worship, weekly LDS worship services have very little ritual or ceremony. The general pattern (other than the first Sunday of the month worship service) is to begin with a welcome by the bishop or one of his counselors, followed by an opening hymn and prayer. Then comes the administration of the Lord's Supper, or "sacrament." After the deacons serve the congregation the bread and water, they are dismissed, and the speakers then present their "talks" (which by their very name resist the formalism of sermonizing). Often one of the number will be a youth speaker, and sometimes an intermediate hymn precedes the closing speaker. Topics are generally assigned by the bishop or counselor.

With its calendar of conferences, member ministering, and fast meetings, the LDS Church resembles Methodism. In its antiformalism, LDS worship may be closest to Quakerism, having no liturgy, calendar of worship, service books, or lectionaries. Scriptures are often employed in the talks, but there is no formal requirement to do so, and there are no readings or recitations. Topics may include grace, or resurrection, or the beatitudes but may also focus on practical matters of self-reliance or thrift. A comment by Wilford Woodruff may shed light on the antiformalism of most LDS worship patterns and the pragmatism of many sermon topics. "Strangers and the Christian world marvel," he said, at the LDS emphasis on "temporal work." He explained: "we can't build up Zion sitting on a hemlock slab singing ourselves away to everlasting bliss."[3]

Although the Saints have no paid or trained clergy at the local level, that in itself does not explain the practice of rotating the speaking duty among all adult members of the congregation.

In theory, particularly gifted congregants might be selected as lay preachers, but that does not happen. The results are legendary in LDS culture (Saints feel particular empathy for Paul, the first preacher on record as having bored a congregant to death—Acts 20:9). Not only does rotating participation engage all adult congregants in the worship service; it demonstrably privileges community forbearance and support over personal, self-directed edification. Women now give talks about as frequently as men, though they apparently rarely spoke in the nineteenth century. Like the early Methodists from whom they drew so many converts, the Saints have consistently valued exhortation and the low style of preaching over rhetorically elegant homiletics. The labor of preparing and delivering a "talk" outweighs in devotional value, in the LDS conception, the contribution of a more polished and qualified sermonizer.

The sacrament prayers, pronounced by youths holding the office of priest or mature men holding the Melchizedek priesthood, are the only formal prayers a Latter-day Saint hears in the weekly public worship service. And although priests pronounce the prayer, the administration of the sacrament is effected by all the members, who pass the bread and water to each other.

The first Sunday of every month is designated "Fast and Testimony Meeting." In lieu of assigned talks, members rise as they feel prompted by the Spirit and bear witness of particular gospel principles and truths or share personal experiences for the edification of the congregation. Frequently lacking both polish and concision, it is likely that such public, spontaneous professions of personal belief, which generally involve the most intimate spiritual experiences and feelings, are another practice that forges the powerful communal bonds for which Latter-day Saints are known.

What is a temple?

From the earliest years of the Restoration, Latter-day Saints, like the ancient Israelites before them, have made the temple a focal point of their worship, considering the temple a site of especial sanctity. They attend Sunday meetings in meetinghouses, reserving the temple for occasions of special worship where "higher" ordinances—or sacraments—are performed. In the book of Exodus (25:8), the Lord commands the Israelites to "make Me a sanctuary," suggesting that a temple is a place not just where worshipers find refuge from, and transcendence of, the evils of the world but also where Jehovah himself comes to find refuge from his pain and from the sorrow inflicted by the evils of his creation. In recognition of the temple as a literal "house of the Lord," Smith enjoined in a dedicatory prayer that "no unclean thing shall be permitted to come into thy house to pollute it" (D&C 109:20).

The temple ordinances make much greater demands on discipleship than a casual Christianity, including very specific injunctions and commitments that are explicitly accepted along with sacred oaths and covenants. The LDS sacraments (with their accompanying covenants) channel and concretize human love and devotion to God and fellow humans into durable relationships. Through baptism, Saints formally and publicly accept Christ's invitation to be their spiritual Father, thus signaling a desire to be adopted into his family. Through further covenantal gestures, Saints affirm their commitment to bind themselves more closely to him and establish a relationship of reciprocity through progressively greater demonstrations of love and obedience, including principles of sacrifice, chastity, and selfless consecration of time, talents, and resources. And in temple marriage, individuals enact their willingness to expand the intimate association with the Divine, both laterally through marriage and vertically through posterity. These examples illuminate Joseph Smith's cardinal insight and most fundamental theological claim: Elijah, he came to believe, was going to "reveal the covenants to seal the hearts of the fathers to the children and the children to the fathers."[4] Smith later claimed that a resurrected Elijah did in fact appear to him and convey to him the priesthood "keys" or powers pertaining to temple sacraments.

Many writers have noted that the LDS heaven is anthropocentric rather than christocrentic or theocentric. In other words, heaven seems more about eternal families than about heavenly choirs adoring the ineffable divine. Such a characterization perpetuates a false dichotomy. For in the LDS conception, the ideal of all godly striving is eternal communion with spouse, family, friends—and a Heavenly Father and Mother. It is not either/or, but both/and. Considering themselves literal progeny of heavenly parents, Saints aspire to fully realize a web of kinship in the next life that incorporates virtually everyone into the heavenly family. Another way of saying this is that for Latter-day Saints, heaven is relational, not situational. It is not where you are but in what kind of relationship you find yourself that determines the degree of blessedness or perdition. The temple, through its series of covenants and ordinances, frames and promotes an ideal human and divine interconnectedness and interdependency.

Why do Latter-day Saints wear special underwear?

Many faith traditions employ particular modes of dress with special religious significance. LDS garments have biblical roots. They are less conspicuous than a Jewish yarmulke or Muslim hijab, but are no less religiously significant. Washing, clothing oneself in special garments, and anointing with oil were important ritual forms with both priestly and royal functions among the Israelites. In early Christian practice, after being washed and anointed the baptismal candidate was clothed in new garments. Scholars note an array of early Christian texts that refer to "rites of washing and anointing" and clothing in "a symbolic but real and tangible garment."

For some early Christians, the white robes received by converts at the time of baptism represented "the garment worn by Adam before his fall, a return to that pre-transgression state of glory and grace,"[5] although in the Genesis narrative God clothes Adam and Eve after they eat the fruit, not before. This makes good sense in LDS theology, however, for Latter-day Saints deny that the action was sinful. And so, in Joseph Smith's reworking of Genesis, God clothes Adam and Eve in special garments and initiates them into the gospel plan after they partake of the fruit and are enlightened as a consequence.

According to Carlos Asay, an LDS Seventy, "prior to their expulsion from the Garden of Eden [but after partaking of the forbidden fruit], Adam and Eve were clad in sacred clothing. . . . They received this clothing in a context of instruction on the Atonement, sacrifice, repentance, and forgiveness. The temple garment given to Latter-day Saints is provided in a similar context."[6] This garment is not a symbol of either a lost Eden or a past premortal glory; it is the sign of entrance into a covenant relationship under conditions that were fully anticipated and divinely sanctioned, leading to the embodiment of the human family as Adam and Eve's posterity. "They were born into the world by the fall," in the words of LDS scripture (Moses 6:59, 1851 ed.). In Adam's words: "blessed be the name of God, for because of my transgression . . . in this life I shall have joy, and again in the flesh I shall see God" (Moses 5:10). Adam and Eve were clothed in a garment that signified their recognition of Christ's atoning sacrifice and a commitment to abide by gospel principles; Latter-day Saints are similarly clothed in imitation of that event. Wearing such garments next to the body, concealed from public view, emphasizes the personal and sacred nature of their significance.

Why can't non-Mormons enter temples?

Many Latter-day Saints themselves do not have permission to enter their temples; simple membership is not a sufficient condition for entrance. If worship is understood as reverencing of the Divine, relishing and celebrating God's goodness and expressing adoration, then it would seem unreasonable to exclude any who wish to participate. And indeed, this is why all LDS meetinghouses bear the words "All are welcome." They are places of public worship.

In the Old Testament, God is described as "a consuming fire" (Deuteronomy 4:24), and for the Jews, the Holy of Holies represented a Divine Presence that could only be approached after extensive preparation and purification. Consistent with this background, LDS temples are not places of public worship or casual approach to God. Rather, they are the site of the most sacred personal covenant-making with God. Only those who are willing, disposed, and prepared to enter into binding commitments with the Divine are candidates for this particular variety of worship. Members decide when they are ready to take this step into a more total immersion in the life of discipleship. In the Puritan system, members chose to be either "brethren" in full fellowship or less committed "disciples," that is, those qualified and those not qualified to participate in the holy sacrament of the Eucharist.[7] In such cases, the separation relied not on arbitrary exclusion but on self-selection according to the seriousness of purpose with which one desired to pursue a personal faith commitment at a particular time in one's faith journey. The LDS hope is that all members of the human family would desire to make those covenants and commitments that inculcate principles of virtue and holiness and that they believe bind humans more closely to their heavenly parents. And all who are desirous to do so may qualify to worship in the temple. To expose the public to the appeal of such sanctuaries, while allaying concern and curiosity about the temple's inner workings, the church generally opens all new temples to the public for a period prior to their dedication. After the dedication, public tours would detract from the purposes of the temple: to provide a locus of sacred worship in a place of holiness pervaded by the divine presence.

Do Latter-day Saints believe in and practice the gifts of the Spirit?

Jesus Christ taught that signs would follow those who believed. He specifically named exorcisms, speaking in tongues, handling dangerous serpents, and healing the sick as examples. The believers of Christendom can be divided into cessationists and noncessationists: those who believe that these and other spiritual gifts—or "charismata"—were confined to the apostolic age and those who believe that gifts of the Spirit will always be in evidence among true believers. Latter-day Saints are unambiguously in the latter group. In the early years of the church, members drew attention to—and were widely ridiculed for—their insistence that gifts were prevalent among them and were an indispensable sign of their movement's divine origins. (An article of faith {7} still affirms belief "in the gift of tongues, prophecy, revelation, visions, healing, interpretation of tongues, and so forth.") And so one finds numerous accounts in the first decades of the church of many spiritual manifestations, but two in particular: speaking in tongues and miraculous healings (exorcisms have occurred as well). Both Joseph Smith and Brigham Young spoke in tongues, and it was not uncommon for others, men and women alike, to be moved to speak in tongues at baptisms, worship services, or prayer meetings. Not as common, and hauntingly beautiful to those who witnessed it, was "tongue-singing," which could also occur with both genders.

By the late decades of the nineteenth century, the LDS pattern was following that of earlier Christian history. Young preached that after the Restoration had taken root, there was less need for miraculous displays of glossolalia (speaking in an unknown tongue). More relevant, he said, was the capacity to speak in an actual language one hadn't studied when it was necessary for evangelizing (xenoglossia). With the fading—and discouragement—of glossolalia in the early twentieth century, focus shifted to the operations of the Spirit in aiding the preparations of missionaries now entering foreign fields by the tens of thousands. And so some Latter-day Saints assert that the gift of tongues persists, though to less dramatic but more useful effect, on a widespread basis today.

Healing followed a similar trajectory. Early Latter-day Saints performed many acts of healing among themselves as well as those to whom they taught and ministered. One of the more famous episodes from Joseph Smith's own life was when he arose from his sickbed during a malaria outbreak in Nauvoo, Illinois, and raised many others from their sickbeds in a "day of God's power." Often performed dramatically in the name of Jesus Christ, such healings were often publicized and even collected, documented, and published in church newspapers as signs to unbelievers and to strengthen the faithful. Soon, however, healings became formalized as a priesthood ordinance, following the pattern laid down by James to call the elders and anoint the sick with oil (James 5:14). Today, the ordinance of healing is widely practiced, though with minimum fanfare, albeit associated with many anecdotal accounts of miraculous results.

What is baptism for the dead?

Along with the doctrine of original sin, the damnation of the uncatechized and unbaptized is one of the most distressing—and ancient—problems in the history of Christian thought. The author of the *Clementine Recognitions*, a fourth-century narrative, put the question: "if those shall enjoy the kingdom of Christ, whom His coming shall find righteous, shall then those be wholly deprived of the kingdom who have died before his coming?"[8] Historically there have been at least two approaches to the problem. The first is to insist that God's justice is inscrutable and affirm that outside belief in Christ and the sacraments of the church, no salvation is possible. Hence, heaven will be the destination of a fortunate few. A second is to deny the indispensability of the sacraments and a specific confession of Christ, believing that God will find ways to accommodate good souls in a more ample heaven.

The Church of Jesus Christ charts a third way. Finding support in both the epistle of Peter that references gospel instruction of the dead (1 Peter 3–4), and Paul's first letter to the Corinthians, with a cryptic reference to baptism for the dead (1 Corinthians 15:29), Latter-day Saints believe that the program of evangelization continues in the world of spirits and that living persons may be baptized on behalf of the deceased. For Latter-day Saints, Christ and his sacraments remain the vital conduit to reunion with God, but the time and place of one's birth in the world is no barrier to those conditions.

The effect of posthumous baptisms is not conversion; only a personal, conscious decision to accept the baptismal covenant, in this life or the next, constitutes conversion. The intention in baptizing on behalf of dead persons is to provide an opportunity for their participation in that whole and complete and perfect union of the human family. The scheme reflects an LDS vision of the eternities, but many are not happy to be put on a guest list for a party they have no intention of attending. Some, on the other hand, can appreciate the motive if not the substance associated with the ordinance. Krister Stendahl, Lutheran bishop of Stockholm and dean of Harvard Divinity School, expressed "holy envy" for a practice so conspicuously rooted in love for one's ancestors. He recognized in this practice, with its hints of ancient origins, acts of devotion performed across a veil of silence, a reaching after our dead in the hope of uniting them to us.

Baptism for the dead is the best-known of LDS temple rituals for the deceased, but all ordinances that are essential for salvation are also performed in the temple on behalf of the dead. That includes priesthood ordination for men, receipt of the Holy Ghost, the "endowment," and sealing as couples and/or families.

Why are Latter-day Saints so interested in genealogy?

The LDS Church's colossal program of genealogical research is explained by belief in a virtually universal salvation predicated—in part—on vicarious sacraments. When Smith revealed the principle of baptism for the dead in 1840, excited members responded by immediately having themselves baptized on behalf of deceased relatives who had lived and died outside the church's boundaries. With time, the practice became systematized, and the project of performing vicarious baptisms on behalf of the deceased grew to include the entire range of saving ordinances, culminating in "sealing ordinances," which bind families into eternal relationship. In 1894, church president Wilford Woodruff framed the implications of LDS theology of salvation as a simple if daunting imperative: "we want the Latter-day Saints from this time to trace their genealogies as far as they can, and to be sealed to their fathers and mothers . . . and run this chain as far as you can get it."[9]

The purpose of this research is hence twofold. Temple ordinances both give individuals access to those covenants and spiritual powers that facilitate their quests to acquire "the divine nature" and organize those individuals into durable, eternal family relationships. Smith had laid the foundations for this endeavor when he preached: "the greatest responsibility resting upon us is to look after our dead," later adding in a paraphrase of Paul that "we cannot be made perfect without [each other]."[10] More is involved here than a requirement that the living act charitably to perform ordinances on behalf of the deceased. The active work of excavating one's family's history and performing ordinance work on their behalf is not a gauge of unselfish service that *qualifies one* or is a *requirement* for salvation; the incorporation of the deceased into sacred relationship with the living is—like the binding of living families through ordinance work—*constitutive* of heaven.

Saints see their project as the organizing of their family lines into eternal chains of belonging. An Old Testament scripture deemed so important to Latter-day Saints that it is repeated in each of their other three books of scripture is the Lord's promise in Malachi that "I will send you Elijah the prophet before the coming of the great and dreadful day of the Lord: And he shall turn the heart of the fathers to the children, and the heart of the children to their fathers, lest I come and smite the earth with a curse" (Malachi 4:5–6). The Saints believe that this "spirit of Elijah" is an inspired recognition of the critical importance of their ancestors and the consequent responsibility to "search out our dead" and bind them to themselves through the ordinances of the temple.

Following Woodruff's announcement, the church sponsored the Genealogical Society of Utah to facilitate the task. Today, the renamed Family History Department, with its thousands of satellite libraries, provides access to over two billion names, found in sources from fourteenth-century English church records to African oral histories. Those records and resources are available to all individuals, not only members of the LDS faith.

What is a patriarchal blessing?

In the concluding chapters of Genesis, the patriarch Jacob gathers his posterity about him in order to tell them "that which shall befall [them] in the last days" (49:1). He then dispenses both blessings and prophecies pertaining to them and their posterity. The rights of kingship will be part of Judah's inheritance; Joseph will have a posterity as abundant as boughs overflowing a wall.

A few years after organizing the church, Joseph Smith instituted the office of patriarch, comparing it to the position Jacob occupied, and made it a hereditary calling. As the church grew, additional patriarchs were called to administer blessings locally. Consequently the office of patriarch over the entire church became redundant and was eliminated in 1979.

The patriarch's calling is exclusively that of a blessing-giver. Every member of the church is entitled—and encouraged—to receive a patriarchal blessing, which is generally a one-time occurrence.

If the sacrament of the Lord's Supper is the most communal of LDS rituals, participated in jointly with a congregation, often while remembering covenants associated with baptism that unite the membership in mutual mourning, grieving, and comforting, then the patriarchal blessing might be considered the most private and personal ordinance. Speaking under the influence of the Holy Spirit, the patriarch gives a blessing that is specifically tailored to the needs and concerns of the individual. A typical blessing may include words of encouragement, identifying special gifts and talents to be employed in serving one's family and the larger world. It may also include words of warning or counsel regarding particular weaknesses or temptations, as well as specific promises of blessings contingent on faithfulness. The recipient and the patriarch generally fast and pray in preparation. There is no prescribed age for the recipient, but the norm is to receive the bishop's recommend (or authorization) for such a blessing in one's midteen years.

One feature of the blessing that connects the practice and the office to its Old Testament precedent is the identification of the person's ancient Israelite lineage. Latter-day Saints believe that the Abrahamic covenant is one in which all of Israel—literal or adoptive—is invited to participate. For Latter-day Saints, the promises of particular importance are those relating to numerous posterity, redefined as an eternal posterity and "the blessings of . . . life eternal" (Abraham 2:11) in an LDS revision of the promises made in Genesis. (This is the basis of the LDS conception of eternal marriage and forever families.) Hence, the patriarchal blessing designates the particular tribe of Israel to which one belongs, or is adopted into, and by virtue of which one is a child of those promises. The particular lineage with which one is identified is immaterial. Nor is it important whether the blessing identifies literal descent or simply assigns the blessed person to a tribe. What matters is the emphatic affirmation of one's position in the household of faith and one's right to the promises of eternal life and eternal posterity that the Saints associate with the Abrahamic covenant.

Are Saints required to pay a tithe to the church?

"Let us here observe," Joseph Smith wrote, "that a religion that does not require the sacrifice of all things never has power sufficient to produce the faith necessary unto life and salvation."[11] For a time, the Latter-day Saints experimented with the Law of Consecration, a principle of communalism such as the early Christians are described as living by in the book of Acts ("they had all things in common"; 4:32). After the Saints had failed to successfully live such a challenging principle, the law of tithing was first given as the standing law of the church in July 1838, to the members in Missouri. The principle, as the etymology of the term suggests, enjoined members to "pay one-tenth of all their interest annually," with "interest" interpreted to mean income. That practice is alluded to in the Bible (as when Abraham paid tithes to Melchizedek and in Malachi's call to ancient Judah to remember the obligation to tithe), and those allusions are the precedents for the LDS practice.

The law of tithing is an efficient system of church finance, as well as a continuing principle by which individual commitment to the gospel is both measured and fostered. Originally, tithes were frequently paid in kind, with members contributing 10 percent of their produce or new livestock. Goods were gathered in the bishop's storehouse, whence they were dispensed to the poor and needy under the authority of the bishop. Today, members generally make cash payments through their local bishop or, increasingly, directly to the church online. All decisions pertaining to the disposition of tithing funds are made from church headquarters.

No collection plate is passed, and donations are not solicited. The principle is taught frequently in church sermons, however, and members must pay a full tithe to be eligible for temple worship. Some people think that is disturbingly close to coercion, but Latter-day Saints see it as a litmus test of real commitment before one undertakes the deepest spiritual obligations associated with temple worship. The consequence is that Saints donate funds to their church at a substantially higher rate than is seen in other faiths. In one study, the number of those donating a full 10 percent of their income to the LDS Church ranged from 40 to 80 percent of the sample, depending on educational level.[12] The church does not release financial figures, so the total income from tithing (and from other sources as well) is not known, though it is a subject of widespread speculation.

Why do Latter-day Saints have large families?

Large family size—in America at least—frequently prompts the assumption that the parents are either Catholic or LDS, and LDS family size is indeed larger than the national average (though the discrepancy is shrinking). Contrary to what some might think, this is not a result of either doctrinal or cultural prohibitions against birth control. The practice is not officially discouraged (though it once was), and LDS married women use contraception at a rate comparable to the national average. As President Gordon B. Hinckley said in 1984: "the Lord has told us to multiply and replenish the earth that we might have joy in our posterity, and there is no greater joy than the joy that comes of happy children in good families. But he did not designate the number, nor has the church. That is a sacred matter left to the couple and the Lord."[13] The official statement of the church includes this language: "husbands must be considerate of their wives, who have the greater responsibility not only of bearing children but of caring for them through childhood, and should help them conserve their health and strength."[14]

Large family size among members of the Church of Jesus Christ is probably attributable to three factors. Historically, the Saints have seen procreation as the conduit through which "noble spirits, that have been waiting for thousands of years," come into mortality, as Orson Pratt taught in 1852.[15] Procreation becomes coparticipation with God in the peopling of the earth according to a plan that preceded the earth's creation. Large families were explicitly encouraged by Brigham Young as a kind of spiritual lifeboat for souls who could otherwise founder on the rocks of uncertain family environments and circumstance, and the pattern became entrenched in LDS culture.

A second reason for larger family size is the LDS theological tenet that families have eternal duration. Marriage solemnized in a temple results in children being born "in the covenant," that is, with the provisional promise of eternal connection to siblings and parents. Church teachings, rhetoric, and programs all make the family the principal unit not just of social organization but of eternal standing. This does not necessarily entail that parents have large numbers of offspring; however, the ubiquitous preoccupation with families and a theological emphasis on their eternal standing cannot help but make bearing children a gesture with more than usual significance.

A third factor would be an official espousal of traditional gender roles in LDS marriages. Until very recently, LDS women were discouraged from working outside the home unless financial necessity dictated otherwise. The official 1995 "Proclamation on the Family" teaches that "mothers are primarily responsible for the nurture of their children," though such language is increasingly tempered with the caveat that "fathers and mothers are obligated to help one another as equal partners."[16] LDS culture has not been insulated from larger cultural trends; fewer LDS women are now stay-at-home mothers than in years past, and they have fewer children, though still more than most (at least in America)—3.4 versus 2.2 for other Christian households.[17]

What is the church's teaching on abortion?

Abortion has been consistently condemned in LDS thought. Many nineteenth-century figures—including feminists like Susan B. Anthony and Cady Stanton—used the terms "abortion," "foeticide," "infanticide," and "child-murder" interchangeably or as near equivalents. This idea likely lies behind the LDS Church's first oblique reference to abortion in 1831: "thou shalt not . . . kill, nor do anything like unto it" (D&C 59:6).

Many liberal Protestants have moved in recent decades to elevate women's reproductive rights above any rights of the unborn child, but the LDS Church has resisted this development. The modern LDS Church officially treats most abortions as "like unto" (but not the same as) murder; one may repent after abortion and be baptized, but not (without special dispensation) after murder. Exception may be made in cases of threat to the mother's health, rape, incest, or nonviability of the child. Though the doctrine of premortality has bearing on LDS ideas about procreation generally, it is not typically invoked as having bearing on abortion. Precisely when the soul enters the body is for Latter-day Saints, as for Christians generally, a matter of speculation rather than dogma.

For a minority of Saints, the theological emphasis on choice offers a persuasive rationale for supporting abortion rights, even if one is personally opposed to the practice. The current leadership has explicitly condemned this rationale. President Russell Nelson, who was a surgeon before his call to the apostleship, has spoken in harsh terms against the "baleful war being waged on life" and "odious carnage."[18] And First Presidency member Dallin Oaks has criticized the "personally opposed but . . ." reasoning in public discourses: the sanctity of one agent's choice can never trump the sanctity of the other's life, he argues. Given the status of the unborn child as a human individual in LDS thought, two human agents, and two vested interests, must be weighed accordingly. Oaks's comments highlight a particular LDS understanding of choice. In this view of moral freedom, there exists a sacrosanct link between choice and consequence. Freedom, in other words, is grounded in a framework of natural law. As Oaks reasons, "the effect in 95% of abortions is not to vindicate choice but to avoid its consequences; using arguments of choice to try to justify altering the consequences of choice is a classic case of omitting what the Savior called the 'weightier matters of the law.'"[19] From this perspective, ironically, those who seek to protect the unborn child are actually defending the principle of choice by protecting the consequences of that choice.

Church policy and member practice are often out of sync. In the case of Latter-day Saints, most members are in accord with church teachings against abortion. A significant majority of Latter-day Saints think abortions should be illegal in all or most cases—a higher percentage than for Catholics and all mainline Protestant groups according to American surveys.[20] Saints have abortions at extremely low levels.

Why do Latter-day Saints stockpile food and other goods?

For some decades, church members have been urged to set aside what they refer to as "food storage" or a "year's supply." (It used to be two years but is now more frequently limited to a goal of one year or less.) The emphasis on temporal self-sufficiency grew out of the experience of the Great Depression, under the leadership of Harold B. Lee. At the height of the practice, in the 1970s, the motivation was often associated with a sense that the Second Coming was imminent and anticipation of the travails and disruptions expected to precede that event. Stockpiling foodstuffs, fuel, clothing, and medical supplies was deemed a prudent precaution for whatever might unfold in the "last days." In more recent years, the practice persists, though with less intensity and fewer references to what evangelicals call a coming "Rapture." (Some of the apostles have even expressed the belief that Jesus will not return in their or their grandchildren's lifetimes.) A wider range of rationales are now invoked for putting aside food: buying in bulk and when on sale makes good financial sense; economic booms and busts, in America and abroad, lend great uncertainty to financial security and employment. And the coronavirus pandemic of 2020 lent particular weight to the practice. Even in the absence of natural disasters, events from power outages to truckers' strikes make a nonagricultural society increasingly vulnerable to short-term shortages.

Having several months' worth of provisions seems reasonable and prudent and can be an invaluable resource at times of personal crisis or need. Members are urged to store what they eat and eat what they store; to garden and can and lay up their own produce when possible; and to adapt their rate and volume of storage to their financial and spatial resources, as well as in ways consistent with cultural practice.

In rural communities, members' basements are often lined with home-canned fruits and vegetables. Urban dwellers maintain whatever surplus is possible in their more spatially constrained circumstances. Those with room to spare often have garages or basements containing large buckets of wheat and freeze-dried food purchased from suppliers that cater to the LDS practice (as well as to survivalists!). Members also often avail themselves of church-run canneries to purchase and dry-pack foods from beans to pasta. Leaders emphasize that home storage should be part of a larger lifestyle of "provident living," in which members do all they can to make themselves emotionally, financially, and spiritually independent. Historically, one can easily see the larger principle as well as the particular form it takes as emerging naturally among a people whose history involved so much displacement, deprivation, and imposed self-sufficiency.

If Latter-day Saints are Christians, why don't they display the cross?

The cross is the universal symbol of Christians. Why, then, do Latter-day Saints neither employ the cross in their worship nor wear the cross on their persons? The explanation is more to be found in culture and history than theology. Theologically, the cross is at the center of LDS religion. As Catholic theologian Steven Webb recognized, "Mormonism is obsessed with Christ, and everything that it teaches is meant to awaken, encourage, and expand faith in him."[21] Latter-day Saints believe that their resurrection and salvation are utterly dependent on the willing suffering and death of Jesus Christ. They may differ from other Christians in believing that such suffering was initiated—and more pronounced—in Gethsemane than on Calvary, but there is no ambiguity in the LDS position: Christ's salvific offering culminated on the cross. According to Joseph Smith, "the fundamental principles of our religion are the testimony of the Apostles and Prophets, concerning Jesus Christ, that He died, was buried, and rose again the third day, and ascended into heaven; and all other things which pertain to our religion are only appendages to it."[22] Brigham Young reaffirmed to his missionaries that if their minds were not "riveted on the cross of Christ, you will go and return in vain."[23]

Wearing a cross was not common among Mormon pioneers, although Young's own daughters were photographed wearing them. In the nineteenth century the cross was typically associated with Catholicism. Latter-day Saints and Protestants alike tended to avoid displaying or wearing it. Protestants gradually adopted the symbol of the plain cross (although not the crucifix with the body of Christ), but Latter-day Saints never did. Perhaps the reason was rooted in the mutual antagonism between Saints and Protestants during most of the nineteenth and early twentieth centuries. Latter-day Saints were largely shunned as both un-American and un-Christian, and they in turn considered Catholic and Protestant alike to be heirs of the universal "Great Apostasy" of Christianity. Avoiding a symbol that was associated in their minds with Protestantism *and* Catholicism was a natural choice.

In more recent decades, Latter-day Saints have officially proffered an explanation related to the focus on Christ's resurrection. "Because the Savior lives, we do not use the symbol of his death as the symbol of our faith."[24] Paul wrote that "as in Adam all die, so in Christ shall all be made alive" (1 Corinthians 15:22). An emphasis on resurrection over crucifixion, life over death, is fully in keeping with Latter-day Saints' cultural disposition to manifest their religiosity in ways more joyful than pious. Nevertheless, no church policy actually forbids the practice, and a growing number of Latter-day Saints do in fact wear a cross.

Why don't the Latter-day Saints drink?

Like devout Jews, Hindus, Muslims, and members of some Christian denominations, Latter-day Saints abide by a dietary law that forbids the ingestion of certain substances. While the revelation known as the Word of Wisdom also enjoins the eating of fresh fruits and grains ("in the season thereof"), it is the prohibitions that dominate LDS—and public—consciousness regarding this law. Tradition holds that Joseph Smith was prompted to inquire of the Lord regarding tobacco use in response to his wife's complaints about the unsavory aspects of the practice as evidenced in the stained floor of their Kirtland, Ohio, home above the Whitney store, used by Smith's School of the Prophets (a forum of both gospel and secular instruction). The ensuing revelation singled out the use of tobacco, alcohol ("wine and strong drink"), and "hot drinks," which the prophet's brother Hyrum (and subsequent leaders) interpreted to mean tea and coffee, as "not good . . . for the body neither for the belly" (D&C 89:7–8). In the 1970s, the church counseled that caffeinated beverages fell under the same proscription, due to their addictive properties. Leaders have since indicated that the caffeine proscription is not a doctrinal stance;

hence, abstaining from cola drinks has become one of the readiest indices of the degree of orthodoxy in Word of Wisdom observance. A substantial minority of Saints still think that cola violates the spirit of the law, and it is noteworthy that BYU did not serve caffeinated beverages on campus until 2018.

Received in 1833, the principle was framed as coming neither by way of "commandment [n]or constraint, but by revelation and the word of wisdom" (D&C 89:2). Apparently, few members or even leaders of the church felt constrained by the revelation, since the prohibited substances continued to find fairly general use among them all. Brigham Young gave new emphasis to the revelation in 1851, and abstinence became a requirement for temple attendance some decades later.

The same revelation also encouraged the sparing use of meat, advising it be limited to "times of winter, or of cold, or famine" (D&C 89:13). If the past is any predictor, perhaps at some future time leaders will move Latter-day Saints to embrace more fully the quasi vegetarianism the law mandates as they did in the case of the other prohibitions—but at present Latter-day Saints around the world probably consume Big Macs and steaks as often as their peers.

In LDS thought, the Word of Wisdom forms part of a theology of the body that has roots in Paul's admonition to treat one's physical self as a "temple of God," with reverence and care (1 Corinthians 3:16). Accordingly, in the spirit of the Word of Wisdom, any substance—or quantity of substance—that is detrimental to health or the independence of the spirit is to be shunned. Clearly, that proscription applies to illegal drugs, prescription drug abuse, vaping, and kindred practices. The addictive nature of caffeine is the reason it is shunned by many of the Saints.

Do Latter-day Saints practice excommunication?

Like most of the Christian world, LDS theology envisions both an invisible, or spiritual, congregation of the elect, as well as a visible body of believers belonging to its temporal version. And while God knows his own, the Church of Jesus Christ is among those institutional churches that have followed New Testament precedent in determining the parameters of its membership. Organizational identity presupposes boundaries, lines of demarcation, and criteria by which membership is achieved or maintained. As William Temple declared centuries ago, "there must always be a tension between the right of the individual to freedom and the right of the institution to have a determinate character."[25] Theologian Timothy Keller has recently observed that "any community that did not hold its members accountable for specific beliefs and practices would not have a corporate identity and would really not be a community at all."[26]

Boundary maintenance, therefore, constitutes a virtually inescapable dimension of ecclesiology. The motive in this practice goes beyond the mere maintenance of a "corporate identity" that Keller has suggested. The concern is clearly for the well-being of disciples who are vulnerable to the influence of those who would corrupt them intellectually or morally. Such persons might "draw away disciples after them" like "grievous wolves" coming in "among you, not sparing the flock," in Paul's analogy (Acts 20:29–30).

Excommunication for heresy has been more common, or perhaps more publicized, in the modern Christian world than excommunication for moral turpitude. The twentieth century saw a number of prominent disciplinary actions for heresy: the Reformed, Presbyterian, Episcopalian, Lutheran, Baptist, and Catholic churches have all held church courts or imposed discipline in the last century and up to today. Joseph Smith, from the Church of Jesus Christ's inception, gave great latitude to unorthodox belief: "I never thought it was right to call up a man and try him because he erred in doctrine," he said, "I want the liberty of believing as I please, it feels so good not to be trammeled."[27] However, the leadership drew the line at *teaching* doctrine deemed injurious to the church.

Judicial proceedings were outlined in early LDS revelations and are conducted by the bishop or by the stake president in cases where a Melchizedek priesthood holder is the offender. Such councils can result in no action, in disfellowshipment (a kind of probationary state in which one is barred from full participation), or in excommunication (resulting in loss of membership and nullification of sacraments performed). The late twentieth and early twenty-first centuries saw a handful of LDS excommunications of vocal critics and dissenters from orthodoxy. Following one such highly publicized episode involving "the September Six," a group of feminists and scholars disciplined by church councils in 1993, the church affirmed that the relevant criterion for church discipline was promulgating, not holding, heretical beliefs. As they clarified in an official statement, "we have the responsibility to preserve the doctrinal purity of the Church. . . . Apostasy refers to Church members who (1) repeatedly act in clear, open, and deliberate public opposition to the Church or its leaders; or (2) persist in teaching as Church doctrine information that is not Church doctrine after being corrected by their bishops or higher authority; or (3) continue to follow the teachings of apostate cults . . . after being corrected by their bishops or higher authority."[28]

Early Christian documents urge restraint in "casting out" offenders, and one of the responsibilities of bishops, harking back to at least the early third century, was to "bring again that which is driven away, that is, do not permit that which is . . . cast out by way of punishment, to continue excluded." Perhaps marking a shift from sanctions to nurture, the LDS Church has changed the name of church courts to "disciplinary councils," suggesting that reintegration rather than punishment is the objective. (Excommunication and disfellowshipment are not irreversible.) Nonetheless, excommunication carries powerful cultural connotations of shunning and cultural banishment, and perhaps for that reason the number of both local and high-profile excommunications seems to be diminishing.

8

CULTURE

How homogeneous are the Latter-day Saints?

Latter-day Saints do not constitute an ethnicity; however, they do diverge—in the United States at least—from national norms across a broad spectrum of cultural and social characteristics. Saints in the United States tend to be overwhelmingly white (86 percent, according to one recent survey). This is doubtless due in part to the fact that until 1978, Blacks were prohibited from holding the priesthood or participating in temple rites. Only after that year did active proselytizing of Blacks even begin. Both the absence of Blacks from the convert pool and the legacy of race-based policies doubtless are causes of that disproportion.

The average level of schooling attained is higher for LDS men and women alike than the national average. The Saints have a long history of supporting educational institutions, founding schools in their first places of gathering, and establishing universities both in Nauvoo, Illinois, in the 1840s and in Utah a decade later. Today, BYU is one of the largest church-sponsored universities in the world. The LDS scriptures encourage intellectual pursuits and the seeking of wisdom "out of the best books" and proclaim that "the glory of God is intelligence." Higher educational levels do not translate to higher economic status, however; LDS incomes are comparable to those of other Americans.

Women in the LDS Church are considerably less likely than their counterparts to be employed full-time outside the home. (A substantial number of LDS women do remunerative work from home.) This is consistent with a faith tradition that has long emphasized the priority of the family in all matters and has recently issued a proclamation that reasserts traditional gender roles. The rates of marriage are also distinctive. Latter-day Saints have the highest marriage rate of any Christian denomination in the United States, as well as the highest rates of endogamy, that is, marriage within the faith. Some studies also show that Saints marrying Saints have the lowest divorce rates of any demographic; Saints marrying outside the faith have among the highest. In both cases, these figures reflect the extent to which Mormonism embodies a pervasive, all-encompassing form of lived religion that thrives in a setting of mutual reinforcement and creates conflict in mixed-faith marriages. Large LDS families are legendary, although here the gap between the Saints and the wider public has decreased; LDS families on average have about one more child than the national average.

One area where divergence between Latter-day Saints and Americans may be realigning is attitudes toward sexual mores. Latter-day Saints have steadfastly maintained a very conservative morality regarding premarital, extramarital, and homosexual relations. The first two prohibitions prevail with virtually no public dissent and unite the Saints in a sexual culture at pronounced odds with dominant trends. As the wider population has grown more accepting of gay marriage, however, many Latter-day Saints feel the personal tension between the appeal of a more accepting social policy and a theology deeply invested in heterosexual marriage now and hereafter. Finally, Latter-day Saints are overwhelmingly supportive of the prolife position regarding abortion, both personally and politically. In sum, there is a statistically manifest homogeneity in LDS culture that is striking even if it is far from absolute.

Some scientists in the 1860s actually argued that Mormons constituted a new racial group. This was all nonsense, since most LDS converts of that era came from British or American backgrounds, with a smattering of members from other nations. However, the consequence of their history and distinctive practices is a certain bewilderment about exactly how to label them. Religious scholar Sydney Ahlstrom observes: "one cannot even be sure if the object of our consideration is a sect, a mystery cult, a new religion, a church, a people, a nation, or an American subculture."[1] Some scholars have called them a "global tribe" and others "a religion that became a people"; the *Harvard Encyclopedia of American Ethnic Groups* even has an entry devoted to Mormons as an ethnicity. What is clear is that to be a Latter-day Saint is to identify with a faith tradition that transcends simple denominational status. Comparisons are sometimes made with Judaism, together with the (not perfectly accurate) observation that Judaism represents a people who became a religion, while Mormonism represents a religion that became a people.

What was the role of education and the intellect in the early church?

A signal characteristic of Joseph Smith's ministry at the head of the LDS Church was his synthesis of the two poles of knowledge acquisition. Smith himself enjoyed very limited formal education. Nevertheless, he was at one and the same time a visionary, given to rapturous epiphanies, angelic visitations, and the gift of seership and an enthusiastic and devoted student of languages, history, and culture. His liberal eclecticism was marked by a confidence that worldly and spiritual learning were mutually reinforcing, and he initiated a "School of the Prophets" to bring his vision of such a happy confluence to fruition. An early revelation directing the establishment of the former mingled unblinkingly an admonition to study "the law of the gospel" with a directive to gain knowledge of "things which are at home; things which are abroad" (D&C 88:78–79). So in the School of the Prophets, "Lectures on Faith" mingled with the study of geography and languages. Smith also organized a Hebrew class attended by nearly a hundred students.

In Nauvoo, Illinois, Smith founded a university with an ambitious curriculum that included courses in chemistry, geology, several areas of mathematics, literature, philosophy, history, religion, music, and foreign languages (German, French, Latin, Greek, and Hebrew). Girls had attended Kirtland High School alongside boys, and in Nauvoo girls filled over half the school's seats. In 1850, only three years after settlement in the Salt Lake Valley, the Saints opened the University of Deseret (later the University of Utah), the first university west of the Missouri. It was a false start, not getting seriously under way for two decades, but the will was there if not yet the means. Brigham Young sent John Bernhisel to New York to spend $5,000 the Saints had secured from Congress to stock a territorial library. It opened in 1852 with 1,900 volumes, about the same time Boston's first public library opened and before Chicago had one. In 1875, the church founded Brigham Young Academy (now BYU), subsidizing the education of hundreds of thousands of Saints at a cost of millions. One hundred years later, a researcher analyzing the origins of American scientists and scholars found that "the most productive state is Utah, which is first in productivity for all fields combined in all time periods. It is first in biological and social sciences, second in education, third in physical sciences, and sixth in arts and professions."[2] Early years in Utah also saw the organization of several independent organizations dedicated to intellectual and cultural improvement, such as the Polysophical Society, the Universal Scientific Society, the Wasatch Literary Association, and assorted reading clubs.

The catalyst behind the early church's emphasis on education was largely theological. The church's doctrine collapsed the sacred distance between the earthly and the heavenly and envisioned an eternity of active learning reflecting earthly models. As Orson Pratt held, "the study of science is the study of something eternal. If we study astronomy, we study the works of God. If we study chemistry, geology, optics, or any other branch of science, every new truth we come to the understanding of is eternal; it is a part of the great system of universal truth. It is truth that exists throughout universal nature; and God is the dispenser of all truth—scientific, religious, and political."[3] Young opined that "when the elements melt with fervent heat, the Lord Almighty will send forth his angels, who are well instructed in chemistry, and they will separate the elements and make new combinations thereof."[4] The image is startling; however, it reflects an LDS perspective that virtually all secular learning has value in the eternities.

What is the role of education in the contemporary church?

A turning point in the LDS Church's relationship to the secular world of learning came in the 1920s and 1930s. In the early years of the twentieth century, the church valued and trusted its most highly educated leadership, assigning them the task of writing the bulk of church curricular materials. Autodidact B. H. Roberts, along with James Talmage and John Widtsoe, apostles holding doctorates, produced a steady stream of manuals and monographs. Beginning in 1925, however, a number of teachers from the Church Educational System were graduating from Chicago Divinity School. Many of them brought back not just impressive degrees but the influence of secular and higher critical methodology. At the same time, surveys conducted at BYU revealed a startling lack of orthodoxy among the church's young. These facts, combined with an influx of newly appointed and deeply conservative apostles, moved the church abruptly in the direction of retrenchment. Church educators, especially, were advised to beware of secular learning. Whereas Smith had labored diligently to integrate mind and spirit, the secular and the sacred realms of knowledge, the new generation of teachers was directed to emphasize the divide between "the natural world" and "the spiritual world": a pivotal discourse ("The Charted Course of the Church in Education," by J. Reuben Clark) directed to all church educators insisted that "the things of the natural world will not explain the things of the spiritual world; that the things of the spiritual world cannot be understood or comprehended by the things of the natural world." Caution and suspicion, in many quarters, replaced hopeful integration.

Some of the more outspoken leaders began exhibiting hostility toward science and "intellectuals," and except for a brief period of openness in the 1970s, the most sensitive aspects of church history contained in church archives were closed to scholars. Even the most prominent defender of church intellectuals, the apostle Neal Maxwell, sounded a warning: "the LDS scholar has his citizenship in the kingdom, but carries his passport into the professional world—not the other way around." Revisionist histories, emerging in the late twentieth century and supplemented by an unfiltered Internet, aggravated a widening gulf. Gradually, the impossibility of controlling or avoiding the flood of contentions unleashed by mass media in an information age became apparent to church leadership, and in the early twenty-first century they proactively launched a number of projects that showed support for more vigorous engagement with the best scholarship across a range of disciplines, especially history. Frank responses to challenging criticisms, documentary editing of the entire Joseph Smith corpus, and an unsanitized new official church history emerged. A new note for a new millennium was authoritatively voiced by senior apostle Russell Ballard in 2016: "gone are the days when a student raised a sincere concern and a teacher bore his or her testimony as a response intended to avoid the issue. . . . If you have questions, then please ask someone who has studied them and understands them."

How do Latter-day Saints balance reason and faith?

The relationship between faith and intellect has been variously understood by Christians and variously depicted by outsiders. The church father Tertullian famously asked "what does Athens have to do with Jerusalem, the Church with the academy?" intimating that the worlds of faith and of intellect may not overlap. The furthest extreme of this position, fideism (the idea that knowledge depends on faith or revelation), maintains that faith and reason are actually hostile to each other. In today's secular age, it is easy for skeptics to dismiss religion wholesale as the refuge of fideists, irrationalists, and worse. In actual fact, Christianity has a much stronger tradition of fostering education, research, and intellectual inquiry than of suppressing them. (Universities in the American colonies, like those of the Middle Ages, were conceived and built and sponsored by churches, after all.) And this is certainly true of the Church of Jesus Christ, although outliers in the faith have always existed. Smith proclaimed that "the glory of God is intelligence." Another revelation holds that "whatever principle of intelligence we attain unto in this life, it will rise with us in the resurrection; and if a person gains more knowledge and intelligence in this life through his diligence and obedience than another, he will have so much the advantage in the world to come" (D&C 130:18–19).

The Church of Jesus Christ was founded in the industrial age, but it went against contemporary liberalizing trends by emphasizing, rather than downplaying, supernatural aspects of the faith. Angels, spiritual gifts, and miraculous healings and visitations featured prominently in the early years especially. The question of how to balance the supernatural and the rational emerged at the beginning, when charismatic manifestations threatened to get out of hand. In response, Smith inquired of the Lord, and in May 1831 produced a revelation that six times invoked the criterion of rationality for ascertaining the legitimacy of spiritual gifts (D&C 50:2, 4).

The apostle Neal A. Maxwell provided an additional principle that governs LDS apologetics to this day. Quoting the Anglican theologian Austin Farrer, he said: "though argument does not create conviction, lack of it destroys belief. What seems to be proved may not be embraced; but what no one shows the ability to defend is quickly abandoned. Rational argument does not create belief, but it maintains a climate in which belief may flourish."[5] The synthesis of Athens and Jerusalem is rooted in the conception that Latter-day Saints have of heaven as a domain of eternal learning and growth, and their conflation of spiritual and secular learning as compatible dimensions of a holistic enterprise. Hence, "for a disciple of Jesus Christ," wrote a modern LDS apostle, "academic scholarship is a form of worship."[6]

Do you have to be a member of the church to attend Brigham Young University?

One does not have to be a member of the church to attend BYU; however, students are required to abide by the BYU honor code. In addition to the principles of honesty that most honor codes embody, the LDS version addresses several aspects of conduct. Alcohol, tobacco, tea, coffee, and drugs are prohibited. Chastity for heterosexuals and gays is mandatory. Shorts and skirts must be at least knee-length. Men are forbidden to have face or body piercings or beards. Women may not have body or multiple ear piercings.

In some regards, standards are laxer for non-LDS than LDS students. Members of the church are required to attend services and keep church standards, and an ecclesiastical leader must attest to their compliance. Nonmembers are simply "encouraged to participate in services of their preferred religion."[7]

For more than two decades, the *Princeton Review* has named BYU the number 1 "stone-cold sober" school in America. That is a source of pride to the Saints but, along with the prohibition against sexual relations, is probably one of the most important reasons for the small number of non-LDS students who apply—between 1 and 2 percent of the student body typically do not identify as members of the church.[8]

For nonmembers who are comfortable being a tiny minority in a fairly homogeneous culture and who share the values of the LDS Church, BYU can be a good home. Tuition is higher for nonmembers, based on the fact that most LDS students tithe (in the same way citizens of a state pay taxes that support a state university), so they or their families have effectively subsidized the lower rate they are charged as students. Even for nonmembers, the tuition is a bargain ($5,790 per semester for the 2019–2020 year). In one typical recent year, the student body included Buddhists, Hindus, Muslims, Bahai, Jews, Catholics, and Protestants.[9] Some nonmembers report feelings of isolation and misunderstanding, and the student body is sometimes disparaged as too culturally homogeneous. In some respects, however, the BYU student body is conspicuously diverse. Nearly 65 percent of the students speak a second language, and 128 languages are spoken on campus, with 62 taught.[10] A substantial portion of the men and many of the women have served missions in foreign countries. (In 2014, almost seventeen thousand students were returned missionaries, most having served abroad.)[11] Between one and two thousand of those students are internationals from nearly fifty countries.[12]

Why do Latter-day Saints in America trend Republican?

The tendency for most American Saints to identify as Republican (over two-thirds, according to surveys) is certainly ironic given the party's history. In its first-ever platform, in 1856, the party undertook to rid the United States of twin evils: slavery and Mormon polygamy. Fourteen years later, the church formed its own political party, called the People's Party, but it had negligible involvement in or impact on national politics. As part of their "Americanization" campaign to achieve statehood, the Saints disbanded their political party in 1891 and engaged the two major national parties. Given the Republican Party's hostility to the church and to its efforts toward statehood, most Latter-day Saints inclined toward the Democrats. According to LDS folk history, in some congregations leaders went down the aisles apportioning the members evenly between the parties in order to avoid the appearance of collective partisanship. Utah trended Democratic over the succeeding decades through midcentury. From that point on, the pendulum began to swing the other way. The most popular church president of the modern era was David O. McKay, a Republican. He approved of the appointment of the church apostle Ezra Taft Benson as President Dwight D. Eisenhower's secretary of agriculture. Another Republican of the church gained even more national attention when George Romney campaigned for the presidential nomination in 1968.

In this same decade and into the 1970s, America fractured over a host of social issues as antiwar protests, feminism, the sexual revolution, abortion rights, and drug use reshaped the culture. In each of these areas, LDS moral conservatism—reinforced by official church statements on these themes—aligned squarely with Republican Party platforms. As a consequence, by the 1980s the LDS electorate in America had moved overwhelmingly into the Republican column.

A number of church members have argued that equally important moral imperatives receive greater attention in the Democratic Party: generous immigration policies and care for the poor especially. That party does find significant representation among citizens and politicians alike: Harry Reid, Democrat from Nevada, was the senate majority leader from 2007 to 2015. In 2018, the LDS First Presidency released a statement that said: "principles compatible with the gospel may be found in the platforms of each of the various political parties."[13] Donald Trump, the most polarizing political figure of the modern era, presented LDS voters with a dilemma that manifested itself in obvious cognitive dissonance and perplexity.

Midway into the 2016 campaign, one pundit called Mormons "the conscience of the nation" for their opposition to a figure notorious for his moral failings;[14] Utah Republicans polled the lowest level of support of any red state. On election day, however, the specter of the Democratic alternative proved decisive, and Utah responded with a plurality—though it was less than the total for the two alternative candidates.[15] Nationally, about half of Latter-day Saints voted for Trump.[16]

What is the place of women in the church?

The role of women in the LDS Church is something of a paradox. Historically, Latter-day Saints have been remarkably progressive in some areas of women's issues while remaining one of the few Christian denominations to preserve church leadership and the priesthood as exclusively male domains. Women exercised the right to vote in Utah before they did in any other state in the union.[17] As a territory, Utah granted women suffrage in 1870, and LDS women served on the executive committees of the church's political party at both the local and territorial levels. (When, contrary to all non-Mormon expectations, LDS women did not use their new political power to oppose polygamy, the US Congress rescinded their right to vote.)

Brigham Young encouraged LDS women to secure an education and develop careers not typically open to women in the nineteenth century, including business, accounting, medicine, and law. "They should stand behind the counter," he urged, "study law or physic, or become good bookkeepers and be able to do the business in any counting house, and all this to enlarge their sphere of usefulness for the benefit of society at large."[18] Outside Utah, such encouragement for women was rare.

The church had inaugurated a women's organization, the Relief Society, in Nauvoo in 1842; it was disbanded in the turmoil that followed. Young reestablished it in 1867 under the leadership of the dynamic Eliza R. Snow. Soon the organization spread to every LDS community, making valuable contributions to the economic self-sufficiency of the Saints. Women church members soon launched a grain storage program, began an ambitious silkworm industry, and in 1872 inaugurated a journal, the *Women's Exponent,* which was unabashedly feminist in its orientation. Anticipating much of the twentieth-century feminist agenda, the *Exponent* proclaimed sexual equality and lobbied for gender equity in pay.

In the contemporary church, LDS female stereotypes are upheld in some regards and upset in others. Not surprisingly, given the emphasis on marriage and family, LDS women who give birth are more likely to be married than their counterparts. In addition, LDS mothers are more likely to be professionally employed if they work outside the home.[19] Research suggests that "LDS women report levels of life satisfaction similar to other women, have higher levels of global happiness, and . . . their levels of mental depression are significantly below those reported by other women throughout the United States."[20]

The American feminist movement of the 1960s had some impact on LDS culture, registering on the pages of some of the independent LDS journals and more particularly in the founding in 1974 of *Exponent II,* a quarterly magazine targeting readers who share "a connection to the Mormon Church and a commitment to women." (The original publication had ceased in 1914.)[21] But the LDS Church first confronted feminism directly in 1976, when the First Presidency issued a statement opposing passage of the Equal Rights Amendment. The document cited the amendment's encouragement of a "unisex society" and potential to threaten the family as an institution by failing to recognize traditional gender roles and differences. The church's ability to mobilize member opposition to the amendment was seen by many as decisive in its 1982 defeat, although support for passage was by then waning nationally.

How is third wave feminism impacting the church?

In the late twentieth century, many LDS women were still reluctant to embrace the label "feminist." In 1993 an influential apostle named feminism as one of three major threats to the church,[22] lending authority to a suspicion already harbored by many Latter-day Saints who saw feminism as hostile to the traditional values of family, gender roles, and sexuality that the church espoused. Fewer LDS women—or leaders for that matter—see those same tensions the same way at present. Women in the church today are explicitly articulating feminist ideals within a framework of orthodox belief. The focus of attention is not the male monopoly on priesthood, although in 2013 some feminists did engage in direct action demanding priesthood ordination; but in a church predicated on revelation, such direct action tends to be seen as seeking to undermine revelatory authority; the leader was excommunicated, and the movement dissipated. More moderate feminists set their sights on creative approaches to change. Several blogs sprang up where feminist ideals could be discussed and debated, such as "Mormon Feminist Housewives" and "The Exponent." In 2010, the Mormon Women Project was founded, with the mission to collect and publish interviews with LDS women across the globe. This project typifies the principal thrust of contemporary LDS feminism: to give women a greater voice in the institution. Other women undertook to eliminate what were perceived as gratuitous norms of gender differentiation. In 2012, a group organized a "Wear Pants to Church Day," resisting a cultural practice that struck many as groundless and needlessly constraining.

The church has responded to the felt need to address inequalities and inequities not tied to priesthood ordination. In 2013, women began to offer prayers in the worldwide General Conference. In 2015, the church acknowledged on an official website that belief in the Heavenly Mother, though seldom addressed in public venues or published materials, was in fact a "cherished doctrine." That same year, the church placed women in its general church councils for the first time (the Priesthood and Family Executive Council, the Missionary Executive Council, and the Temple and Family History Council). Meanwhile, the LDS Historical Department committed resources to promoting the study and publication of women's history.

In 2017, female church employees were permitted to wear slacks, as were sister missionaries the year following. That same year, another kind of parity was achieved when the General Women's Session of the General Conference was made an annual meeting, alternating biannually with the men's Priesthood Session. The next year, the church's Priesthood Executive Committees were disbanded and replaced at the ward levels with councils that included women. Women leaders also began to attend stake leadership training sessions. In 2019, more substantive changes occurred. Wording in the temple endowment was changed to effect greater equality in the ceremony. The character of Eve was given greater prominence. Later that year, the budgets of the young men's and the young women's organizations were formally equalized, and women qualified as witnesses in temple ceremonies. The Young Women's theme now explicitly acknowledges heavenly "parents," not only a Heavenly Father.

Several other changes are on the LDS feminist wish list: holding their infants during baby blessings; participating in sacrament preparation (and occupying more callings that are similarly not relegated to males by scripture); serving as ushers; more gender equity in the way "virtue" is preached; more parity between mission presidents' wives and their husbands; and, for the Relief Society, more of the autonomy it knew in Joseph Smith's day. At present, the rate of such changes, however slow in isolation, suggests a growing momentum of efforts to balance theologically rooted norms of gender difference with gender equality.

What is the history of Latter-day Saint women and education?

As early as 1842 in the Latter-day Saint capital of Nauvoo, a lyceum was held on the question "should Females be educated to the same extent as Males?" The verdict was not recorded, but evidence of the consensus reached is pretty strong. According to county records, over half the students enrolled in Nauvoo's schools were female. Slightly earlier, a witness to the migration of the Saints into Illinois had observed that "the women were generally well educated and as a rule were quite intelligent." In fact, it has been suggested that the Saints' liberal views on the equality of the sexes were in part responsible for hostility to the church in Illinois.[23]

Shortly after the Saints entered the Salt Lake Valley, they founded the University of Deseret (now the University of Utah). After a brief existence in the 1850s, it reopened in 1868, with women making up almost 50 percent of the students.[24] After Brigham Young advised women to attend medical schools, the Relief Society supported a number of sisters in going East to obtain training. With Relief Society support, Romania B. Pratt Penrose, Ellis Shipp, and Margaret Shipp Roberts (sister wives), together with Martha Hughes Cannon and many others, returned with degree in hand to establish practices and teach classes. Eliza Snow even attempted to establish a "Female Medical College" so Utah could train its own women doctors.[25]

By the turn of the century, more female American medical students hailed from Utah than from any other state in the union.[26] After 1890, when the church's earlier stand discouraging novel-reading had softened, LDS women published fiction in three LDS youth magazines as well as writing their own novels and short stories.[27] Editing and producing their own journal and literature was but one indication of the independent mentality of LDS women. In the educational realm, the LDS people had already shown themselves unusually progressive with regard to women. They now graduate from college and have postgraduate training at a higher rate than their Protestant and Catholic counterparts.[28] Recent studies affirm that "education . . . is more consistent with marriage, childbearing, and church activity for Mormons than is the case nationally."[29]

Does the church have anything unique to contribute to feminist theology?

Suffragist leaders of the nineteenth century deplored plural marriage, and it was easy to see polygamy and political equality as incompatible. However, LDS women actually found in their religion a basis for aspirations to full equality and self-realization. One reason for this can be found in the LDS scriptures' radical reinterpretation of the Fall. Latter-day Saints see in this primordial transgression a cause for celebration and not lament. And since it was Eve whose initiative set the whole process in motion, she is venerated rather than reviled in LDS thought. Church leaders have consistently taught that "Mother Eve bestowed upon her daughters and sons a heritage of honor, for she acted with wisdom, love, and unselfish sacrifice."[30] The LDS people thus circumvent a historical tradition that sees Eve as the prototype of vulnerable, fallen woman, as Milton's weaker vessel and the universal temptress.

The feminist Elizabeth Cady Stanton wrote: "the first step in the elevation of woman to her true position, as an equal factor in human progress, is . . . the recognition by the rising generation of an ideal Heavenly Mother."[31] Leaders of the LDS Church have affirmed that they worship God the Father but recognize as well the Heavenly Mother. This teaching appears to have been first officially promulgated by President Wilford Woodruff in an 1893 church conference, when he said: "with regard to our position before we came here, I will say that we dwelt with the Father and with the Son, as expressed in the hymn, 'O my Father,' that has been sung here. That hymn is a revelation, though it was given unto us by a woman—Sister Snow."[32]

The verse in the hymn to which he referred asks "in the heavens, are parents single?" and continues, "no the thought makes reason stare: truth is wisdom, truth eternal tells me I've a mother there." Eliza R. Snow, LDS poet and author of that hymn, was a plural wife of Joseph Smith, and some sources indicate that it was from Smith that she received the idea.

This doctrine remains largely undeveloped and unheralded. Some LDS feminists have argued for the belief as a justification for praying to the Heavenly Mother and criticize the church for its failure to celebrate and worship two deities. No LDS scripture or revelation addresses the subject, however, and in the absence of a tradition of speculative theology, LDS leaders generally refrain from elaboration. As one LDS scholar observes, "the widening 'theology' [concerning the Heavenly Mother] which is developing is more of a 'folk,' or at least speculative, theology than a systematic development by theologians or a set of definitive pronouncements from ecclesiastical leaders. For the moment, Mother in Heaven can be almost whatever an individual Mormon envisions her to be." [33] In the 1990s, the church acted to discipline some for their public advocacy of views that were deemed unacceptable, including promotion of prayer to the Heavenly Mother.[34] At the same time, the church now publicly owns the doctrine of the Heavenly Mother in an official webpage, calling it "a cherished and distinctive belief among Latter-day Saints."[35] LDS doctrine also affirms that separate and apart from a woman to whom he is sealed, no man can achieve salvation, and vice versa.

How was polygamy compatible with nineteenth-century Latter-day Saint feminism?

Polygamy represents an instance of tremendous irony. To outsiders, the institution was prima facie evidence of an oppressive inequality. In popular fiction of the era, polygamous brides were depicted as the victims of raiding parties or kidnappers, coerced into a version of white slavery. Literary heroes were defined by their daring exploits in saving Mormon women from this version of "oriental despotism." American demagogues and preachers mobilized a public campaign of denunciation that matched abolitionism in moral fervor, scope, and resources. And yet, in some ways polygamy advanced Utah women's self-reliance.

At one point in the late 1880s, the federal government funded the construction of a huge "Industrial Christian Home" as a sanctuary for escaped plural wives. The expected waves of fugitives never materialized, and the home closed down a few years later. The public should not have been surprised. In 1870, in response to proposed antipolygamy legislation, thousands of LDS women gathered in Salt Lake City to demonstrate in support of the practice. With eloquence and surprising solidarity, they passionately attacked federal intervention in their supposed behalf. This is not to say that LDS women found plural marriage especially congenial or emotionally satisfying. But if it was a trial, it was a trial they believed they were called by God to endure, and many prided themselves on the higher spiritual qualities of selflessness and sacrifice the practice required.

And in reality, plural marriage turned out not to be the degrading institution of fiction and *Punch* cartoons. Perhaps unexpectedly, the social reality was that polygamy by its nature engendered independence and resilience on the part of women necessarily deprived of the constant presence of a provider and companion. One historian has commented that "Mormon women in pioneer Utah had social power that was unavailable to other women throughout the United States and Europe. Polygamous wives often had sole responsibility for months or years to manage their households, farms, or family businesses. Monogamous wives did likewise whenever their husbands were called on two-year proselytizing missions (a very common practice until the 1900s)."[36] Plural marriage may have been painful and even demeaning, but such negative repurcussions often were accompanied by a legacy of resilience and independence.

What about Latter-day Saint women and the priesthood?

The most pressing questions about the church and women ultimately come down to the exclusion of women from the priesthood. Women may pray and preach in LDS worship meetings, they may give counsel in the worldwide General Conferences of the church, and they may preside over local or global auxiliaries of the church. But they cannot sit in the leading councils with apostles and prophets or administer baptism and sit at the sacrament table to administer the Lord's Supper.

One traditional LDS explanation for a gender-restricted priesthood is that the privileges and obligations of motherhood balance the obligations and privileges of priesthood. Joseph Fielding Smith wrote: "a woman's calling is in a different direction. The most noble, exalting calling of all is that which has been given to women as the mothers of men. Women do not hold the priesthood, but if they are faithful and true, they will become priestesses and queens in the kingdom of God, and that implies that they will be given authority."[37] "Our roles and assignments differ," was how President Spencer W. Kimball put it more simply."[38]

That rationale sounds unsatisfactory to some LDS women who feel this role differentiation diminishes women in the here and now (and potentially hereafter) to merely bodily beings. Studies indicate that LDS women would like to be more involved with decision-making in the church,[39] and in recent years, especially at the local level, "ward councils," leadership meetings in which women are represented, have played an increasingly emphasized role in ward governance. Many LDS women appear satisfied with the status quo regarding access to the priesthood itself. This is most likely a reflection of a theology that is, at its heart's core, radically egalitarian and marriage-centered. Marriage in LDS thought need not be of merely temporal duration. That the marriage relationship can be of eternal duration may in itself be unique among Christian belief systems. But the LDS scriptures also affirm that marriage is indispensable—not just permissible—as a prelude to eternal life. Joseph Fielding Smith put it succinctly: "a man cannot be exalted singly and alone."[40] Perhaps this explains a response typical of rank-and-file LDS women. "To tell you the truth, the whole issue of women and the priesthood really isn't very high on my spiritual 'worry list,'" writes one woman (a world-renowned radiologist and wife of a General Authority). "I think no religion holding as one of its fundamental tenets that the seed of godhood is in every man and every woman and that neither can achieve it without the other could by any reasonable, fair definition be called sexist."[41]

At the same time, with each rising generation LDS women are more "bothered" that they don't hold the priesthood (24 percent of the Boomer and Silent generations, 48 percent of Gen Xers, and 59 percent of Millennials).[42] Latter-day Saints recognize the potential for abuse in a patriarchal system. Joseph Smith spoke feelingly of having learned "by sad experience that it is the nature and disposition of almost all men, as soon as they get a little authority, as they suppose, they will immediately begin to exercise unrighteous dominion." Thus the scriptural injunction to men that "no power or influence can or ought to be maintained by virtue of the priesthood, only by persuasion, by long-suffering, by gentleness and meekness, and by love unfeigned." As for those who undertake to "exercise control or dominion or compulsion upon the souls of the children of men, in any degree of unrighteousness, behold, the heavens withdraw themselves; the Spirit of the Lord is grieved; and when it is withdrawn, Amen to the priesthood or the authority of that man" (D&C 121:39, 41, 37).

That it will continue to be a priesthood of men for a long while to come—perhaps permanently—seems likely. President

Howard W. Hunter said in 1994 that "there isn't an avenue of ever changing. It's too well defined by revelation, by Scripture. . . . I see nothing that will lead to a change of direction at the present time—or in the future."[43] There is nothing in LDS scripture that explicitly precludes such a possibility; Hunter was apparently referring to the scriptural pattern of a male-only priesthood. Tradition does not trump revelatory novelty in LDS thought, however, and in theory, at least, the possibility is always there of a change that could take everyone by surprise.

What is the Latter-day Saint attitude toward the environment?

At the present day, there are clearly discrepancies between prophetic priorities and the Utah record of environmental stewardship. President Spencer W. Kimball expressed great concern in this regard, when he decried pollution not only of mind and body but also of humans' surroundings. "When I review the performance of this people in comparison of what is expected," he told his people, "I am appalled and frightened."[44] Avid environmentalist and gadfly of the church Hugh Nibley pointed out that in recent years critics had declared the congressional delegation from Utah the most antienvironmentalist in the nation. "Ecology and environment are dirty words in Utah," he lamented."[45] At the turn of the twenty-first century, the League of Conservation Voters ranked the state's legislators near the bottom on environmental issues. For the 107th Congress (2001–2002), both senators scored 4 percent, and the two Republican congressmen scored 5 percent and 9 percent. (The lone Democrat, Jim Matheson, scored 68 percent.)[46] More recent data is little changed. Polling results in the United States indicate a higher level of concern about the environment among the Saints than Republicans generally, but lower than among Democrats. Compared to other religious groups in the United States, they rank 59 out of 61 in terms of actual support.[47]

In 1996, President Bill Clinton invoked the 1906 Antiquities Act to declare 1.7 million acres of southern Utah lands the new Grand Staircase-Escalante National Monument, a move largely interpreted locally as vindictive and autocratic. The incident certainly echoed a legacy of federal intervention and antagonism that has made Utah culture more resistant than most to government oversight of personal and local property rights. William B. Smart, former editor of the church-owned *Deseret News*, has written that "in the past half century, no issue has torn apart my state as the use of the land that once seemed so limitless."[48] Acclaimed environmental author (and Latter-day Saint) Terry Tempest Williams has teamed with other LDS writers to urge fellow Saints to "change our behavior of inactivity toward the earth, personally and collectively," reminding readers of how inconsistent with the heritage of Brigham Young and Joseph Smith are the affluent lifestyles and environmental apathy of today's LDS community.[49]

During the 1834 march of Zion's Camp, an expedition mounted by Ohio Saints to assist their persecuted brethren in Missouri, someone spotted several rattlesnakes at a resting spot. A man was about to kill the snakes when Joseph Smith reprimanded him: "how do you expect enmity to cease between man and beast," he asked, "if men continually seek to kill the animals?" He went on to say that if humans "would banish from our hearts this spirit to destroy and murder, the day would soon come when the lion and the lamb would lie down together."[50] A century and a half later, LDS president Spencer W. Kimball caused consternation among Utah sport hunters when he admonished members to heed the words of the children's song Mormon pioneers used to sing, "Don't kill the little birds."[51]

Given the strictures of the Word of Wisdom, which admonished Latter-day Saints to eat meat sparingly, and the pronouncements of Joseph Smith, one might expect the Saints to espouse a quasi vegetarianism. The beasts John saw in his Revelation, Joseph wrote, were actual individual creatures, who represented "the glory of the classes of beings in their destined order or sphere of creation, in the enjoyment of their eternal felicity" (D&C 77:3). "Always keep in view," Brigham Young wrote, "that the animal, vegetable, and mineral kingdoms—the earth and its fulness—will all, except the children of man, abide their creation—the law by which they were made, and will receive their exaltation."[52] More recently, LDS scriptorian and future prophet Joseph Fielding Smith clearly affirmed that "animals do have spirits and that through the redemption made by our Savior they will come forth in the resurrection to enjoy the blessing of immortal life."[53]

In LDS thought, human dominion over the earth should be a call to reverence, an obligation to stewardship, not a license to exploit. In LDS culture, the conflict between a tradition of frontier individualism and wilderness-taming on the one hand and environmental progressivism on the other has not found satisfactory resolution. As one observer has written, "it should be of the greatest interest and importance to see if the LDS Church is able to incorporate in any formal sense the enormous, revitalizing energy which is being generated by ecologically-minded Mormons in Utah and elsewhere today."[54]

What is the Latter-day Saint legacy regarding war and peace?

In the early history of the LDS Church, violent opposition repeatedly forced the leadership to choose between the path of armed resistance or sacrifice of personal rights. The Saints usually chose the latter as a simple matter of self-preservation. In 1833, their numbers were insufficient to resist their forcible expulsion from Jackson County, Missouri. The next year, Smith mounted a paramilitary relief expedition from Ohio, called Zion's Camp, but the Saints, weakened by sickness and internal dissension and faced with overwhelming opposition from Missourians, returned east without waging battle. Again in 1836, the Saints submitted to removal from Clay County, Missouri. In 1838, they fought limited battles against opponents in Caldwell County but were quickly overwhelmed and exiled once more. Once established in Nauvoo, Smith commanded a militia of three to five thousand trained Latter-day Saints under arms. But even this impressive force never engaged in major conflict. Smith submitted to an imprisonment he sensed would end in his death rather than ignite a civil war by summoning the Nauvoo Legion to defend him.

During the Mexican-American War, and in the midst of their flight to Utah, hundreds of Latter-day Saints volunteered for service in a "Mormon Battalion" that made the longest infantry march in American history (from Council Bluffs, Iowa, to San Diego) but engaged in no combat. Their motives were transparently economic (they needed money to fund the trek to the West), not civic. During the Civil War, the Latter-day Saints kept themselves mostly aloof from military involvement. But this was not a studied pacifism. Near neutrality (Saints did protect Union mail routes) stemmed more from an unwillingness to involve themselves in a quarrel between southern slaveholding rebels, with whom they would have had little affinity, and a federal government that had recently invaded their own territory and could therefore make little claim on their allegiance. A generation later, however, Utah had achieved statehood, and the church responded to the next conflict with patriotic zeal: once war was declared against Spain in 1898, the First Presidency issued a statement urging the youth of the church to support the national cause. In the war's aftermath, and as a global conflict neared, apostle Anthony W. Ivins explained the church's position at a General Conference: "we do not hasten into war, because we do not believe in it; we believe it to be unnecessary; but, nevertheless, if it shall come, we believe it to be our duty to defend those principles of liberty and right and equality which were established by the Father."[55]

With the outbreak of World War I, Latter-day Saints were anxious to prove their loyalty to a still dubious American public. More than twenty thousand members served in Allied armies, and about 650 died.[56] As America's involvement in

World War II approached, church leaders urged caution; prominent member of the First Presidency J. Reuben Clark was especially outspoken against US involvement. Even as church leaders expressed misgivings about the prospect of large standing armies on American soil, they once again exonerated individual members of bloodshed committed in response to obligations imposed even by unrighteous governments or those opposed to American forces: "God . . . will not hold the innocent instrumentalities of the war, our brethren in arms, responsible for the conflict."[57]

Can Latter-day Saints be pacifists?

At the time of World War I, church leaders urged respect for both conscientious objectors and enemy combatants who, as subjects of their leaders, were themselves innocent. During World War II, counselor in the First Presidency J. Reuben Clarke espoused a pacifist position—as he did to the end of his life—but it never became the majority stand of LDS leaders. The official LDS position at the time of the Vietnam War was that "membership in the Church of Jesus Christ of Latter-day Saints does not make one a conscientious objector. . . . [But] there would seem to be no objection . . . to a man availing himself on a personal basis of the exemption provided by law."[58] In practice, fewer Latter-day Saints tend to serve in the armed forces than their counterparts.[59] This is probably a result of the fact that most active LDS young men already commit two years of their lives to full-time missionary service, and additional service in the military would be burdensome. Nevertheless, patriotism continues to run high among Latter-day Saints, and Saints have served honorably in every major American war.

At a time when some Christian churches are moving toward military isolationism and even embracing pacifism, LDS leaders have repudiated militarism while continuing to defend the concept of "just war." Spencer W. Kimball surprised the public—and much of his own constituency—when he spoke out in opposition to the Reagan administration's plan to base an MX missile system in Utah. "We are a warlike people, easily distracted from our assignment of preparing for the coming of the Lord. When enemies rise up, we commit vast resources to the fabrications of gods of stone and steel—ships, planes, missiles, fortifications," he wrote. "When threatened, we become anti-enemy instead of pro–kingdom of God, we train a man in the art of war and call him a patriot, thus, in the manner of Satan's counterfeit of true patriotism, perverting the Savior's teachings."[60] Still, with rare exceptions, LDS leaders have been firm supporters of American military involvements, believing, as Gordon B. Hinckley said, that "until the Prince of Peace comes to reign, there always will be tyrants and bullies, empire builders, slave seekers, and despots who would destroy every shred of human liberty if they were not opposed by force of arms."[61] During the controversies surrounding America's involvement in the second Persian Gulf war, President Hinckley said: "there are times and circumstances when nations are justified, in fact have an obligation, to fight for family, for liberty, and against tyranny, threat, and oppression," warning further that "it may even be that He will hold us responsible if we try to impede or hedge up the way of those who are involved in a contest with forces of evil and repression."[62]

What do Latter-day Saint scriptures teach about peace and war?

Latter-day Saints, like the Puritans before them, saw the founding of America as a chapter in providential history. The Book of Mormon suggested that the American Revolution was a divinely ordained prelude to the Restoration of the gospel. The Book of Mormon prophet Nephi apparently saw the revolutionaries in vision and said that "the power of God was with them" (1 Nephi 13:18). Revelation to Joseph Smith characterized the Founding Fathers as foreordained by God to frame the Constitution. In addition, the Book of Mormon, a record replete with catastrophic conflicts, validates defensive warfare even while condemning a certain form of passivity in the face of evil. At a time of national crisis, Captain Moroni erects a battle standard to rally his people, "the title of liberty," on which he writes: "in memory of our God, our religion, and freedom, and our peace, our wives, and our children." The record's editor later says of this Nephite freedom fighter that "if all men had been, and were, and ever would be, like unto Moroni, behold, the very powers of hell would have been shaken forever" (Alma 48:17). When Lamanite armies threaten to overwhelm the land, Nephite dissenters who sympathize with the invaders refuse to take up arms. Moroni obtains permission to "compel those dissenters to defend their country or to put them to death" (Alma 51:15). Time and again Book of Mormon prophets remind the reader that the spirit of liberty is wedded to principles of righteousness.

At the same time, as Gordon B. Hinckley and other church leaders have urged, Latter-day Saints are commanded by modern revelation to "renounce war and proclaim peace" (D&C 98:16). The Book of Mormon describes righteous war but also describes a group of Lamanites who repent of their past bloodshed and repudiate every form of violence, even taking an oath to that effect: "if our brethren seek to destroy us, behold, we will hide away our swords, yea, even we will bury them deep in the earth, that they may be kept bright, as a testimony that we have never used them, at the last day; and if our brethren destroy us, behold, we shall go to our God and shall be saved" (Alma 24:16). When they are attacked by their former brethren, they submit passively, like Gandhi's benign resisters, and are hewn down by the hundreds. Their pacifism is lauded and their salvation affirmed by the admiring chronicler of the wars. Yet later in the saga, it is the children of these same pacifists who become a mighty army of "stripling warriors." At a time of national crisis, they fight ferociously for their people, helping to win a decisive war against invaders to their homeland. And in recognition of their valiant participation they are miraculously preserved: "there were two hundred, out of my two thousand and sixty, who had fainted because of the loss of blood; nevertheless, according to the goodness of God, and to our great astonishment, and also the joy of our whole army, there was not one soul of them who did perish; yea, and neither was there one soul among them who had not received many wounds. . . . Now this was the faith of these of whom I have spoken" (Alma 57:25–27).

The moral of the Book of Mormon, where righteous pacifism and righteous warfare find comfortable coexistence, would seem to be that faithfulness to covenants righteously entered into trumps both. The peace-loving anti-Nephi-Lehies "had entered into a covenant and they would not break it" (Alma 43:11). By the identical token, their sons "entered into a covenant to fight for the liberty of the Nephites" (Alma 53:17) and risked their lives doing so. Both were singled out for particular approbation. In the Book of Mormon, covenant-keeping is the thread of safety by which the survival, spiritual safety, and very identity of the people hang.

The Doctrine and Covenants tilts more toward endurance of evil than armed self-defense. In an 1833 revelation, the Saints are encouraged to "bear it patiently" when "your enemy shall smite you." Three assaults they are enjoined to suffer, "and then if thou wilt spare him, thou shalt be rewarded for thy righteousness." Only subsequent to such patient and repeated indulgence, the Lord directs, does he "deliver . . . thine enemy into thine hands" (D&C 98:23–30).

Is there such a thing as a secular or cultural Mormon?

In every religion in every time and culture, there have probably been adherents who went through the motions with little or no commitment to the dogmas and doctrines of their professed faith tradition. This has always been true of Latter-day Saints, with pressures going in both directions, centripetal and centrifugal. On the one hand, because the Church of Jesus Christ is such a high-demand religion and generally requires such extensive investment—spiritually, financially, and temporally—it is difficult to live the religion casually. The strict health code, the prohibition on premarital and extramarital sex, the tithing requirement for temple access, and the eighteen to twenty-four months of self-supported mission work expected of men (and, increasingly, women) make it unlikely that anyone comes along just for the ride. In addition, the truth claims of the church go so far beyond normative Christianity as to make a commitment taxing on one's faith as well as conduct. Joseph Smith's first vision of God and Christ, his miraculous translation of the Book of Mormon and the Book of Abraham, living prophets who commune with God—these and many other propositions are nonnegotiable, foundational tenets.

On the other hand, those same enormous costs add up to a huge investment of self, and that emotional (not to mention financial) capital, combined with intense social and familial bonds, makes disaffiliation a particularly daunting, even devastating, prospect. Like a marriage, such deep levels of commitment and investment can easily transform feelings of disappointment or dissatisfaction into feelings of deception or betrayal. Hence, ex-Latter-day Saints commonly manifest greater hostility toward their former church than is typical of lapsed Presbyterians or Catholics—as a browse of the internet quickly reveals.

Given these strong family and social bonds, significant numbers of Saints do continue to participate without feeling a deep commitment to the truth claims of the church. Some find a compromise position by embracing the spiritual value of the teachings and scriptures but without believing in Smith's visions or the reality of the gold plates. "Temple Mormons" are those who are willing both to contribute financially to the church and to affirm belief in God and in Joseph Smith and subsequent prophets as called by God to restore and administer his church. Aside from virtuous moral conduct, little else in the way of assent to truth claims is required. A significant portion of Latter-day Saints are fully active and engaged members without holding temple recommends (ecclesiastical endorsements permitting entry to the temple).

When the burden of belief or practice becomes too great, disaffiliation is common. In many cases, however, some combination of a pioneer heritage, family connections, or indelible feelings of belonging in a tightly knit community has led a good many people to continue to claim their status as (cultural) Mormons, in spite of no formal affiliation or faith commitment whatsoever.

What is the Latter-day Saint position on homosexuality?

The LDS Church website "Mormon and Gay" is meant to succinctly convey the position that one may identify as a gay person and be a Latter-day Saint in full faith and fellowship. However, there is a clear distinction between condition, predisposition, or identity, on the one hand, and behavior or actions, on the other. The LDS faith holds no position on the causes of same-sex attraction. Apostle Dallin Oaks acknowledged that homosexuality may be related to a genetic predisposition to which no judgment should attach: homosexuals "may have certain inclinations," and their origin is a "scientific question." The church does not consider homosexuality to be a choice one makes, with moral implications. However, it does consider acting on those inclinations to be a violation of God's law. Oaks has taught that "we have the agency to choose which characteristics will define us; those choices are not thrust upon us."[63]

In the public realm, the church supports full civil rights for LGBTQ+ persons. As the *New York Times* reported in 2015, a Utah bill banning "discrimination against lesbian, gay, bisexual and transgender people in housing and employment" passed the legislature "with the backing of Mormon Church leaders."[64] However, in the moral sphere, the church teaches that sexual relations are only permissible between a man and a woman within the bonds of marriage.

The LDS leadership has no developed theology of sexual orientation. What is implicit is the critical distinction in the church's doctrine between the eternity of the soul, which comes with its own distinct eternal identity, and that soul's mortal embodiment in a tabernacle, which is the product of heredity, the laws of nature, and the contingencies of fetal development, environment, and early childhood. One does not experience one's sexual orientation as a contingent rather than essential facet of one's identity. Gays may well feel that one's identity as gay is an intrinsic part of one's eternal self. The LDS Church's theological pronouncements, like the Proclamation on the Family, indicate that "gender is eternal," leaving open the nature of sexuality and sexual attraction in the hereafter. Whether gender and sexuality are coterminous in the eternal worlds is likewise nowhere explicitly stated. Here some gay advocates find an opening for same-sex unions in heaven. However, LDS scripture indicates that the union of male and female is the precondition for all exalted beings (D&C 131:2; 132:4), and that is the principal constraint on the further liberalizing of LDS sexual theology. However, the church insists that the plan of salvation encompasses all persons living and dead within its orbit.

Some progressive members of the church are convinced that with time the softening of the church's antigay rhetoric—which has become more welcoming and compassionate in recent years—will eventuate in more liberal policies in regard to gay sexuality and gay marriage in this lifetime at least. Indeed, the church has recently posted articles and interviews, published books, and produced films encouraging a more loving acceptance of gay members and even sanctioned gay support groups at its church-owned and -administered universities. The church also maintains the website "Mormon and Gay" to support gay members who desire to find a path of faithful commitment to the church. In a church guided by continuing revelation, shifts in policy—as happened with polygamy and the priesthood ban—are certainly possible, although no changes in doctrine are on the horizon.

Why does the church oppose gay marriage?

Since marriage is both a civilly recognized institution and a church sacrament, there are really two questions involved: social policy and sacramental doctrine. The LDS Church opposed the legalization of gay marriage on both sociological and theological grounds. The church supported the Proposition 8 (gay marriage ban) campaign in California on the same grounds cited by the lone dissenter when the proposition was struck down on appeal: Judge N. Randy Smith argued that "the family structure of two committed biological parents—one man and one woman—is the optimal partnership for raising children."[65] An official church statement in support of Proposition 8 declared: "children are entitled to be born within this bond of marriage."[66] The church also put forward the theological position that marriage is "ordained of God" and the "formation of families is central to the Creator's plan."[67]

With gay marriage now a court-mandated right, the only pertinent question concerns the church's refusal to perform gay marriages in its own churches and temples and the church sanctions placed on gay members who do marry. And here the rationale is more complex than the invocation of biblical prohibitions. Some mainstream Protestant churches have found ways around those apparent scriptural obstacles, but LDS doctrine presents additional difficulties. First and most vital is the conflict with the fundamental LDS doctrine of a dual-gendered godhead. As LDS apostle Erastus Snow put the case, "there never was a God, and there never will be in all eternities, except they are made of these two component parts; a man and a woman; the male and the female."[68] What Snow is saying, and what has been reaffirmed repeatedly in official church pronouncements, is that human beings are children of heavenly parents, and those parents consist of two exalted divinities, Heavenly Father and his exalted eternal companion, Heavenly Mother. Human families—here and in the eternities—are modeled on the parental template and involve a companionate marriage in the eternities and "a continuation of the seeds forever and ever," that is, a creating and nurturing of "the souls of men" for aeons into the future.

In addition, the Church of Jesus Christ may be unique in positing gender differentiation rather than sexual differentiation as the basis of marriage. "Gender is eternal," reaffirms the 1995 "The Family: A Proclamation to the World," reiterating a position that has never varied in LDS theology.[69] Gender, in this statement, but not sexuality, is coeternal with core human identity. This semi-canonical position has been repeatedly reaffirmed, in spite of modern belief that gender is a social construct. In LDS doctrine, conjugal complementarity is more than sexual or biological. As Elder Jeffrey Holland states, "sexual union is also, in its own profound way, a very real sacrament of the highest order, a union not only of a man and a woman but very much the union of that man and woman with God."[70] The LDS Church's rejection of gay marriage as a sacramental—if not a legal—possibility moves beyond biological arguments (which underlie Catholic natural law arguments) with this substitution of gender for sex. In LDS belief, the essential element of eternal human identity is gender, not sexual orientation, and the place of gender as a constituent of eternal human identity suggests that the complementarity of eternally gendered agents is nonsubstitutable and provides the basis for the fullest human flourishing.

At the same time, LDS leaders have acknowledged that LDS theology is not—or not yet—fully adequate to address a range of sex and gender issues that have become urgent in the contemporary environment. The apostle Dallin Oaks readily admitted that "the unique problems of a transgender situation is something we have not had so much experience with, and we have some unfinished business in teaching on that."[71] The same is doubtless true for other hard cases, like intersex births, which assertions of premortal gendered identity do not resolve.

What are some practical implications of the Latter-day Saint teaching on chastity?

Latter-day Saints place enormous emphasis on temple marriage, a requirement for which is sexual chastity before marriage (or repentance for any breach thereof). Sexual chastity is a mainstay of the LDS moral code, and sexual fidelity after marriage is a requirement for temple attendance and participation in the highest sacraments of the church. As a consequence, many church teachings and practices are designed to reinforce and support individuals in their pursuit of virtue so defined. ("Virtue" encompasses far more than sexual chastity, but in LDS culture the two have traditionally been synonymous.) Modesty in dress is emphasized and is part of the BYU honor code (with a disproportionate share of the burden borne by LDS women and girls). Consistently with this theme of sexual purity, leaders inveigh against pornography, and publications and guides have counseled the youth to avoid R-rated movies (at least in America, where such a prohibition is relevant). In recent years, such printed counsel has shifted to the injunction to "choose wisely" when viewing media. The LDS emphasis on premarital chastity and marital fidelity appears to bear measurable fruit. Studies reveal LDS youth to have a significantly lower incidence of premarital sex than their non-LDS counterparts.[72] In fact, Latter-day Saints register rates consistently lower than national averages for premarital sex, teen pregnancy, and extramarital relations.[73]

Surprisingly, perhaps, the prohibitions against sex and alcohol and much of popular entertainment do not extend to the realm of dance, as they do for some fundamentalist Christians. Latter-day Saints danced in Joseph Smith's Mansion House, they danced in their first temples, they danced on the trail west, and they opened dancing schools once in the Salt Lake Valley.

In 1952 the *New York Times Magazine* reported that "Mormon liberalism" was shocking to other denominations because of their excessive indulgence in dancing, and in 1959 *Time* thought them "the dancingest denomination in the country."[74] Currently, more than twelve thousand BYU students enroll every year in a range of dance classes from ballroom to aerobic. Given that pool to draw on, it is hardly surprising that BYU's Ballroom Dance Company has won numerous US and British championships.

Why does the church still try to convert people?

In Matthew 28, Jesus delivered what Christians refer to as "the Great Commission": "go ye therefore, and teach all nations, baptizing" and "teaching them to observe all things whatsoever I have commanded you" (19–20). Following this directive, the first apostles and early missionaries spread the Christian gospel throughout much of the ancient world, missionaries from Europe accompanied explorers and colonizers centuries later, and Catholics and Protestants have vied for converts since the Reformation. With the recent decline of religious fervor in the face of secularism's encroachments, and given greater awareness of the evils of colonialism and ideological imperialism, religious evangelizing has become both less popular and more politically suspect.

Latter-day Saints, however, believe that the original commission to share the gospel is still in force; indeed, they believe that the imperative has been reaffirmed repeatedly in the modern age through Joseph Smith and subsequent prophets. As a consequence, the church has devoted extensive resources to training and supporting missionaries, most of them young men (eighteen and up) and women (nineteen and up), at any one of a dozen Missionary Training Centers. Most missionaries undergo three to twelve weeks of preparation at the Missionary Training Center in Provo, Utah, where one studies evangelizing materials and methods and one of fifty languages.

Others go to centers in Argentina, Brazil, Colombia, Ghana, Mexico, New Zealand, Peru, the Philippines, South Africa, or the United Kingdom.

Serving a mission is emphasized as a duty and responsibility for the men of the church (pertaining to a range of priesthood responsibilities) and as an opportunity for women who choose that path of service. In 2018, there were over sixty-five thousand full-time missionaries and another thirty-eight thousand service missionaries. Many of the latter are senior missionaries, usually retired couples. Missionaries are usually self-funded, although wards can provide support for those who are financially unable to support themselves. Full-time missions generally last two years for men, eighteen months for women, and six to twenty-four months for service missionaries. For full-time missionaries, the work is arduous, with long days, no vacations (just a half day for weekly "preparation"), no dating, and no movies, television, or other entertainment. Only personal devotion—or the intense cultural pressure within the LDS community—can explain such sacrifice by teenagers at a time when the enticements of sex, pop culture, and educational/career preparations are at their peak.

It would be a mistake, however, to assume that missionary efforts are entirely a matter of fulfilling a religious obligation—personal or institutional. A Book of Mormon scripture suggests that one should "consider on the blessed and happy state of those that keep the commandments of God" (Mosiah 2:41). In the best scenario, missionaries are seeking to share a set of values and beliefs that they believe will be of inestimable benefit—here and now—to those who embrace them.

What is the historical place of Blacks in the church?

Joseph Smith's views on Blacks were progressive for his era. A revelation declared as early as 1833 that "it is not right that any man should be in bondage to another" (D&C 101:79), and under his leadership, a few Black members were ordained to the priesthood alongside whites. Intemperate LDS praise for "the wonderful events of this age," in which "much is doing towards abolishing slavery,"[75] fueled anti-Mormon violence in slavery-leaning Missouri, and Joseph Smith himself campaigned for US president in 1844 on a platform that advocated a federal buyout of all slaves by 1850. The situation changed abruptly with the Saints' removal to Utah. While making no specific claim of revelation, in 1852 President Brigham Young declared a prohibition on Blacks receiving the priesthood. It seems to have been justified by inherited Christian beliefs regarding the curse of Cain and of Ham, reinforced by Young's own reading of the Bible. Decades later, the leadership would find further support in an Abrahamic text produced by Smith that referred to a "lineage" with no "right of priesthood" (now understood as having no reference to race).

From that time on, Blacks were accepted as members but denied both priesthood and temple sacraments. Opposition to the church's position grew—from within and outside the church alike—during the civil rights era. It was only after most of the storm had passed, however, in 1978, that President Spencer W. Kimball claimed a revelation declaring that "every faithful, worthy man in the church may receive the holy priesthood, with power to exercise its divine authority, and enjoy with his loved ones every blessing that flows therefrom, including the blessings of the temple." Shortly thereafter influential apostle Bruce R. McConkie advised the church membership to "forget everything that I have said, or what President Brigham Young or President George Q. Cannon or whomsoever has said in days past that is contrary to the present revelation. We spoke with a limited understanding and without the light and knowledge that now has come into the world."[76]

Evangelization in Africa has yielded hundreds of thousands of converts, but growth among American Blacks remains tepid. Commemorations of black history, sponsorship of LDS symposia on African American relations, and outreach (as in the aftermath of the 1992 Los Angeles riots) have contributed somewhat to mending the damaged relations of the past, with three particularly striking developments. First, in April 1988, church president Gordon B. Hinckley received the NAACP Distinguished Service Award from Julian Bond. In 2001, the church made public, with great fanfare, the records of the Freedman's Bank. The extensive records from this Reconstruction-era institution, organized under church sponsorship during an eleven-year period, make it possible for millions of African Americans to connect their family histories to the half million names indexed in the collections. In this way the church furthered its mission to connect the human family through genealogical research, while providing a significant service to the African American community. And in 2019, President Russell Nelson was invited to address the annual meeting of the NAACP.

From the church leadership, condemnations of racism are frequent, and the church aspires to embody the principle first printed in the 1830 edition of the Book of Mormon: "he inviteth them all to come unto him and partake of his goodness; and he denieth none that come unto him, black and white, bond and free, male and female" (2 Nephi 26:33). Still, the sting of the more than century-long ban remains, and many still await a formal apology for a policy that has never been clearly repudiated as prophetic error.

Why are there so many Latter-day Saints in America's FBI and CIA?

As in most voluntary relationships, motives for the association are to be found in both parties. From the government's perspective, LDS agents would tend to be immune to many of the practices that can render an agent vulnerable to disloyalty. The perception of Latter-day Saints as sexually chaste before marriage and generally faithful within makes it less likely that they will be vulnerable to "honeytraps" or similar seduction schemes. Practicing abstinence from alcohol eliminates one more potential source of impaired job performance or judgment. A final bonus when hiring a Latter-day Saint is the likelihood that one is acquiring a candidate with foreign language skills and experience living in a foreign culture. The vast majority of LDS adult males—and a rapidly growing number of LDS women—have served as missionaries abroad. They bring to their new employment what is often a near-native fluency in a language and a familiarity with and love of a culture outside their own.

As for motives on the other side of the equation, American Latter-day Saints by and large are strongly patriotic. This is ironic, because Latter-day Saints experienced a degree of both state and federal opposition and persecution without parallel in American religious history. They were deemed enemies of the state and forcibly expelled from Missouri in 1838. And they were effectively exiled from the United States after Smith's murder in 1844. Petitioned formally and recurrently for redress, officials at all levels refused all aid and compensation. Determined to leave the country that had so abused them, Latter-day Saints fled to Mexico, but found themselves in an American territory—later Utah—as a consequence of the Mexican War. In their quest to achieve statehood in the last decades of the nineteenth century, the Saints acquired the habits of patriotic citizens. They abandoned their own political party for national ones, scaled back their rhetoric, and abandoned polygamy. The imperative to convince a skeptical government passed, but the shift from contempt to patriotism, maybe oddly, persisted. This was aided by scriptural declarations that the United States had a special role in providential history. One revelation to Joseph Smith declared: "I established the constitution of this land, by the hands of wise men whom I raised up unto this very purpose" (D&C 101:80). So while the administrators of state and national government have not always treated the Latter-day Saints with tolerance or justice, members of the church have historically revered the nation itself and the Constitution on which it was founded.

What explains the Latter-day Saints' high rate of growth?

Through the twentieth century, the Church of Jesus Christ maintained a consistent, impressive rate of growth. It has tapered off in the first years of the new millennium but still surpasses that of virtually all the Protestant groups. Doubtless some of this success is attributable to a missionary force larger than those of the rest of the Protestant world combined—over sixty thousand men and women serving full-time. Sociologists of religion have pointed to two other factors found in successful religious movements: maintaining an optimum level of tension with the surrounding culture and qualifying as a high-demand religion.

In the case of Latter-day Saints, members find a comfortable place in the world of contemporary commerce, politics, and public life generally. Saints have run for president, led the Senate, and chaired many Fortune 500 corporations and are overrepresented in cultural forums from boy bands to *Dancing with the Stars*. Ever since winning the Silver Medal at the 1893 World's Fair, the Mormon Tabernacle Choir (now the Tabernacle Choir at Temple Square) has been an American staple, and your favorite sci-fi writer, like your NFL team's quarterback, has a decent chance of being LDS. At the same time, Latter-day Saints have enough cultural distinctives—such as Sabbath observance, sexual chastity, abstinence from alcohol and tobacco, modesty in dress—to be identifiable as a people out of sync with dominant cultural mores. In other words, Latter-day Saints are familiar enough to fit in but different enough to be recognizable as a distinct people. The same holds true for their religious beliefs: they are recognizably Christian, as the name implies: the Church of Jesus Christ of Latter-day Saints. At the same time, they are more unlike Methodists, Baptists, and Catholics than Methodists, Baptists, and Catholics are unlike each other. Their belief in additional scriptures, like the Book of Mormon, a godhead consisting of separate and distinct members, and modern prophets and apostles sets them apart from all other

Christians. What this means in practice is that those looking for, or open to, new ways of thinking about religion find a clear—but not incomprehensible—alternative in the LDS belief system.

The Church of Jesus Christ is also a high-demand faith. It is perhaps counterintuitive but nonetheless true that those religions most likely to thrive are those that require the most, not the least, of their members. Saints' financial commitment to their church is generally much higher than for their counterparts. Latter-day Saints are expected to donate a full 10 percent of their income to the church for the Lord's work. The time commitment is also unusually high. The LDS youth donate two years (eighteen months for women) of their lives to full-time, unremunerated mission service. And in a lay ministry, most members are expected to serve weekly as teachers, youth leaders, or bishops—expending up to twenty hours a week. And all members, young and old, attend two hours of worship services every Sunday, while most teens spend one hour each weekday morning in religious instruction called "seminary." The sacrifice of personal appetite is also a high demand: fasting once a month; no alcohol, tobacco, coffee or tea; no sexual relations before or outside of marriage.

One additional feature of the church has often been cited as a likely factor in areas where the convert growth is highest, that is, Latin America and Africa. The faith is structured, in terms of programs, organization, and theology, around the centrality of the family. It is probably no coincidence that missionary work is most successful in those places where the institution of the family is, and has long been, particularly strong.

Does Mormonism have its own literary tradition?

As branches of Christianity go, the Church of Jesus Christ is quite young, not having yet reached the end of its second century. Yet already in the late nineteenth century, the leadership called for a literary tradition that would reflect the unique doctrine and culture of the LDS people. As one apostle put it, "our literature must live and breathe for itself. Our mission is diverse from all others; our literature must also be. . . . In God's name and by his help we will build up a literature whose top shall touch heaven."[77] The results were mostly unimpressive and didactic. A few decades later, the tradition produced its first nationally acclaimed works by authors like Marjorie Whipple and Virginia Sorenson. In the 1970s, Richard Cracroft and Eugene England pushed again for a very self-consciously LDS literature—and literary appreciation. One of England's contributions was his recognition of the personal journal as a particularly potent form of LDS expression; he excavated marvelous examples even as he practiced the personal essay himself to great effect. Since that time, many LDS writers have produced fine work, but none has yet achieved a status comparable to the greatest Catholic writers, like Flannery O'Connor or Graham Greene.

Orson Scott Card—followed to a lesser extent by Brandon Sanderson and Larry Correia—are probably the most recognized American writers in the faith whose work is occasionally infused—explicitly or implicitly—with LDS themes. The fact that all three write in the science fiction genre is not accidental: LDS writers are overrepresented in that genre, for reasons that may have to do with a highly developed and highly unconventional cosmology. LDS authors are also well represented within the genre of young adult fiction. (Think James Dashner, author of the *Maze Runner* series, and Shannon Hale, Newberry Honor Book winner for *Princess Academy*.)

By far the bestselling LDS writer is Stephanie Meyers, of *Twilight* fame. Critics claim to detect submerged Mormon themes throughout her work; however, apart from themes of sexual purity and abstinence from unhealthy substances, nothing clearly LDS in sensibility pervades the text. The same is true of bestselling mystery writer Anne Perry.

At BYU and other Utah institutions, Mormon literature is a common course offering, reflecting a growing body of work that, however limited in its broader appeal, has found substantial recognition within "the Mormon corridor," that is, regions of Western North America settled by members of the church and still hosting a high LDS population.

9

QUESTIONS ON THE PERIPHERY

Who are the three Nephites?

In the closing passages of the Gospel of John, there is a cryptic exchange involving Peter, Jesus, and John. Looking at John, Peter asks Jesus: "what shall this man do? Jesus saith unto him, If I will that he tarry till I come, what is that to thee? follow thou me. Then went this saying abroad among the brethren, that that disciple should not die" (John 21:21–23). In the Book of Mormon, this story is interwoven with a New World version. After his Jerusalem death and subsequent resurrection, Jesus appears to a group of his disciples in the Western Hemisphere. There, he shows them the marks of his crucifixion, preaches to them, and organizes them, calling twelve to be their leaders. Before he departs, he asks each of the twelve what they most desire of him. Nine ask to join him upon their deaths, but three are hesitant to express their wish—which he discerns. "I know your thoughts, and ye have desired the thing which John, my beloved, who was with me in my ministry, before that I was lifted up by the Jews, desired of me. Therefore, more blessed are ye, for ye shall never taste of death; . . . And again, ye shall not have pain while ye shall dwell in the flesh, neither sorrow save it be for the sins of the world" (3 Nephi 28:6–9). The chronicler of the story, Mormon, writing over three centuries later, adds the detail that the three remained on earth as immortal emissaries and ministers, and then says: "I have seen them, and they have ministered unto me" (3 Nephi 28:26).

Like all religious traditions, the Church of Jesus Christ has spawned a vast legacy of myth, folklore, and anecdotal narratives, interwoven with their history and doctrinal roots. In this category is a robust corpus of stories that recount personal encounters with one or more of these "three Nephites."

Are Jesus and Satan brothers?

The eternal nature of human spirits is a foundational doctrine of the church. All those born into the world were at one time spirit children of God. Smith taught that spirit is eternal—there was never a time when humans' spirits did not exist. In the modern church, that doctrine has evolved into a doctrine that eternal "intelligence" was created or fashioned or birthed into spirit persons by heavenly parents. In either case, all those entities known as spirits, angels, or other heavenly beings were in some sense children of God, and siblings all. Those premortal ranks included Jesus Christ, who held a privileged position and was, as the Gospel of John indicates, God even before he was made flesh. Lucifer, the light bearer, was also a son of God of high status. After he rebelled against God, he became known as Satan and put himself into opposition to God's purposes and the human family. So Latter-day Saints believe that the devil is a real personage, with an ancestry as an angelic being. In the sense that all beings subordinate to God were—and are—his children, then that would make Jesus and Satan brothers, sons of the same divine parents.

What is Kolob?

Many ancient Christian and Hebrew traditions recount ascension narratives, in which a prophetic figure is taken up to heaven and there a cosmic vision is revealed to him, often spanning time and space alike. Enoch is one such figure, appearing in a number of pseudepigraphical texts, and in the Book of Abraham (which Smith produced in portions in the 1830s and 1840s) his encounter with God, whom he sees weeping, is recounted. But the Book of Abraham also includes a visionary experience in which Abraham himself is tutored in the order of the cosmos. He records, in part: "I saw the stars, that they were very great, and that one of them was nearest unto the throne of God; and there were many great ones which were near unto it; And the Lord said unto me: These are the governing ones; and the name of the great one is Kolob, because it is near unto me, for I am the Lord thy God: I have set this one to govern all those which belong to the same order as that upon which thou standest" (Abraham 3:4).

Latter-day Saints posit no more nor less than this striking reference to a cosmic order beyond humans' ken; they derive neither their astronomy nor any particular doctrine from this account. To outsiders, it is a curiosity; to Saints, it is an intriguing detail in a narrative whose emphasis is on the fact that Abraham, like many other prophets before and since, "talked with the Lord, face to face" (Abraham 3:11). Much more central to the LDS Restoration doctrine was Abraham's subsequent vision of a premortal council, in which human spirits participated as God revealed his intention of creating a world to be inhabited by his embodied children.

Do Latter-day Saints believe that the Garden of Eden is in Missouri?

Again and again, one finds a pervasive pattern in LDS theology of taking seriously what other Christians often see as biblical allegories and mythologies. While they do not believe that Eve was fashioned from Adam's rib, they do believe that Adam was a real person and, in some essential sense, the head of the human family. This belief is derived not solely from the Genesis account but also from revelations Smith received that identified Adam as the archangel Michael in his human form, a soul of immense significance for the past and future of the Lord's plan currently unfolding. Consequently, Smith wrote that "Adam was the first member of the church of Christ on earth" and referred to father Adam as the supreme priesthood authority in the human family, who held "the keys of the universe" and who would personally deliver up his stewardship to Christ preparatory to the Second Coming.[1] Adam, in other words, possessed the fullness of priesthood keys (or authority) to administer the ordinances of salvation. And to him was given responsibility to reveal to humankind those ordinances at the appointed times, either in his angelic role as Michael or through the intermediation of other celestial messengers.

In May 1838, after finding refuge in Caldwell County, Missouri (after expulsion from Jackson County), Smith identified an area near "Wright's Ferry" as the location at which Adam offered sacrifice after his expulsion from the Garden of Eden. Subsequently, he declared that nearby "Spring Hill is named by the Lord Adam-ondi-Ahman, because, said he, it is the place where Adam shall come to visit his people, or the Ancient of Days shall sit, as spoken of, by the prophet Daniel" (D&C 116). The prophecy referenced, from Daniel 7, refers to the apocalyptic vision of Daniel in which the thrones of the world "were cast down, and the Ancient of days did sit" and "ten thousand times ten thousand stood before him: the judgment was set, and the books were opened" (7:9–10). Prophets of the LDS tradition have interpreted these texts to point to an end-time event in which Adam, or Michael, the Ancient of Days, assumes his role as steward, under Christ, of the human family.

Finding a concrete geographical site associated with the biblical Adam is, of course, highly unusual. It serves as one more example of an intractable pattern in LDS thought: taking the preeminent figures of the Bible as real individuals, who often appear in more than one guise, either as premortal angels or resurrected angels or both. And real individuals inhabit real places.

10

CONFLICTS AND CHALLENGES

If the church is led by revelation, why has its position on many issues (race, marriage, homosexuality) changed?

Latter-day Saints tend to see developments in their church as reflecting changes in policy or practices or procedures rather than doctrines. And those changes occur in accordance with LDS belief that God continues to guide and direct the institution as a "living church" and a Restoration that is still underway. The distinction between doctrine and policy is debatable in cases where practices were explained in theological terms: polygamy was depicted by some leaders as grounded in a heavenly order wherein women served as eternal soul-bearers and men presided; the racial ban pertaining to priesthood and temple privileges was interpreted by some leaders as reflecting differing conduct (or neutrality) in the premortal war in heaven. Such doctrinal explanations, however, were not codified in scripture or official church declarations, even if some (like Brigham Young's teaching that Adam was God) emanated from a prophet speaking in a general conference.

In the aftermath of the revocation of the priesthood ban, the apostle Bruce R. McConkie gave the following statement:

> people write me letters and say, "You said such and such, and how is it now that we do such and such?" And all

> I can say to that is that it is time disbelieving people repented and got in line and believed in a living, modern prophet. Forget everything that I have said, or what President Brigham Young or President George Q. Cannon or whomsoever has said in days past that is contrary to the present revelation. We spoke with a limited understanding and without the light and knowledge that now has come into the world. We get our truth and our light line upon line and precept upon precept. We have now had added a new flood of intelligence and light on this particular subject, and it erases all the darkness and all the views and all the thoughts of the past. They don't matter anymore.[1]

The LDS myth of prophetic infallibility can be traced to the nineteenth-century statement of Wilford Woodruff, who assured the Saints: "The lord will never permit me or any other man who stands as President of this Church to lead you astray" (D&C Official Declaration 1). Smith himself had been insistent that he was subject to error and referenced his own foibles and missteps in canonized scripture. However, many members have taken Woodruff's words as an assurance of the prophet's infallibility, which has caused no end of disharmony in the church. Modern leaders continue to disavow infallibility and urge on members personal responsibility. "Not every statement made by a Church leader, past or present, necessarily constitutes doctrine," Elder Todd Christofferson reminded the Saints.[2] When a member of the First Presidency recently expressed what should have been an unexceptional truism—"leaders in the Church have simply made mistakes"—the *New York Times* found it striking enough to devote two articles to it.[3]

It would seem that, like biblical figures who could err and argue even as they moved forward the building of the church (compare for instance Moses's sin at the waters of Meriba and Peter and Paul's sharp discord—Numbers 20:12; Galatians

2:11–14), LDS prophets believe that they are called of God but nonetheless receive God's word according to their inspired but human capacity, "precept upon precept, line upon line" (Isaiah 28:13).

Is the Church of Jesus Christ an American church?

The church's beginnings did not portend a successful internationalization of the membership. First of all, this is because Joseph Smith established a dramatic series of connections between the restored gospel and a very particular idea of place—American place. Moroni, he related, was an angel who had inhabited *this* hemisphere. The artifacts of Nephite civilization and the icons of God's reemerging covenant were emphatically local. The Book of Mormon was uncovered in upstate New York. Its contents chronicled three ancient civilizations that had inhabited the Americas. And the most quoted Book of Mormon passage in early church publications was Ether 13:4–8, which predicts "a New Jerusalem upon *this* land." Even the abode of Adam, Smith revealed, was in the land of Daviess County, Missouri.

What this means, of course, is that the Book of Mormon was physically connected as an actual artifact and ancient history, in the minds and the tactile experiences of early Saints, with this land. And the history in the Book of Mormon was explicated in terms of that physical terrain over which the Saints themselves trekked and camped. America was the abode of Adam and Moroni, the cradle of American independence and the Restoration, and the future home of the inhabitants of Zion. Certainly, Harold Bloom's identification of Mormonism as "the American religion" finds ample validation in the intensely American complexion of Mormonism's early elaboration.[4]

Locale was not the only American feature of Mormonism. Historians have long construed the church as an expression of a particular American cultural climate and Joseph Smith as a quintessentially American prophet. Indeed, many of the church's features were especially appealing in light of an ethos that worked to democratize religious experience in the postrevolutionary period. "The disintegration of older structures of authority," writes historian Gordon Wood, was part of a "democratic revolution" that profoundly affected American culture. "Countless numbers of people were involved in a simultaneous search for individual autonomy," and "people were given personal responsibility for their salvation as never before."[5]

"To the honorable men of the world," Smith began one of his open letters, "we . . . say unto you, Search the Scriptures search the revelations which we publish, and ask your heavenly Father . . . to manifest the truth unto you. . . . You will then know for yourselves and not for another: You will not then be dependent on man for the knowledge of God; . . . Every man lives for himself."[6] LDS culture, in other words, may be seen as the religious anticipation of Emerson's 1837 "American Scholar" speech, wherein the sage admonished his Harvard audience to establish an authentically American expression of culture. Mormonism represented such an original, indigenous expression of American piety, claiming direct authorization from God without the need of mediating Old World customs, traditions, authority, or scriptures.

On the other hand, a principal lesson of the Book of Mormon is that a covenant people is defined by their discipleship, not their location in one particular promised land. The Zion toward which Latter-day Saints aspire is, by definition, a global community of the "pure in heart," and the church can only fulfull its mission to the extent that it is not primarily associated with one country or people. The growing diversity of its leadership, like its membership, underscores that essential fact.

How is the church faring internationally?

The first LDS missionaries to sally abroad went out from Kirtland, Ohio, in 1837. Six months later, they had recorded six hundred baptisms, and for the next two decades the rate only increased until there were over thirty thousand British Saints—more than the entire territory of Utah boasted.[7] As these converts poured into Illinois and later Utah by the thousands, the first cultural amalgamation of the church began—though the common ancestry of most members made the process virtually seamless. But over the next generation, missionary work expanded to other nations as well. Scandinavia was opened for missionary work in 1850 and proved second only to Britain as a source of converts. The same year, missionary work commenced in France and then Italy, followed by Germany. By the turn of the century, over a hundred thousand converts had streamed across the ocean to New Orleans, sailed up the Mississippi to Iowa, and outfitted themselves with wagons or handcarts before the last leg of the trek across the prairies and mountains to Salt Lake City. Some sailed to New York first and others directly to California.

Until about 1900, converts abroad were urged to migrate, or "gather," to Utah. Consequently, at the turn of the century (1900), 90 percent of the LDS membership resided in the United States. By 1960, that percentage was little changed. Then the internationalization of the Church of Jesus Christ began in earnest. Over the next thirty years, South America's share went from 1 to 16 percent, Mexico and Central America from 1 to 11 percent, and Asia from virtually 0 to 5 percent.[8] In 1961, the first non-English-speaking stake of the church was organized in the Netherlands, and a few months later the first Spanish-speaking stake was organized in Mexico City. In just three decades, the church was transformed. By 1990, there were seventeen hundred stakes, with more than three-quarters outside Utah. Active in fifty nations in 1950, the church was now organized in 128, and over a third of the church members lived outside the United States. By the year 2000, a watershed demographic shift had occurred—over half of the Church's members spoke a tongue other than English as their native language.

The internationalization of the church has not unfolded evenly around the globe. The vast majority of members (85 percent in 1995) reside in the Western Hemisphere,[9] where the phenomenal growth rate continues to be centered. It may be more accurate to refer to the Church of Jesus Christ as a "New World" religion rather than a new "world religion." The reasons for the rapid success of the church in Latin America and Africa, and its more labored growth in Europe and Asia have not been fully explored but derive, at least in part, from the fact that the United States and increasingly Latin America are less secularized and have a more open religious-market mentality than is the case in Asia and elsewhere.[10] It also appears, as Rodney Stark has argued, that for a new religious movement to succeed it must maintain a balance between cultural continuity with its host societies and a certain degree of tension with them. Cultural factors like a Christian heritage and strong family ties, for example, seem especially relevant to the church's success in Latin America. The church has long been justly noted not just for its family-centered doctrines but also for providing an unusually powerful community that is, essentially, a vastly enlarged family.

The major locus of rapid growth outside the New World is Africa. When the priesthood ban was lifted in 1978, evangelizing of Africa (and northern Brazil) began almost immediately. The 7,500 African Saints of 1978 grew to almost half a million by 2014,[11] with continuing consistent growth down to the present. If China were to open its doors to evangelizing, the dominance of Western world Mormonism could be further altered.

How are Latter-day Saints weathering secularization?

Recent surveys indicate that the fastest growing category of religious affiliation, at least in America, is "none," as in "none of the above." Historically, Latter-day Saints have fared better than most denominations in maintaining their young people through the transition into adulthood. Now, however, the tides of disaffiliation and religious disillusionment are hitting the church fairly hard. Several factors are probably contributing. First is generational skepticism regarding large institutions generally. Millennials and Gen Xers have shifted dramatically away from a "religious" orientation and toward a so-called spiritual one, emphasizing the personal over the collective. Because the LDS religion has always been "high demand," members have historically felt more a part of a people than a church institution. With the increasing corporatization of the church, that may no longer be true. Millennials especially are less tolerant of the forms the corporatization of the church has entailed. The drive for "correlation," which went into overdrive in the 1960s, created a hypercentralized bureaucracy, standardization of all programs and curricula globally, and priesthood oversight of all church entities, resulting in vastly diminished autonomy for local leaders and the women's organization in particular.

Second, the Church of Jesus Christ is rooted more deeply than other Christian denominations in a particular historical narrative surrounding its founding, one that includes Joseph Smith's First Vision, his reception and translation of the Book of Mormon, visitations of angels that conferred on him priesthood "keys," and other particular events and transactions. In the last few generations, LDS historiography has become highly professionalized. The traditional narrative has been deepened but also complicated and, in parts, challenged. In the high-speed information age, members have unprecedented access to these competing versions of their history. Multiple accounts of Smith's First Vision; his use of a peep stone in translating the Book of Mormon; his plural marriages to young teens; Brigham Young's racist statements; these and other details of the LDS past suggest to some people deliberate obfuscation or deception on the part of the institutional church.

Third, Smith's translation of the Book of Abraham has garnered particular attention. Non-Mormon Egyptologists assert that his rendering of hieroglyphs on facsimiles that he published in the 1840s is entirely fallacious. Surviving fragments of the papyri he worked from have been identified as funerary texts, whereas he claimed that at least some of the ones he translated were authored by Abraham and described his own life and visions. Since the Book of Abraham has been canonized as scripture, attacks on its authenticity threaten to undermine the foundations of the church itself.

Fourth, the Church of Jesus Christ rests on the premise of inspired prophetic leadership. Racial politics have divided this country going back to its origins, but public intolerance of racism has reached new heights in American society (witness the NFL protests, Black Lives Matter, and public figures discredited over blackface). Racial tensions are particularly challenging for a church that revoked a policy of excluding Blacks from priesthood and temple blessings only in 1978. The nation was then still in the throes of systemic racism, with busing controversies and recent riots in Houston and Chicago—but the church's prophetic leadership, presumably, should have put it ahead, not behind, the curve. What now appears to be a legacy of racism combined with the prospect of prophetic error is particularly disturbing in the current environment.

Fifth, feminism, like the war against racism, has found new energies and forms of expression in the twenty-first century. (The 2017 Women's March and the Me Too movements are two examples.) Some LDS women (and men) find it difficult to remain faithful to an institution that allows only boys and men to hold the priesthood and to preside over wards, stakes, and the church. The issue for many is not sacerdotal power per se but the social power that accompanies priesthood authority.

Finally, the most dramatic and rapid shift in contemporary cultural mores has occurred with the legal and societal acceptance of not just homosexual practice but also gay marriage. The church encountered enormous and widespread hostility as a consequence of its support for the Proposition 8 (gay marriage ban) campaign in California. In 2015, the church further alienated the gay community and its supporters by declaring gay marriage equivalent to apostasy, meriting excommunication (the policy was reversed in 2019). Taken together, these six areas of contention constitute a perfect storm of discontent. Future prospects for the church depend almost entirely on the nature of its reponse to that set of challenges.

What has catalyzed the shift from a fringe society and a "peculiar people" to a relatively more mainstream faith?

Latter-day Saints existed at the fringes of the American mainstream from early in their history, both geographically and theologically. They lived on the frontier in closely knit communities and believed in additional scripture, angels, and modern prophets. Starting from the fringes, they then took on a new status as exiles, as they were forced out of Illinois in 1846. Beginning in the 1850s, journalists and fiction writers launched a moral crusade against the Saints for their practice of polygamy; though the church sanctioned that practice for less than fifty years, the label and image took deep root in the public imagination. In order to gain statehood for Utah, the Latter-day Saints there engaged in a deliberate campaign of "Americanization," working to minimize political and cultural differences. With the cessation of the practice of plural marriage and admission to statehood near the end of the nineteenth century, the Saints' core values of self-reliance, hard work, and family-centeredness began to gradually displace the more negative stereotypes.

With the coming of the sexual revolution and the protest movements of the 1960s, these values, added to a staunch patriotism and uncompromising conservative sexual morality, moved Latter-day Saints toward the center of mainstream American culture. The Mormon Tabernacle Choir had become a beloved and nationally celebrated institution, entertainers from the King Sisters in the 1940s to the Osmonds in the 1980s epitomized a clean-cut ethos, while Ezra Taft Benson as Eisenhower's agricultural secretary and George Romney as a governor of Michigan, president of American Motors, and then cabinet secretary and presidential candidate gave the church further recognition and respect. By the 1980s, Reagan was publicly touting the church's welfare system and practice of caring for their own. In that same decade, the prominent public intellectual Harold Bloom, in an astonishing and historic reversal of fortune, could refer to Mormonism as "the American religion."

The shift has not been without its obstacles and setbacks. Following widespread public denunciations of its temple and priesthood racial ban, the church belatedly removed all such restrictions in 1978. And at the moment in the early twenty-first century when gay marriage was coming to be embraced by virtually all politicians and most of the public, the Latter-day Saints incurred enormous ill will for their very public support of California's Proposition 8, which banned same-sex marriage (2008). As one of few churches (along with the Catholic Church) that retained a male monopoly on the priesthood, the LDS church is also increasingly out of alignment with prevailing notions of gender equality. By the time of Mitt Romney's campaigns in 2008 and 2012, with prominent journalists and talking heads declaring that Latter-day Saints were inherently disqualified for office, it was clear that the old hurdles were not fully overcome.[12]

How is the church responding to the challenges of the new millennium?

In a move to deepen young people's commitment to the church during the vulnerable late teen years, the church lowered the mission age for both men and women (eighteen for the former, nineteen for the latter). Women especially have responded to the new policy in substantial numbers; the long-range consequence for member retention remains to be seen. The most pervasive and far-reaching institutional developments of recent decades have taken place in the Church History Department. A new official church history (*Saints*) addresses with frankness and transparency the sticky wickets of the LDS past and incorporates the best scholarship available. A series of "gospel topics" essays discuss in detail the most challenging questions about LDS history, including the racial exclusion, multiple accounts of the First Vision, and Joseph Smith's polygamy. And a large team of scholars has produced the *Joseph Smith Papers*, a definitive, unexpurgated documentary account of Smith's letters, revelations, and journals—including even the heretofore publicly inaccessible minutes of the secret Council of Fifty—forecast to comprise some two dozen volumes when complete.

When the Joseph Smith papyri were reacquired in 1966, the church moved quickly to publish them for public and professional scrutiny. For over a century (dating to 1913), the church has acknowledged that what Smith produced are not translations in the conventional sense of the term. The editor of the *Deseret News* readily admitted that Smith might have erred in his rendering of the Egyptian. But, as B. H. Roberts affirmed, "in those translations are truths that are part of a mighty system of truth."[13] The recently published gospel topic essay on the subject[14] suggests that the papyri might have been more a catalyst than a direct source for Smith's words. Such views going back to 1913 were not widely known to contemporary Saints, however, who have typically believed that the Book of Abraham was a straightforward translation of an ancient text.

Similarly, regarding the priesthood ban, the church has acknowledged in print that the historical record provides no evidence of a revelatory basis for the practice and that there is no official explanation to account for its implementation. Smith advocated emancipation and ordained Black members to the priesthood. Older rationalizations for Young's policy, the essay admits, echo widespread racial ideas of the time. In LDS scripture and current policy, "all are alike unto God" (2 Nephi 26:33).

Although there seems little likelihood of female ordination to the clergy, movement has been conspicuous in other ways. Women are now involved in church leadership councils, from the ward level through the highest echelons. Lowering the missionary age for sisters from twenty-one to nineteen has resulted in a balance much closer to parity in the mission fields. Most significantly, the temple ceremonies were reconfigured in 2019 to address phrasing and depictions that were seen to unduly subordinate and silence women.

In the area of same-sex attraction, too, the church has made numerous modifications to rhetoric, policy, and practice. Homosexuality as an orientation is now sharply differentiated from homosexual behavior. The leadership has acknowledged that same-sex attraction may indeed have a genetic component and no guilt or sanctions attach to such a status. The church supports a number of gay support organizations and supported Utah legislation outlawing discrimination on the basis of sexual orientation.

Perhaps the greatest cultural shift of all, in response to the crisis of secularism, is the church's move to decriminalize doubt. Latter-day Saint culture has been immersed in a rhetoric of certainty. Members are long accustomed to bearing personal witness that they "know" the church is true, "know" that Joseph Smith was a prophet, "know" the Book of Mormon is true, and so forth. Recently, apostles have acknowledged the simple fact that faith and belief are, like spiritual knowledge, gifts of the spirit. And for those who can do no more than desire to believe, the church is taking steps to become a more welcoming place.

Appendix

THE ARTICLES OF FAITH

1 We believe in God, the Eternal Father, and in His Son, Jesus Christ, and in the Holy Ghost.

2 We believe that men will be punished for their own sins, and not for Adam's transgression.

3 We believe that through the Atonement of Christ, all mankind may be saved, by obedience to the laws and ordinances of the Gospel.

4 We believe that the first principles and ordinances of the Gospel are: first, Faith in the Lord Jesus Christ; second, Repentance; third, Baptism by immersion for the remission of sins; fourth, Laying on of hands for the gift of the Holy Ghost.

5 We believe that a man must be called of God, by prophecy, and by the laying on of hands by those who are in authority, to preach the Gospel and administer in the ordinances thereof.

6 We believe in the same organization that existed in the Primitive Church, namely, apostles, prophets, pastors, teachers, evangelists, and so forth.

7 We believe in the gift of tongues, prophecy, revelation, visions, healing, interpretation of tongues, and so forth.

8 We believe the Bible to be the word of God as far as it is translated correctly; we also believe the Book of Mormon to be the word of God.

9 We believe all that God has revealed, all that He does now reveal, and we believe that He will yet reveal many great and important things pertaining to the Kingdom of God.

10 We believe in the literal gathering of Israel and in the restoration of the Ten Tribes; that Zion (the New Jerusalem) will be built upon the American continent; that Christ will reign personally upon the earth; and that the earth will be renewed and receive its paradisiacal glory.

11 We claim the privilege of worshiping Almighty God according to the dictates of our own conscience, and allow all men the same privilege, let them worship how, where, or what they may.

12 We believe in being subject to kings, presidents, rulers, and magistrates, in obeying, honoring, and sustaining the law.

13 We believe in being honest, true, chaste, benevolent, virtuous, and in doing good to all men; indeed, we may say that we follow the admonition of Paul—We believe all things, we hope all things, we have endured many things, and hope to be able to endure all things. If there is anything virtuous, lovely, or of good report or praiseworthy, we seek after these things.

NOTES

Chapter 2

1 Arthur Masson, ed., *A Collection of English Prose and Verse for the Use of Schools*, 7th ed. (Edinburgh: 1773), 196.

2 Martin Luther, quoted in Roland Bainton, *Here I Stand: A Life of Martin Luther* (New York: Abingdon, 1950), 65.

3 John Wesley, May 24, 1738, in *The Heart of Wesley's Journal* (New Canaan, CT: Keats, 1979), 43.

4 *Joseph Smith Papers: Histories*, ed. Karen Lynn Davidson, David J. Whittaker, Mark Ashurst-McGee, and Richard L. Jensen (Salt Lake City: Church Historian's Press, 2012), 1:11.

5 *Joseph Smith Papers: Histories*, 1:13.

6 *Joseph Smith Papers: Histories*, 1:10–13.

7 *Joseph Smith Papers: Histories*, 1:211–215.

8 See Newell G. Bringhurst and John C. Hamer, eds., *Scattering of the Saints: Schism within Mormonism* (Independence, MO: John Whitmer Books, 2007), 7–9.

9 Robert V. Remini, *Joseph Smith* (New York: Penguin, 2002), 6.

10 *Elders Journal of the Church of Jesus Christ of Latter-day Saints* 1.3 (July 1838): 43.

11 *The Joseph Smith Papers: Administrative Records: Council of Fifty Minutes*, ed. Ronald K. Esplin, Matthew J. Grow, Matthew C. Godfrey (Salt Lake City: Church Historians Press, 2016), 95–96.

Chapter 3

1 Brigham Young, in Brigham Young et al., *Journal of Discourses*, 26 vols., reported by G. D. Watt et al. (Liverpool: F. D. and S. W.

Richards et al., 1851–86; reprint, Salt Lake City, 1974) (September 21, 1856), 4:55–56.

2 It is "fornication for the man to cohabit with his wife after she had thus become alienated from him." *Complete Discourses of Brigham Young*, ed. Richard S. Van Wagoner (Salt Lake City: Smith-Petitt Foundation, 2009), 4:1916–1917.

3 Romania B. Pratt Penrose, "Memoir of Romania B. Pratt, M.D." (1881), in Kathleen Flake, "The Emotional and Priestly Logic of Plural Marriage," Leonard J. Arrington Lecture, October 1, 2009 (Logan: Utah State University Press, 2009).

4 Helen Mar Whitney, *Plural Marriage as Taught by the Prophet Joseph* (Salt Lake City: Juvenile Instructor, 1882), 27.

5 Whitney, *Plural Marriage*, 48.

6 Quoted in Richard S. Van Wagoner, *Polygamy: A History* (Salt Lake City: Signature, 1989), 100.

7 Quoted in James Parton, *The Life of Horace Greeley: Editor of the New York Tribune* (New York: Derby and Miller, 1868), 459.

8 "Minutes of a Ladies' Mass Meeting," *Latter-Day Saints' Millennial Star* 32 (Liverpool: H. S. Eldredge, 1870), 102.

9 Brigham Young, "Plurality of Wives," *Contributor* 5.2 (Salt Lake City: Deseret News, 1884), 58.

10 B. H. Roberts, *The Life of John Taylor: Third President of the Church of Jesus Christ of Latter-day Saints* (Salt Lake City: George Q. Cannon & Sons Co., 1892), 100.

11 B. Carmon Hardy, ed., *Doing the Works of Abraham. Mormon Polygamy: Its Origin, Practice, and Demise* (Norman: University of Oklahoma Press, 2007), 356.

12 The Kimball story is recounted by Jake Garn, *Why I Believe* (Salt Lake City: Aspen, 1992), 13. Cited in Robert E. Wells, "Uniting Blended Families," *Ensign* 27.8 (August 1997), 28.

13 Wells, "Uniting Blended Families," 28.

Chapter 4

1 "President Hinckley's Speech at the National Press Club," *Deseret News*, March 27, 2000.

2 "LDS Church Has Spent 1.2 Billion on Welfare and Humanitarian Efforts," World Religion News, https://www.worldreligionnews.com/?p=29124.

3 Sarah Jane Weaver, "LDS Charities Was Involved in Over 2,800 Projects during 2018. Here's a Look at Their World Impact," *Church News*, March 2, 2019, https://www.thechurchnews.com/global/

2019-03-02/lds-charities-was-involved-in-over-2800-projects-during-2018-heres-a-look-at-their-worldwide-impact-4450.

4 David and Bonnie Kenison, *Kenisons in Argentina* (blog), October 30, 2019, https://kenisonsinargentina.blogspot.com/2019/10/humanitarian-projects-our-initial.html#more.

Chapter 5

1 Joseph Smith History 1:60, Pearl of Great Price.

2 The sources are given in John A. Tvedtnes, "Jeremiah's Prophecies of Jesus Christ," in *The Most Correct Book* (Salt Lake City: Cornerstone, 1999): 101–102.

3 "Journal of Reuben Miller," October 21, 1848; for background see R. L. Anderson, "Reuben Miller, Recorder of Oliver Cowdery's Reaffirmations," *BYU Studies* 8 (1968): 277.

4 "Reuben Miller Journal," October 21, 1848, in Dan Vogel, *Early Mormon Documents* (Salt Lake City, Utah: Signature, 1998), 2:494.

5 "Letter of John H. Gilbert to James T. Cobb," February 10, 1879, in Vogel, *Early Mormon Documents*, 2:522–523.

6 *Joseph Smith Papers: Documents*, vol. 1, ed. Michael Hubbard MacKay, Michael Hubbard MacKay, Gerrit J. Dirkmaat, Grant Underwood, Robert J. Woodford, and William G. Hartley (Salt Lake City: Church Historian's Press, 2013), xxix.

7 Hugh W. Nibley, "Lehi in the Desert; The World of the Jaredites; There Were Jaredites," ed. John W. Welch, Darrell L. Matthews, and Stephen R. Callister, in *The Collected Works of Hugh Nibley* (Salt Lake City: Deseret Book and FARMS, 1988), 5:4.

8 Wilfred Cantwell Smith, "The Study of Religion and the Study of the Bible," in Miriam Levering, ed., *Rethinking Scripture: Essays from a Comparative Perspective* (Albany: State University of New York Press, 1989), 26.

9 Carl Mosser and Paul Owen, "Mormon Scholarship, Apologetics, and Evangelical Neglect: Losing the Battle and Not Knowing It?," *Trinity Journal* (1998): 181, 185, 189.

10 Austin Farrer, "Grete Clerk," in Jocelyn Gibb, ed., *Light on C. S. Lewis* (New York: Harcourt Brace, 1966), 26.

11 "Extract from Stephens' 'Incidents of Travel in Central America,'" *Times and Seasons* 3.22 (September 15, 1842), 914.

12 John W. Welch and David J. Whittaker, *Mormonism's Open Canon: Some Historical Reflections on Its Religious Limits and Potentials* (Provo, UT: FARMS, 1986), 10.

13 These lectures, presented at the School of the Prophets in Kirtland, Ohio, were probably not authored by Joseph Smith, though he doubtless approved of their published form.
14 Andrew F. Ehat and Lyndon W. Cook, eds., *The Words of Joseph Smith* (Orem, UT: Grandin Book Company, 1991), 211.
15 *Joseph Smith's New Translation of the Bible: Original Manuscripts*, ed. Scott H. Faulring, Kent P. Jackson, and Robert J. Matthews (Provo, UT: Religious Studies Center, 2004), 450 (compare John 4:24).
16 *Joseph Smith's New Translation*, 701 (compare Exodus 33:20).
17 *Joseph Smith's New Translation*, 443 (compare John 1:18).
18 Joseph Smith History 1:12.

Chapter 6

1 "Theology," in *Oxford Dictionary of the Christian Church*, ed. F. L. Cross and E. A. Livingstone (Oxford: Oxford University Press, 1997), 1604.
2 Andrew F. Ehat and Lyndon W. Cook, eds., *The Words of Joseph Smith* (Orem, UT: Grandin Book Company, 1991), 234.
3 Ehat and Cook, *Words, 285.*
4 *Millennial Star* 3.11 (March 1843): 177.
5 John Taylor, in Brigham Young et al., *Journal of Discourses*, 16:197–198.
6 Henry B. Eyring, "The True and Living Church," *Ensign* 38.5 (May 2008): 20, 22.
7 Ehat and Cook, *Words*, 34.
8 "United Methodists Adopt Guidelines for Mormons Joining Church," 2000 United Methodist General Conference, May 10, 2000, http://gc2000.org/gc2000news/stories/gc052.htm.
9 1 John 3:2–3; Lecture Seventh, Doctrine and Covenants (Kirtland, OH: F. G. Williams, 1835), 66–67.
10 E. Brooks Holifield, *Theology in America: Christian Thought from the Age of the Puritans through the Civil War* (New Haven: Yale University Press, 2003), 335.
11 The text is corrupt, but the sense is plain: "Presbyterians any truth. embrace that. Baptist. Methodist &c. get all the good in the world. come out a pure Mormon." Ehat and Cook, *Words*, 234.
12 Soren Kierkegaard, *The Essential Kierkegaard*, ed. Howard V. Hong and Edna H. Hong (Princeton: Princeton University Press, 2000), 344.
13 Ehat and Cook, *Words*, 353.

14 *Complete Discourses of Brigham Young*, ed. Richard S. Van Wagoner (Salt Lake City: Smith-Petitt Foundation, 2009), 3:1378.

15 All versions of the creeds and confessions in this section are from Philip Schaff, ed., *The Creeds of Christendom with a History and Critical Notes*, 6th ed. (Grand Rapids: Baker Book House, 1990).

16 Stephen Webb, *Jesus Christ, Eternal God: Heavenly Flesh and the Metaphysics of Matter* (New York: Oxford University Press, 2011), 249.

17 "To Isaac Galland," in *Personal Writings of Joseph Smith*, ed. Dean C. Jessee (Salt Lake City: Deseret, 2002), 458.

18 See the discussion, and the fact that this text was published in an 1831 newspaper under the title; "The Mormon Creed," in Gerald Smith, *Schooling the Prophet* (Provo, UT: Neal A. Maxwell Institute, 2015), 54–55.

19 Parley P. Pratt, "Immortality and Eternal Life of the Material Body," in *An Appeal to the Inhabitants of the State of New York; Letter to Queen Victoria; The Fountain of Knowledge; Immortality of the Body; and Intelligence and Affection* (Nauvoo, IL: John Taylor, [1844]), 30.

20 Roger E. Olson, *The Story of Christian Theology* (Downers Grove, IN: InterVarsity Press, 1999), 277.

21 Cardinal Walter Kasper, *Mercy: The Essence of the Gospel and the Key to Christian Life* (New York: Paulist Press, 2013), 44.

22 The 1878 edition varies slightly: "by reason of transgression cometh the fall, which fall bringeth death." Robert J. Matthews, "How We Got the Book of Moses," *Ensign* 26.1 (January 1986): 46.

23 W. W. Phelps, "The Answer" [to William Smith], *Times and Seasons* 5.24 (January 1, 1844): 758.

24 Brigham Young et al., *Journal of Discourses*, 26 vols., reported by G.D. Watt et al. (Liverpool: F.D. and S.W. Richards, et al., 1851–86; repr., Salt Lake City: n.p., 1974) 26:214.

25 "Becoming a God," Gospel Topics, churchofjesuschrist.org, February 25, 2014.

26 Athanasius, *Incarnation of the Word* 54.3, in Philip Schaff, ed., *Nicene and Post-Nicene Fathers of the Christian Church*, 2nd ser. (Peabody, MA: Hendrickson, 1999), 4:65; Clement of Alexandria, *Exhortation to the Heathen* 1, in Alexander Roberts and James Donaldson, eds., *The Ante-Nicene Fathers* (Grand Rapids, MI: Eerdmans, 1977), 2:174.

27 Clement of Alexandria, *Stromata* 7.10, in Roberts and Donaldson, *Ante-Nicene Fathers*, 2:539; Saint Basil the Great, *On the Spirit* 9.23,

in Schaff, *Nicene and Post-Nicene Fathers,* 8:16; Gregory Nazianzen believed that through the incarnation Christ would "make me God." Fourth Theological Oration (Oration 30) 14, in Schaff, *Nicene and Post-Nicene Fathers,* 7:315.

28 Dionysius the Areopagite, *On the Ecclesiastical Hierarchy* 1.3, in Norman Russell, *The Doctrine of Deification in the Greek Patristic Tradition* (New York: Oxford University Press, 2006, 1.

29 Parley P. Pratt, *Key to the Science of Theology* (Liverpool: F. D. Richards, 1855), 33.

30 Henry Denzinger, *Sources of Catholic Dogma,* 30th ed., trans. Roy J. Deferrari (Fitzwilliam, NH: Loreto, 2007), no. 39, p. 15.

31 Orson F. Whitney, *Conference Report* (April 1928): 59–60.

32 *Times and Seasons* 5.24 (January 1, 1845): 758.

33 "'1931 Statement of the First Presidency,' written to the Quorum of the Twelve, the first council of the Seventy, and the presiding bishopric," April 5, 1931, http://www.scottwoodward.org/Talks/html/FIRST%20PRESIDENCY/FirstPresidency_1931Statement_pre-adamites.html.

34 "What Does the Church Believe about Evolution?," *New Era* (October 2016), https:/www.churchofjesuschrist.org/study/new-era/2016/10/to-the-point/what-does-the-church-believe-about-evolution?lang=eng.

35 Gary James Bergera and Ronald Priddis, *Brigham Young University* (Salt Lake City: Signature, 1985), 163.

36 John Bradford, *Works,* 2 vols., 1:82, cited in Horton Davies, *Worship and Theology in England: From Cranmer to Baxter and Fox, 1534–1690* (Grand Rapids, MI: Eerdmans, 1996), 34.

Chapter 7

1 "The Latter-day Saint Woman: Basic Manual for Women, Part A," https://www.churchofjesuschrist.org/study/manual/the-latter-day-saint-woman-basic-manual-for-women-part-a/gospel-principles-and-doctrine/lesson-7-reverence?lang=eng.

2 *The Complete Discourses of Brigham Young,* ed. Richard S. Van Wagoner (Salt Lake City: Smith-Petit Foundation, 2009), 88.

3 Wilford Woodruff, in *Journal of Discourses* 16 (October 8, 1873): 268–269.

4 Andrew F. Ehat and Lyndon W. Cook, eds., *The Words of Joseph Smith* (Orem, UT: Grandin Book Company, 1991), 244.

5 Erik Peterson, *Pour une théologie du vêtement*, trans. M.-J. Congar (Lyon: Edition de l'Abeille, 1943), 6–13. Cited in Stephen D. Ricks, "The Garment of Adam in Jewish, Muslim, and Christian Tradition," in Benjamin H. Hary, John L. Hayes, and Fred Astren, eds., *Judaism and Islam: Boundaries, Communications, and Interaction* (Leiden: Brill, 2000), 206–208. See also Bryan Spinks, *Early and Medieval Rituals and Theologies of Baptism* (London: Routledge, 2006), 87.

6 Carlos E. Asay, "The Temple Garment: An Outward Expression of an Inner Commitment," *Liahona* 23.9 (September 1999).

7 Cotton Mather, for example, indicated that "disciples" who had not yet "risen to the . . . state of Brethren" did not enjoy access to the privileges (like Communion) granted full members. Quoted in Edmund Morgan, *Visible Saints: The History of a Puritan Idea* (Mansfield Centre, CT: Martino, 2013), 144.

8 Clementine, *Recognitions* 1.51, in Alexander Roberts and James Donaldson, eds., *The Ante-Nicene Fathers* (Grand Rapids, MI: Eerdmans, 1977), 8:91.

9 Wilford Woodruff, "Discourse by the Prophet Wilford Woodruff," *Millennial Star* (May 28, 1884): 339.

10 Ehat and Cook, *Words*, 346.

11 Joseph Smith, *Lectures on Faith*, comp. N. B. Lundwall (Salt Lake City: Bookcraft, n.d.), 58.

12 Perhaps surprisingly, but consistent with Mormonism's exception to the secularization hypothesis, a higher educational level correlated with more faithful observance of the principle of tithing. Sam L. Albrecht and Tim B. Heaton, "Secularization, Higher Education, and Religiosity," in James T. Duke, ed., *Latter-day Saint Social Life: Social Research on the LDS Church and Its Members* (Provo, UT: Religious Studies Center, Brigham Young University, 1998), 305.

13 Gordon B. Hinckley, *Cornerstones of a Happy Home* (Salt Lake City: Church of Jesus Christ of Latter-day Saints, 1984), 6.

14 Hinckley, *Cornerstones*.

15 Orson Pratt, "Celestial Marriage," *Journal of Discourses* 1.63.

16 Church of Jesus Christ of Latter-day Saints, "The Family: A Proclamation to the World," September 23, 1995, https://www.churchofjesuschrist.org/study/manual/the-family-a-proclamation-to-the-world/the-family-a-proclamation-to-the-world?lang=eng.

17 "Most Churches Are Losing Members Fast—But Not Mormons," *Vox* (March 6, 2019), https://www.vox.com/identities/2019/3/6/18252231/mormons-mormonism-church-of-latter-day-saints.

18 Russell M. Nelson, "Reverence for Life," *Ensign* 15.5 (May 1985): 11.

19 Dallin H. Oaks, "Weightier Matters," speech given at Brigham Young University, February 9, 1999, https://speeches.byu.edu/talks/dallin-h-oaks/weightier-matters/.

20 "Views about Abortion," Pew Research Center, https://www.pewforum.org/religious-landscape-study/views-about-abortion/.

21 Steven H. Webb, "Mormonism: Obsessed with Christ," *First Things* (February 2012), https://www.firstthings.com/article/2012/02/mormonism-obsessed-with-christ.

22 *Elders Journal* 1.3 (July 1838): 44.

23 *Complete Discourses of Brigham Young*, ed. Richard S. Van Wagoner (Salt Lake City: Smith-Petitt Foundation, 2009), 4:2431.

24 "Cross," Gospel Topics, Church of Jesus Christ of Latter-day Saints, https://www.churchofjesuschrist.org/study/manual/gospel-topics/cross?lang=eng.

25 Quoted in G. T. Eddy, *Dr Taylor of Norwich: Wesley's Arch-heretic* (London: Epworth Press, 2003), 39.

26 Timothy Keller, *The Reason for God: Belief in an Age of Skepticism* (London: Hodder, 2008), 40.

27 Joseph Smith, Discourse, April 8, 1843, Joseph Smith Collection, Church History Library, https://www.josephsmithpapers.org/articles/religious-freedom.

28 Statement by the First Presidency and the Quorum of the Twelve, October 17, 1993, https://www.lds.org/ensign/1994/01/news-of-the-church/statement-released-by-first-presidency-and-quorum-of-thetwelve? lang=eng. The definition of "apostasy" is from *General Handbook of Instructions* (Salt Lake City: Church of Jesus Christ of Latter-day Saints, 1989), 10–13.

Chapter 8

1 Sydney E. Ahlstrom, *A Religious History of the American People*, 2nd ed. (New Haven: Yale University Press, 2004), 508.

2 Kenneth R. Hardy, "Social Origins of American Scientists and Scholars," *Science* 185 (1974): 500.

3 Orson Pratt, *Journal of Discourses* (February 12, 1860): 7:157.

4 Brigham Young, *Journal of Discourses* (August 11, 1872): 5:2910.
5 Farrer, "Grete Clerk," in Neal A. Maxwell, "The Disciple-Scholar," in *On Becoming a Disciple-Scholar*, ed. Henry B. Eyring (Salt Lake City: Bookcraft, 1995), 5.
6 Maxwell, "The Disciple-Scholar," 7.
7 "Church Educational System Honor Code," https://policy.byu.edu/view/index.php?p=26.
8 "Religions Represented at BYU, 2002–2014," https://web.archive.org/web/20150221002204/http://yfacts.byu.edu/Article?id=97.
9 "Religions Represented at BYU, 2002–2014."
10 Tom Hollingshead, "BYU One of Nation's Highest Producers of Foreign-Language Degrees," *BYU News*, January 20, 2019, https://news.byu.edu/news/byu-top-producer-foreign-language-degrees-nation.
11 "Enrollment Reports Show More Returned Missionaries This Fall," *BYU News*, September 28, 2014, https://news.byu.edu/news/enrollment-reports-show-more-returned-missionaries-fall.
12 "Brigham Young University—Provo International Student Report," College Factual, 2018, https://www.collegefactual.com/colleges/brigham-young-university-provo/student-life/international/.
13 "First Presidency Issues Letter on Utah Precinct Caucus Meetings," *Church of Jesus Christ of Latter-day Saints Newsroom*, February 13, 2012.
14 Noah Feldman, "Noah Feldman: Utah Is the Political Conscience of the Nation," *Salt Lake Tribune*, October 20, 2016.
15 Donald Trump received 45.5 percent, Hilary Clinton 27.5 percent, and Evan McMullin 21.5 percent. https://en.wikipedia.org/wiki/2016_United_States_presidential_election_in_Utah#cite_note-3.
16 "Romney Is Running for Senate," *Washington Post*, February 16, 2018, https://www.washingtonpost.com/news/acts-of-faith/wp/2018/02/16/romney-is-running-for-senate-even-if-he-wins-the-mormon-church-has-been-losing-powerful-status-in-dc/.
17 Marc Haddock, "Utah Women Voted Earlier Than Most in the U.S.," *Deseret News*, February 8, 2010. Wyoming extended the vote to women a few months before the Utah legislature but held no elections where women could exercise their franchise until after Utah had.

18 Brigham Young, "Obeying the Gospel," *Journal of Discourses* (July 18, 1869): 18:61.

19 Merlin B. Brinkerhoff and Marlene MacKie, "Religion and Gender: A Comparison of Canadian and American Student Attitudes," *Journal of Marriage and the Family* 47 (1985): 415–429

20 Sherrie Mills Johnson, "Religiosity and Life Satisfaction of LDS Women" (Ph.D. diss., Brigham Young University, 2003), 97.

21 From the homepage of *Exponent II*: http://exponentii.org/.

22 Boyd K. Packer, "Talk to the All-Church Coordinating Council," May 18, 1993, http://www.zionsbest.com/face.html

23 George Givens, *In Old Nauvoo: Everyday Life in the City of Joseph* (Salt Lake City: Deseret, 1990), 227–236

24 Leonard J. Arrington and Davis Bitton, *The Mormon Experience* (New York: Random House, 1979), 337.

25 Jill Mulvay Derr, Janath Russell Cannon, and Maureen Ursenbach Beecher, *Women of Covenant: The Story of Relief Society* (Salt Lake City: Deseret, 1992), 107.

26 Claudia L. Bushman, *Mormon Sisters: Women in Early Utah* (Logan: Utah State University Press, 1997), 58–59.

27 Rebecca de Schweinitz, "Preaching the Gospel of Church and Sex: Mormon Women's Fiction in the *Young Woman's Journal*, 1889–1910," *Dialogue* 33:4 (Winter 2000): 29.

28 Brinkerhoff and MacKie, "Religion and Gender," 415–429.

29 Tim B. Heaton, "Familial, Socioeconomic, and Religious Behavior: A Comparison of LDS and Non-LDS Women," *Dialogue* 27.2 (Summer 1994): 177.

30 Beverly Campbell, "Eve," in Daniel Ludlow, ed., *Encyclopedia of Mormonism*, 4 vols. (New York: Macmillan, 1992), 2:476.

31 Elizabeth Cady Stanton, *The Women's Bible* (New York: Prometheus Books, 1999), 14.

32 *Millennial Star* 56 (April 9, 1894): 229.

33 Linda P. Wilcox, in Maureen Ursenbach Beecher and Lavina Fielding Anderson, eds., *Sisters in Spirit: Mormon Women in Historical and Cultural Perspective* (Urbana: University of Illinois Press, 1987), 74.

34 Maxine Hanks, for example, who wrote and lectured on the subject of a Heavenly Mother, was excommunicated in September 1993. In 1997, BYU refused to grant continuing status to Gail Turley Houston, citing her "advocacy" on the issue of

"praying to Heavenly Mother." Kristin Moulton, "Profs Say BYU Short on Academic Freedom," *Denver Post*, September 15, 1997.

35 "Mother in Heaven," https://www.churchofjesuschrist.org/study/manual/gospel-topics-essays/mother-in-heaven?lang=eng.

36 D. Michael Quinn, "LDS 'Headquarters Culture' and the Rest of Mormonism: Past and Present," *Dialogue* 34:3–4 (Fall–Winter 2001): 148.

37 Joseph Fielding Smith, *Doctrines of Salvation*, 3 vols., ed. Bruce R. McConkie (Salt Lake City: Bookcraft, 1954–56), 3:178.

38 *Ensign* 29.11 (November 1979): 102.

39 Studies to this effect have been referred to by Mormon apostle Melvin J. Ballard. Cited in Lynn Matthew Anderson, "Issues in Contemporary Mormon Feminism," in Douglas Davies, ed., *Mormon Identities in Transition* (London: Cassell, 1996), 165.

40 Smith, *Doctrines of Salvation*, 2:65.

41 Anne Osborn Poelman, *The Simeon Solution: One Woman's Spiritual Odyssey* (Salt Lake City: Deseret Book Co., 1995), 4.

42 Jana Reiss, *The Next Mormons: How Millennials are Changing the LDS Church* (New York: Oxford University Press, 2019), 98.

43 "Leader of Mormons Reaffirms Primacy of Church Teaching: Interview: After Being Chosen President and Prophet in June, Howard W. Hunter Reached Out to Disaffected Members. But He Still Upholds Authority of the Hierarchy," *Los Angeles Times*, October 22, 1994.

44 Spencer W. Kimball, "The False Gods We Worship," *Ensign* 6:6 (June 1976): 3–4.

45 Hugh Nibley, in *Approaching Zion*, in *The Collected Works of Hugh Nibley* (Salt Lake City, UT: Deseret Book and FARMS, 1988), 9:480.

46 Terry Tempest Williams, William B. Smart, and Gibbs M. Smith, *New Genesis: A Mormon Reader on Land and Community* (Salt Lake City: Gibbs Smith, 1998), ix.

47 "Mormons and the Environment," *Religion in Public* (blog), https://religioninpublic.blog/2018/12/19/mormons-and-the-environment/.

48 William B. Smart, "The Making of an Activist," in Terry Tempest Williams, William B. Smart, and Gibbs M. Smith, eds., *New Genesis: A Mormon Reader on Land and Community* (Salt Lake City: Gibbs Smith, 1998), 1.

49 Williams et al., *New Genesis*, ix.

50 *Millennial Star* 57.30 (July 25, 1895): 470.
51 Spencer W. Kimball, "Strengthening the Family—The Basic Unit of the Church," *Ensign* 8 (May 1978): 45.
52 Brigham Young, "Blessings of the Saints," *Journal of Discourses* (September 30, 1860), 8:191.
53 Joseph Fielding Smith, *Answers to Gospel Questions,* 5 vols. (Salt Lake City: Deseret, 1957–1966), 2:48.
54 Richard C. Foltz, "Mormon Values and the Utah Environment, Worldviews 4.1 (2000): 16, https://www.jstor.org/stable/43809149?seq=1#page_scan_tab_contents.
55 Anthony W. Ivins, *Conference Report* (Salt Lake City: The Church of Jesus Christ of Latter-day Saints, 1911): April 118–119.
56 D. Michael Quinn, "Conscientious Objectors or Christian Soldiers? The Latter-day Saint Position on Militarism," *Sunstone* 10.2 (March 1985): 19.
57 James R. Clark, ed., *Messages of the First Presidency* (Salt Lake City: Bookcraft, 1965), 6:159.
58 Quinn, "Conscientious Objectors or Christian Soldiers," 21.
59 James T. Duke, "Latter-day Saint Exceptionalism and Membership Growth," in Davies, *Mormon Identities*, 51.
60 Spencer W. Kimball, "First Presidency Message: The False Gods We Worship," *Ensign* 6.6 (July 1976), 3–4.
61 Gordon B. Hinckley, "In Grateful Remembrance," *Ensign* 1.3 (March 1971): 20.
62 Gordon B. Hinckley, "War and Peace," *Ensign* 33.5 (May 2003).
63 "Interview With Elder Dallin H. Oaks and Elder Lance B. Wickman: 'Same-Gender Attraction,'" The Church of Jesus Christ of Latter-day Saints Newsroom, 2006, https://newsroom.churchofjesuschrist.org/article/interview-oaks-wickman-same-gender-attraction.
64 Laurie Goodstein, "Utah Passes Antidiscrimination Bill Backed by Mormon Leaders," *New York Times*, March 12, 2015.
65 "First Presidency (Thomas S. Monson, Henry B. Eyring, and Dieter F. Uchtdorf), 'Preserving Traditional Marriage and Strengthening Families' (2008)," in Terryl L. Givens and Reid L. Nielson, eds., *The Columbia Sourcebook of Mormons in the United States* (New York: Columbia University Press, 2014), 220.
66 Church of Jesus Christ of Latter-day Saints, "The Family: A Proclamation to the World," September 23, 1995, https://www.churchofjesuschrist.org/study/

manual/the-family-a-proclamation-to-the-world/the-family-a-proclamation-to-the-world?lang=eng.

67 Church of Jesus Christ of Latter-day Saints, "The Family: A Proclamation to the World."

68 Brigham Young et al., *Journal of Discourses*, 26 vols., reported by G.D. Watt et al. (Liverpool: F.D. and S.W. Richards, et al., 1851–86; repr., Salt Lake City: n.p., 1974), 19:270.

69 Church of Jesus Christ of Latter-day Saints, "The Family: A Proclamation to the World."

70 Jeffrey R. Holland, "Souls, Symbols, and Sacraments," speech given at Brigham Young University, January 12, 1988, https://speeches.byu.edu/talks/jeffrey-r-holland/souls-symbols-sacraments/.

71 Oaks's words came in a live interview reported in Taylor Petrey, "A Mormon Leader Signals New Openness on Transgender Issues," *Slate*, February 13, 2015, http://www.slate.com/blogs/outward/2015/02/13/mormons_and_transgender_elder_dallin_h_oaks_says_the_lds_church_is_open.html.

72 Brent C. Miller and T. D. Olson, "Sexual Attitudes and Behavior of High School Students in Relation to Background and Contextual Factors," *Journal of Sex Research* 24:194–200; another study indicated that the lowest levels of premarital sexual activity occur among three groups: Latter-day Saints, Pentecostals, and Jehovah's Witnesses. See S. H. Beck, B. S. Cole, and J. A. Hammond, "Religious Heritage and Premarital Sex: Evidence from a National Sample of Young Adults," *Journal for the Scientific Study of Religion* 30:173–180.

73 Tim B. Heaton, "Four C's of the Mormon Family: Chastity, Conjugality, Children, and Chauvinism," in D. Thomas, ed., *The Religion and Family Connection: Social Science Perspectives* (Provo, UT: Religious Studies Center, Brigham Young University, 1988), 107–124.

74 Cited in Dennis L. Lythgoe, "The Changing Image of Mormonism," *Dialogue* 3.4 (Winter 1968): 48.

75 "Free People of Color," *Evening and Morning Star* (July 1833): 109.

76 Bruce R. McConkie, "All Are Alike unto God," speech given at Brigham Young University, August 18, 1978, https://speeches.byu.edu/talks/bruce-r-mcconkie/alike-unto-god/.

77 Orson Whitney, "Home Literature," *Contributor* 9.8 (June 1888): 296–300.

Chapter 9

1 Terryl Givens, "The Book of Mormon and the Reshaping of Covenant," in Elizabeth Fenton and Jared Hickman, eds., *Americanist Approaches to The Book of Mormon* (New York: Oxford University Press, 2019), 354.

Chapter 10

1 Bruce R. McConkie, "All Are Alike unto God," speech given at Brigham Young University, August 18, 1978, https://speeches.byu.edu/talks/bruce-r-mcconkie/alike-unto-god/.

2 D. Todd Christofferson, "The Doctrine of Christ," *Ensign* 42.5 (May 2012): 88.

3 Dieter F. Uchtdorf, "Come, Join with Us," *Ensign* 43.10 (November 2013): 22. The two articles were https://www.nytimes.com/2013/10/06/us/a-top-mormon-leader-acknowledges-the-church-made-mistakes.html, and https://www.nytimes.com/2013/10/09/us/a-leaders-admission-of-mistakes-heartens-some-doubting-mormons.html.

4 Harold Bloom, *The American Religion* (New York: Chu Hartley, 2013).

5 Gordon S. Wood, "Evangelical America and Early Mormonism," *New York History* 61 (October 1980): 368, 367, 361.

6 *Evening and the Morning Star* 1.3 (August 1832): 22.

7 The numbers were 34,299 for 1840–1849 and 43,304 for 1850–1859. Tim B. Heaton, Stan L. Albrecht, and J. Randal Johnson, "The Making of British Saints in Historical Perspective," *BYU Studies* 27.2 (Spring 1987): 119.

8 Tim B. Heaton, "Vital Statistics," in Daniel H. Ludlow, ed., *Encyclopedia of Mormonism*, 4 vols. (New York: Macmillan, 1992), 4:1520.

9 Armand L. Mauss, "Identity and Boundary Maintenance: International Prospects for Mormonism at the Dawn of the Twenty-First Century," in Douglas Davies, ed., *Mormon Identities in Transition* (London: Cassell, 1996), 13.

10 Armand L. Mauss, *The Angel and Beehive: The Mormon Struggle with Assimilation* (Urbana: University of Illinois Press, 1994), 14.

11 Tad Walch, "Major LDS Growth in Africa Unaffected by Priesthood Restriction, Elder Sitati Says," *Deseret News* (October 9, 2015), https://www.deseretnews.com/article/865638671/

Major-LDS-growth-in-Africa-unaffected-by-priesthood-restriction-Elder-Sitati-says.html.

12 See Maureen Dowd and Jane Barnes in the *New York Times*, and Jacob Weisberg in *Slate*, for three examples of high profile voices claiming the LDS religion was a disqualifier for office: See Givens, *Viper on the Hearth: Mormons, Myths, and the Construction of Heresy* (New York: Oxford University Press, 2013), 183–185.

13 B. H. Roberts, "A Plea in Bar of Final Conclusions," *Improvement Era* 16.4 (February 1913): 325.

14 https://www.churchofjesuschrist.org/study/manual/gospel-topics-essays/translation-and-historicity-of-the-book-of-abraham?lang=eng.

INDEX

For the benefit of digital users, indexed terms that span two pages (e.g., 52–53) may, on occasion, appear on only one of those pages.